In Your Garden
with
Percy Thrower

Best Wishes

Percy Thrower

In Your Garden with Percy Thrower

Line drawings by Norman Barber

Hamlyn: London · New York · Sydney · Toronto

Contents

Published by
The Hamlyn Publishing Group Limited
London · New York · Sydney · Toronto
Astronaut House, Feltham, Middlesex, England

Filmset in Great Britain by
Siviter Smith Limited, Birmingham
Printed and bound in The Canary Islands by
Litografía A. Romero, S. A. Santa Cruz
de Tenerife, Canary Islands (Spain)

First published by W. H. and L. Collingridge
Limited in 1959
Revised edition published in 1973
Eighth impression, 1977
© Percy Thrower and The Hamlyn Publishing
Group Limited, 1959, 1973

ISBN 0 600 34840 7
D. L. TF. 27 - 1974

Colour Illustrations

ACKNOWLEDGEMENTS
The Editor would like to thank *Amateur Gardening*, Pat Brindley, Ernest Crowson, Valerie Finnis, Iris Hardwicke, Elsa Megson, Sheila Orme and Harry Smith for the photographs used in this book.

Introduction

Gardening is a joy to me. It is both a satisfying occupation and a rewarding and fascinating hobby. Even before I left school at the age of 14 I longed to start work in the garden with my father, and I spent all my summer evenings and Saturday mornings there.

Interest in gardens and gardening has increased enormously in recent years. And if many of the large and beautiful gardens of the past have disappeared, this is more than made up for by the thousands of smaller but equally lovely gardens which have sprung up all over Britain.

There are multitudes of even smaller gardens, too, in town and country, and many thousands of allotments—all tended by people who cannot find out enough about their hobby. This enthusiasm is wonderful to experience, when I lecture up and down the country.

A gardener is never without friends, and I have made many new ones through my sound broadcasts and television programmes. Television has, I think, taught us that pictures are a marvellous aid to understanding in gardening. In this book, outlining the gardening year, I have tried to give you the best of both worlds by combining reading matter with a wealth of colour pictures and hundreds of clear drawings of plants and gardening operations.

There are no hard and fast rules in gardening. Like the farmer, the gardener is dependant on the weather to a very large extent and he has to learn to take advantage of every favourable opportunity to get on with his cultivations. Times of sowing and planting vary from one part of the country to another, so you must be guided to quite a large extent by local conditions. The information I have given is of necessity general so that it will suit, as far as possible, those gardeners who live in the north of England and Scotland as well as those in the south and the more favoured western parts of the British Isles.

May you derive as much joy as I do from gardening. It is all a great adventure—and it lasts a lifetime.

Percy Thrower

Present-day Gardening

Gardening is an ever-growing interest. Few houses, nowadays, are built without their accompanying garden, and many thousands of young people each year find that they have a garden for the first time in their lives. At first, the garden takes second place to the home, for obvious reasons, and for not a few people, I know, it has little interest. The interest comes later, when the house is ship-shape and the desire is awakened to do something about the garden. For others, though, the garden will always have been of prime importance.

So a garden usually has small beginnings. A lawn is made, probably from seed, then roses are planted and shrubs and other plants are almost certain to follow soon.

Generally speaking, everyone is looking for easier and better ways of running their gardens. The tendency is to concentrate on permanent plants that will provide colour throughout the year in one form or another with little maintenance involved and to rely less on – or do without altogether – bedding plants like geraniums (pelargoniums), salvias, lobelias and begonias.

On the other hand, bedding plants still have their uses, especially where a patio adjoins the house and plants can be grown in tubs or other containers, or in raised beds. Such a sitting-out area can be made very colourful and give great pleasure.

More and more, too, garden owners are using ground-cover plants to keep down weeds and reduce work – plants like the heathers (ericas), vinca (periwinkle), the prostrate juniper, *Juniperus media pfitzeriana*, and perennials such as hostas, ber-

Hosta

Vinca

genias, *Stachys macrantha* and the herbaceous geraniums. Indeed, many shrubs and herbaceous perennials will spread themselves out and give excellent cover and act as weed suppressors. If groundcover plants are introduced into the garden in a sensible way and balanced with plants grown primarily for their colour and other decorative features, then you will find that the garden loses nothing in interest and beauty by adopting such a planting policy.

One of the most interesting developments in recent years has been the widespread adoption of 'island bed' planting for all kinds of plants from shrubs to herbaceous plants and annuals, these often being very attractively mixed together. There are several advantages in this kind of display: for one thing you can shape them to suit your garden's overall layout; you can view the plants all round, and it

makes routine cultivations and plant care quite a lot easier. Also, the informality of it all fits in very well with modern ideas.

It seems to me that garden owners are getting much better at associating different kinds of plants to create special effects. Plants with bold leaves like the mahonias, hostas, bergenias and *Acanthus mollis*, and *Alchemilla mollis*, the Lady's Mantle, so much in demand for flower arrangements, are excellent for planting in prominent positions, and anyone making a new garden or developing an existing one can get a great deal of pleasure out of thinking up suitable planting associations. This is an ideal way, for instance, to deal with the odd corners that are found in most gardens.

Another trend, these days, is to make much greater use of paving and wall screening as well as cavity walls – double walls with soil between them which can be used for planting. And sitting-out areas such as those I referred to previously can be covered with screening materials or at least sheltered from the wind so that they can be used on a greater number of days than would otherwise be possible.

Car ports are commonplace nowadays, and the stark outlines of these can be softened by growing climbing plants like roses, clematis and honeysuckle up the supports. And while on the subject of climbers this is an appropriate time to consider the use of these on house walls. If your home is suited for such display and you, too, are keen on climbing plants as a decoration these can add much to the garden scene in general. Quite apart from the beauty of climbing roses, clematis and so on there is the opportunity it gives one

An attractive combination of foliage plants and paving. Such a grouping would be particularly suitable for a shady corner and could include such plants as hostas, rheums, rodgersias and ornamental grasses

to grow plants like the pineapple-scented broom, *Cytisus battandieri*, and the winter-tasselled *Garrya elliptica* which need a modicum of protection.

Water is also fashionable in today's gardens. A small pool planted with aquatic plants and stocked with goldfish and with moisture-loving plants around its margins is certain to be a centre of attraction. Children, in particular, will delight in the goldfish, but take care if there are really young children in the family. Such garden pools are made with pool liners, black or blue polythene or rigid glass fibre. Pools are still made, too, of concrete, although this is much more a constructional job than the other ways I have just mentioned, where the only preparation is the digging of a hole to the dimensions desired, with the addition afterwards of a stone surround.

The permanent plants I mentioned earlier on are shrubs and, of course, trees which will form the framework of the garden. I find that many not very experienced gardeners fall into the trap of selecting only spring-flowering shrubs, which is a pity because it is so very easy to make a choice which will provide colour and interest of one kind or another during all four seasons. Even in a small garden it is possible to plant the odd tree or shrub which will provide a display of autumn colour with its leaves and/or berries, and winter can be well looked after by planting a selection of winter-flowering ericas (*Erica carnea* and its varieties); *Viburnum fragrans*, with its pale pink, fragrant flowers; the lemon-yellow *Mahonia japonica*, with flowers scented like those of lily-of-the-valley; and *Prunus subhirtella autumnalis*, which blooms intermittently from November to March.

There are many splendid small trees available for providing interest at all times of the year, and I would make a plea that the temptation to plant forest-type trees be resisted. Planting trees like poplar, ash, beech, sycamore and elm in small gardens can only lead to trouble, for when they become too large they have to be pollarded and immediately lose their attraction.

Another tree which is often planted in unsuitable places is the weeping willow. This is all right in a garden of an acre or more but it should never be planted in small gardens. It will grow too large and take the moisture and light from other plants, quite apart from looking out of proportion. If you want a weeping tree then choose a weeping cherry or birch.

Remember also not to plant trees too near to the house for this will keep the light from windows and may also disturb the foundations of the house. In this respect, it is important to visualise the tree at its full height and spread before you decide on the site or, for that matter, buy it anyway. Large shrubs can also keep light from downstairs windows.

If you have the right soil, there is a great deal to be said for making a small heather garden, for this can be planted to provide colour throughout the year. The heaths and heathers (species and varieties of *Erica* and *Calluna*) are marvellous weed smotherers and need relatively little attention. However, all callunas and all the ericas except *E. carnea* and its varieties, *E. mediterranea* and *E. darleyensis* are lime-hating, which restricts your choice if you garden on chalk. All ericas are best in

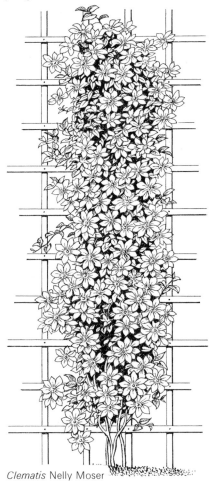

Clematis Nelly Moser

peaty soil, if it comes to that, and they should not be planted too deeply.

Rhododendrons and azaleas are colourful, popular plants but the same applies to these as to the heathers; the soil they are grown in must be lime-free. They can, like other lime-hating plants, be grown in chalky soil if treated at intervals with iron sequestrene, but this is expensive to do on any scale, and plants grown under such conditions are not really healthy.

As a screen within the garden or on the boundary I find hedges make a much better background to the garden than fences or walls. In my own garden I have beech hedges on the road side and within the garden, to provide a backdrop to a border at the side of the drive and to screen off the vegetable garden. On the field side I have a quickthorn hedge, for this forms the best possible cattle barrier, and at the top of the bank on which my house is situated and which is very exposed to wind, I have planted a hedge of *Cupressocyparis leylandii*. This makes a magnificent screen in only a few years from planting and with its deep green foliage is very handsome.

Splendid shrubs for low hedges within the garden include *Lonicera nitida*, box (*Buxus sempervirens*), *Berberis thunbergii*, and lavender, (*Lavandula* varieties), with good subjects for taller internal hedges being *Berberis darwinii* and *B. stenophylla*, various escallonias, forsythia, beech (*Fagus sylvatica*), holly (*Ilex aquifolium*) and such conifers as Lawson's Cypress (*Chamaecyparis lawsoniana*), yew (*Taxus baccata*) and Western Arbor-vitae (*Thuja plicata*).

For a boundary one would normally consider an evergreen hedge essential, but beech is really as effective as an evergreen for the attractive green leaves turn brown in late autumn and are retained throughout the winter. Such a hedge not only provides shelter but also brings colour and warmth to the garden.

An awful headache for many people moving into a completely new home is to know how to start to make a garden from the rough site the builder will have left behind him. My advice would be to sort out, first of all, any bricks, stones and rubbish which may be lying around and place these on one side for later path making. Next, dig over the whole plot or, better still, either hire a cultivator or get a garden contractor to work the ground over initially and level it. This will save time and energy and leave you free to get on with other jobs. If the soil is heavy it is advisable to work in peat, garden compost or straw at this stage to improve its texture and to aid free drainage. Light soils also benefit from such dressings for the texture of these can also be improved in this way and, in this case, they will have their moisture-holding capacity considerably improved.

My next recommendation would be to put the whole area down to grass seed. A good time to do this is between late March and April in the South and in April or May in the Midlands or North. Better still, though, is August or September for at this time there are unlikely to be periods of prolonged drought just when the young grass is becoming established. In the South, sowing can even continue into early October. Within a few weeks from sowing there will be a pleasant green sward around the house and you will then have time to think what else you would like to do.

Flower beds and borders, planting holes for trees, paths, a site for a pool perhaps – all these can be cut out of the grass at a later stage when your plans have been finalised. The attraction of making a garden this way is that you do not have to look at rather depressing bare soil for a long period and it gives you all the time in the world to develop your garden at your own pace without it looking unattractive in the process.

A common fault in garden making is to try and cram too much into a small area. This is never successful and I would strongly recommend concentrating on a few really good features which will be in keeping with their surroundings. And when you buy plants, make sure that they are of high quality. There is no falser economy than to buy inferior plants for not only is it money which is wasted in the long run but time as well, for the lack of success which may follow such purchases takes a year or so in some cases to show.

Somebody coming fresh to gardening will usually be content for a number of years to learn all he or she can on the subject in general, and, naturally, this is the best possible way to set about things; but after that there may well come the desire to take a deeper interest in one particular flower or group of plants. Coming to grips with one narrow aspect of gardening in this

Decorative concrete screening blocks are now available in many designs and may be used for garden walls when complete privacy is not required. They can also be used to divide the garden up into sections, or to hide such things as compost heaps

way can be fascinating and there are many specialist horticultural societies in the country which do a splendid job in promoting such interests. For example, there are societies for roses, dahlias, chrysanthemums, fuchsias, carnations, rock plants, daffodils, sweet peas, auriculas and primulas, and cacti and succulents. As this list shows there is scope for the most varied tastes and interests.

One of the first jobs in a new garden is the laying of paths for these are an absolute necessity – to reach, say, the vegetable garden, the greenhouse, or just to take you to a special garden feature like a small rock garden or pool. Any soil dug out during the construction of the path can be used in other parts of the garden, and the broken bricks, stones, ashes or other rough material which are used to form the base of the path put in its place. The top layer could be gravel, tarmac, concrete, paving stones or crazy paving. If paving stones are laid, set these on a sand base and secure each one with four or five blobs of cement on the base. Such a path always looks attractive.

I like to see small planting areas left in paving where thymes, armerias, dianthus, sempervivums and similar plants can be grown attractively. Such plantings help to give the garden cohesion.

Another very attractive feature is a sink garden, especially if one positions it near the house where it can be viewed as one walks up to the front door or where it can be enjoyed from inside the house. Many popular rock-garden plants of small size and with slow growth are suitable for such

Three styles of paving suitable for garden use. Natural stone, bricks, pebbles and a large range of pre-cast paving slabs can be chosen to give an interesting design. It is unwise, however, to mix too many different types of material

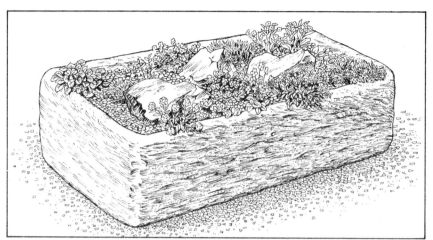

For small, slow-growing rock plants, a sink garden makes an ideal home. The old sandstone sinks are the most attractive for this purpose, but as these are becoming increasingly difficult to find, a glazed kitchen sink may be used instead

a feature – things like *Phlox douglasii* and its varieties, *Primula marginata*, some of the saxifrages and an enormous range of sempervivums, the pretty *Penstemon rupicola*, dwarf narcissi, crocuses, dwarf irises, and a host of other plants with dwarf conifers like the popular *Juniperus communis compressa* to give added interest.

Something which is often overlooked is that the soil in the typical small garden – usually packed with trees, shrubs and other plants – becomes impoverished after a time. It must be kept in good heart by applying humus-forming material like peat, garden compost or farmyard manure, and providing balanced plant foods in the form of fertilisers. The best time to feed plants is in the spring when they are beginning to come into growth. Special fertilisers are available for roses, lawns, shrubs, chrysanthemums, dahlias, vegetables and so on, but this is an expensive way of going about things. If you buy one good general garden fertiliser you can use it for virtually everything in the garden and get more for less money. The only exception to this is treating a weedy lawn. Using a lawn fertiliser with selective weedkillers added enables one to feed the grass and kill the weeds both at once.

The traditional planting seasons for many plants have been vastly altered, if not stood on their heads, by the large-scale introduction of container-grown plants, for these can be planted at any time of year, when weather and soil conditions are suitable. Trees, shrubs, conifers, roses, border plants and fruit trees can all be bought in containers nowadays. Quite

apart from the advantage of being able to plant at virtually any time, it has also given less experienced gardeners the opportunity to see so many flowering plants in bloom – before they make their final choice. Previously, it was a question of ordering from a catalogue and waiting for results. The sale of plants through garden centres and similar outlets has really given gardening a new face, for in addition to seeing a wide range of plants it is also possible to seek advice on what is right for your soil, what height particular plants will grow to eventually and things of that sort.

There are a few simple rules which should be observed when you get container-grown plants home. First, give them a thorough watering before they are removed from their containers. Secondly, remove them from their containers carefully so that the roots are not disturbed. Thirdly, do not plant them too deeply. Mix peat with the soil and add a little bonemeal or general fertiliser but take care that the fertiliser used does not come in direct contact with the roots. Make the soil firm around the plant and water in well. If a dry period follows, the plants should be watered again about a week later. From this stage onwards you are more likely to be successful with container-grown shrubs than with those lifted from the nursery.

In all but the smallest of gardens I feel an area should be screened off for growing vegetables. Fruit too, although this does depend on the kind of fruit you wish to grow and how it is grown (or trained) in relation to the space you have available.

You could grow apples or pears as cordons or espaliers to form a barrier between the vegetable and flower garden – an admirable way to kill two birds with one stone for these fruits are attractive in blossom and produce high-quality fruits in their trained form when well looked after.

But more of fruits later; let us now consider vegetables. The vegetable garden should be used to produce the favourite vegetables of the family, not just stock produce like potatoes, cabbages and cauliflowers but those which are more difficult to buy or have got to be used fresh – young carrots, French beans, broad beans, runner beans, young beetroot, lettuces, radishes and peas. There are also Brussels sprouts, savoy cabbages, broccoli, leeks and celery to consider. The range depends entirely on the size of your garden and your requirements. One thing is certain, bought vegetables – or fruit for that matter – bear no comparison with home-raised produce for flavour.

Always pay attention to continuity and succession with vegetables for there is no profit in having a glut at one moment and little or nothing at another. Intercropping – growing quick-maturing crops between those which need longer to mature – is also profitable. With a little forethought it is possible to have something from the vegetable garden during most of the year, if a reasonable area is devoted to these crops. For example, a plot of 60 ft. by 30 ft. should be enough to satisfy the needs of a family of four during the best part of twelve months, excluding potatoes.

You can advance the season of many crops by making use of plastic cloches, getting produce two or three weeks earlier in the case of vegetables like lettuces, peas, onions and carrots. While on this subject of sowing let me say that I deprecate too-early sowing outdoors. The important thing is to be guided by the soil temperature and weather conditions, rather than a date on the calendar.

Another important point I must also mention is crop rotation. No crops should be grown on the same piece of ground two years running as different crops take different foodstuffs from the soil, and, equally important, pests and diseases are less likely to build up to damaging proportions. The usual plan is to divide the vegetable plot into three sections, one section being devoted to potatoes, root crops and celery, another to onions, leeks, lettuces, beans and peas and the third to cabbages, Brussels sprouts, cauliflowers and other green crops. These sections are moved around the vegetable plot each year.

I suppose the most popular top fruits must be apples and pears, and with space a problem in many gardens nowadays, there is every inducement to grow them as cordons, espaliers, dwarf pyramids (for apples) and dwarf bushes. Appropriate dwarfing rootstocks are available and it is quite easy to obtain the right kind of stock for your conditions. Plums are probably best grown as fan-trained specimens on walls in most gardens – or as bushes – for plum trees take up a lot of room. A warm, sunny wall is an excellent home, too, for a peach or nectarine.

You can grow apples in any reasonably fertile garden soil with good drainage, but for the highest quality results a deep loam is needed. Poor fruits are obtained on very light sandy soil, and if the soil is at the other extreme, very heavy and prone to waterlogging, there will probably be trouble from canker.

Choosing apple varieties, as with those of other fruits, is very much a matter of personal choice, but one of the best known, with a superb flavour is Cox's Orange Pippin (for eating between November and January). James Grieve is a good pollinator for this variety as well as being a fine, juicy apple in its own right, and other excellent dessert varieties for extending the season are Ellison's Orange (September to October), Lord Lambourne (October to November) and Laxton's Superb (November to February).

Lane's Prince Albert (November to

Primula marginata

Saxifraga burseriana

March) is, I would say, the best cooking apple for the small or average-sized garden, and Bramley's Seedling (November to March) and Newton Wonder (suitable for dessert or cooking, November to March) for the larger garden. Lord Derby (October to November) is also a splendid cooking apple and crops well.

Of pears, I would recommend Doyenné du Comice (November maturing) as the finest flavoured variety of all but, alas, a shy cropper; the splendid Conference (October to November) which is a very good cropper; Williams' Bon Chrétien (September) which has excellent flavour and keeps well in store; and Joséphine de Malines (December to January), another fine-flavoured pear which stores well.

There is a good choice of plum varieties including the partially self-fertile Rivers' Early Prolific, a culinary variety maturing in late July which makes excellent jam; the self-fertile dessert varieties Early Transparent Gage and Victoria, both mid-August maturing; and Monarch, a self-fertile culinary variety maturing at the end of September.

I believe in always using the walls of the house and garage whenever possible to grow fruit. A north-facing wall is ideal for a fan-trained Morello cherry. There is no dwarfing rootstock for cherries so the fan method of training is the only practical way of growing this fruit in smallish gardens. Standard cherries can make very large trees indeed.

Soft fruits are an excellent proposition even in a quite small garden for they take up relatively little space and give an excellent return. The most popular kind is undoubtedly the strawberry, followed, I suppose, by the raspberry. One row of

raspberries, say 10 yards long, should provide a family of four with sufficient fruit throughout the summer months. Then there are the currants; black, red and white, and gooseberries and loganberries, too, if you want something a little different.

Strawberries have always been in demand for jam making so it is not only a question of growing the fruit for immediate use. By using cloches, too, it is quite possible to extend the season to six or seven weeks with the first fruit ripening in the most favoured positions in late May (on plants given such cover from March). A sunny position is needed, of course, and a site which is not in a frost pocket. The early to mid-season Cambridge Favourite and the late mid-season Talisman are excellent for cloche cultivation. The early Royal Sovereign, with its delicious flavour, is a splendid variety for ordinary cultivation, but remember that it is susceptible to virus disease. Another good variety is the mid-season Red Gauntlet.

I consider it well worth while growing some perpetual-fruiting strawberries for these fruit in summer and early autumn. Sans Rival and St Claud are two popular varieties of this type.

A sunny open position is also needed by raspberries. This is a very easy fruit to grow and the fruits are splendid for freezing. By growing both summer- and autumn-fruiting varieties it is possible to have this fruit on the table from early July until October. Varieties I favour are Lloyd George, an old variety of good flavour which crops in mid-season and autumn; the early to mid-season Malling Jewel; the vigorous, heavy-cropping Norfolk Giant; and September, an American variety which crops in September and October.

Penstemon rupicola

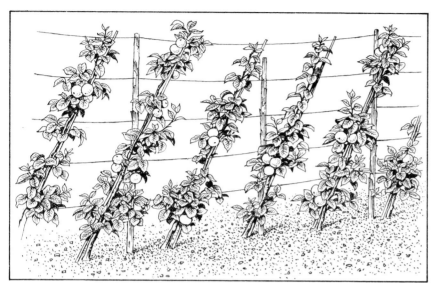

Cordon-trained apples and pears are especially useful in a small garden where space is at a premium. Grown in this way they make an excellent barrier between the vegetable and the fruit garden

Another excellent fruit for home freezing and one with a high vitamin C content is the black currant. The bushes should be protected from wind or they will suffer from 'run off' for bees will not pollinate the flowers in such conditions and the result is a very poor set. A wide range of varieties is available of which I favour the early-fruiting Mendip Cross; the early to mid-season Wellington XXX, a very good cropper; and the late Daniel's September. Black currants like a rich, well-cultivated soil with a good moisture content and they can be grown in sun or partial shade.

Red and white currants and goose-berries are all grown on a short 'leg' or stem. The early-fruiting currant varieties should be grown in sun but the later varieties are better in a shady position. Gooseberries like sunshine but some, like Whinham's Industry, grow well in the shade provided it is not too dense. Examples of good red currants include the early Laxton's No. 1, the mid-season Red Lake and the late Wilson's Long Bunch. White Versailles is a good, early white currant. Recommended gooseberries are Careless, a green, culinary variety; Whinham's Industry, red, culinary or dessert; and Leveller, yellow, culinary or dessert. All are mid-season varieties.

I have quite a lot to say in this book about pest and disease control because this is such an important part of running a really successful garden or greenhouse. I would not wish to over-emphasise this aspect of the gardener's craft but it is, perhaps, timely to say that prevention is better than cure and that good hygiene in garden and greenhouse alike – and particularly in the latter with its enclosed environment – can mean that one avoids a whole host of troubles which afflict less prudent or careful gardeners. The other thing is to grow your plants really well for it is usually the weak or sickly plant which succumbs most easily to pest and disease attack.

Also, when using chemicals in a garden read the manufacturer's instructions carefully, and apply them at the right time. I will agree that it is not always easy for the inexperienced to remember just when to do this and that to prevent damage or an infestation, but it is worth going to some trouble to become well informed on the habits of the most troublesome pests and diseases and know the kind of symptoms to look for.

On timings it is a great help to keep a diary of when particular jobs are done so that this can be referred to in subsequent years. (Such a diary can be fascinating, too, if you also include such details as the flowering times of plants and the kind of results obtained, when seeds were sown or plantings made and other things of that nature.)

The other very important thing is to keep all garden chemicals well out of the way of children – preferably in a locked cupboard, but if this is not possible, at least on a high shelf in the garden shed.

Nowadays it is possible to buy multi-purpose sprays and dusts and these have made things much easier for all of us. Also, modern spraying equipment is easy to operate and light to handle for it is usual for plastic to be used as much as possible.

To have a greenhouse is to open up whole new avenues of enjoyment. To be able to grow plants independent of the weather and plan for interest during all the seasons is a wonderful extension of one's hobby – gardening. With modern equipment and greenhouses the gardener has many options open to him, these ranging from the warm greenhouse which, if fitted with labour-saving equipment, gives the gardener the most opportunities to be adventurous, to the cool greenhouse, the unheated greenhouse, the sun lounge or conservatory. Whichever you choose you can be certain that you will have a lot of pleasure. The only thing I would say at this stage on the question of choice is that a moderately heated greenhouse gives infinitely more scope to the gardener than an unheated one, but such decisions must be taken in the light of how much you are able or prepared to spend.

An important consideration when siting your greenhouse is convenience and access. In other words you should place it as near to the house as possible bearing in mind that you want the best possible light conditions inside the greenhouse and the minimum of distance to walk from the house on cold winter nights and in wet weather. The other important consideration in this respect is the availability of electricity and gas services, electricity for obvious reasons because so much equipment, including lighting and heating, is powered in this way nowadays and gas because there is now a first-class natural gas greenhouse heater of completely new design in addition to the conventional gas-fired boiler heating piped water. I have more to say about heating units on p. 20.

One last word: throughout the text I have made reference to the use of loam in the preparation of composts. As everybody knows this is becoming more and more difficult to obtain so on occasions it may be necessary to substitute good topsoil— as infrequently as possible, though, I would hope.

Equipping your Garden and Greenhouse

THE GARDEN

Deciding what equipment one should have for one's garden is not always the easiest of things – it depends on so many factors. The depth of one's pocket, for instance, as well as the size of one's garden. What I intend to do now is to take a look at the equipment field in general so that you will have some idea of what is available and what would be best suited to your circumstances.

The tools it is impossible to do without are the fork, spade, hoe and rake, and the same can really be said of garden shears and secateurs, the first for grass and hedge cutting and the second for pruning. Small hand trowels and forks are invaluable for the more fiddly jobs and these, like the large cultivating tools I have mentioned, are available in chrome armour or stainless steel if you are prepared to pay the extra cost. The benefits come in easier use, the ease with which they are kept clean and their longer life. A watering-can is also an essential and some kind of sprayer for pest and disease control.

Let us now look at these in detail.

Spades. The most important factor when choosing a spade is to make sure that it is of the right weight for your physical capacity. Nothing is more tiring than to have a spade which is too heavy, for one must remember that it is not only the tool itself which has to be lifted but also the soil. Women gardeners in particular should note this point. Not too large a blade, then, and make sure that the model is nicely balanced and 'sits' well in the hands. T-, Y- and D-handled models are available with wooden or metal shafts and wooden or plastic handles.

Spades are used for digging, preparing planting holes and trenches and many other jobs of a similar nature. They are quite indispensable gardening tools.

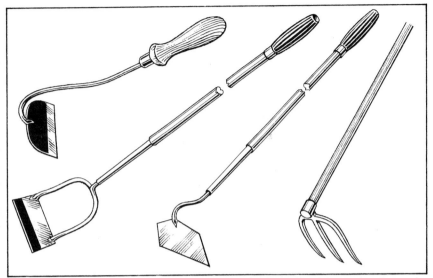

There are many different styles of garden hoe, but the four most commonly used are those shown here. From left to right, a hand or onion hoe, a Dutch hoe, a draw hoe and a Canterbury hoe

Forks. My remarks about size, weight and balance in connection with spades apply equally to forks, which can be used for breaking down the soil, light cultivations, removing weeds from among plants and collecting plant debris, among other things. A light border fork is probably the best choice for most home gardeners and if one of really good quality is obtained this will last for many years. The typical border fork has four square or rounded prongs, and there are also specially designed forks with flat prongs for lifting potatoes.

Hoes. The hoe is a tool used for cultivating the surface soil and many different types are available. I shall have something to say about the four I consider the most important. The Dutch hoe has a narrow, flat blade almost in line with the handle. It is especially useful for eliminating weeds, for the operator walks backwards when using it and so does not walk over the freshly moved soil. Another extremely useful hoe is the draw hoe with the blade set at right angles to the handle. This is used to make drills for seed sowing, to destroy tough weeds by using it with a chopping action, and for such jobs as earthing up potatoes. This tool is available in a swan-necked version or with a straight connection to the handle. The Canterbury hoe has prongs instead of a blade and is a very good tool for breaking down rough soil and for loosening the surface of hard soil. A hand hoe is a tool of the draw hoe type with the typical swan neck but a short handle. This makes it an admirable tool for close work among plants such as thinning rows of seedlings and weeding.

Rakes. Obtaining a fine tilth for seed sowing, levelling and many other jobs like leaf collection would be difficult or impossible without the services of a rake. The ordinary garden rake used for fine soil cultivation consists of a steel head with many teeth (the width can vary and so can the number of teeth) set at right angles to the long handle. Wire-toothed rakes are used for removing debris from lawns, collecting leaves and so on and consist of a fan of curved teeth attached to a long handle. Other designs for use on lawns are more traditional in shape, but with flexible rubber teeth. Another type, which is only needed in larger gardens, is the wooden rake (or hay rake) which can be used for soil levelling, leaf collection and, in orchards, for collecting mown grass.

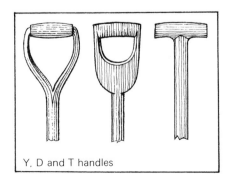

Y, D and T handles

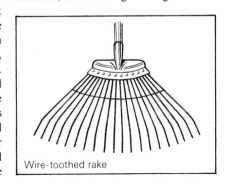

Wire-toothed rake

17

Dibber

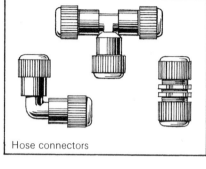

Hose connectors

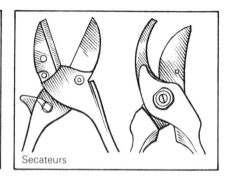

Secateurs

A Dibber. This simple tool has a handle like the end of a spade or fork with a short shaft, pointed at the end, over which a steel cap is fitted. It is usually about 15 in. long overall, and the handy gardener can quite easily make his own – minus the steel cap – from a broken spade or fork handle. All it really requires is a little shaping with a plane or knife. This tool is used to prepare the holes for planting out seedlings – for brassicas and such like plants – and thus does a similar, but quicker job to the trowel. Most gardeners, however, and quite rightly, reserve its use for planting on lighter soils for under heavy conditions there tends to be trouble with compaction as the dibber penetrates, and the result can be air spaces around the roots of the plants when the holes are filled in – a most undesirable state of affairs.

Hand Trowel. This tool should always be used for planting small plants, like pot-raised alpines and bedding plants, where care is necessary to avoid root disturbance.

Hand Fork. A hand fork is another extremely useful tool, mainly for cultivating among small plants where a larger tool could not be used.

Wheelbarrows and Trucks. Many kinds of wheelbarrows and trucks are available nowadays, and the main concern should be to obtain the right size to cope with your needs. As with some garden tools, getting too large a wheelbarrow or truck can be an embarrassment. On the whole I prefer a metal wheelbarrow to one made of wood because it is lighter and stands up to the weather better. Trucks and wheelbarrows are now also made of heavy duty polythene and these, too, are lightweight and strong. When considering which to buy, one would naturally look for good workmanship and, just as important, good balance. With wheelbarrows in particular good balance can make a world of difference. A load

carrier of some kind is essential in all but the smallest of gardens.

A Garden Line. This is another item it would be difficult to do without. Lines can be obtained in hemp or nylon and the best kind has a simple reel which makes letting out and taking in the line very easy.

Measuring Rod. For planting out seedlings at the correct intervals, spacing seed drills and for other jobs where accurate measurements are essential, a measuring rod is invaluable.

Brooms. A besom broom is always a useful aid for clearing lawns of surface debris, and a hard broom of conventional type for use on paving, paths and so on.

Watering Equipment. A good watering-can is a 'must', and again this should be well balanced. Many watering-cans nowadays are made of plastic, and for lightness and long service these have advantages over the metal type. A garden hose, with or without a reel, is another very useful piece of equipment. Ingenious and easily fitted connectors make it a simple matter to run out long lengths of hose to different parts of the garden. Perforated hoses, with which whole areas of the garden can be watered gently, are now commonplace. A water butt in which rainwater is collected is always worthwhile for in periods of water restriction it provides an admirable supply to meet the needs of flagging plants.

Sprayers. A modern, pressurised, portable sprayer is essential unless the garden is quite small. If this is the case, all that will be necessary is a hand sprayer.

Pruning Tools. No professional gardener would be without his pruning knife, for in skilled hands this can be used with precision for all kinds of cutting back, but for amateur gardeners a pair of good secateurs is much easier to use. Secateurs are of two kinds: the parrot's bill type and the anvil type, the first having an action rather like a

pair of scissors and the second having a sharp cutting blade which is brought up against a flat plate. Both do a good job.

For removing unwanted wood on trees well above arm's reach, there are long-arm pruners. One manufacturer, at least, makes a pruner of this kind which comes in three sections (9 ft. in length overall), and it has a useful saw attachment as well.

Long-handled loppers are invaluable for cutting out stouter pieces of wood than a pair of secateurs will cope with, for the purchase the operator can obtain through the long handles is very considerable. Likewise, a pruning saw can be in frequent use in larger gardens.

For hedge trimming, which is, after all, a form of pruning, there are various types of electric hedgecutter, operated from the mains electricity, from the battery of an electric mower or from a portable power pack or a rechargeable nickel cadmium battery. Also, for those with relatively small hedges to keep in order, there are ordinary garden shears, which need to be kept sharp and in good condition if this job is not to become arduous. It should be remembered that hedges of large-leaved evergreens like laurel or rhododendron are best pruned with secateurs, otherwise the leaves are certain to be cut as well as the wood and this will make them turn brown at the edges.

Knives. Whether you use a pruning knife for its correct purpose or for other odd jobs it is a very useful thing to have to hand – to tidy up a broken branch, perhaps, adjust a tree tie and other similar jobs. Likewise, a budding knife, with its tapered bone edge to the handle can be helpful.

Gloves. These are almost essential for jobs such as rose pruning, and the tougher the material they are made of the better.

Lawn Equipment. The major item of equipment needed for lawn care is, of course, a mower, and depending on the size of the area down to grass you will need anything from a simple, two-wheeled, hand-propelled machine or a rather more sophisticated hand-propelled, cylinder-type mower to a powered version of the latter, a rotary grass cutter or, most advanced of all, a ride-on mower. Again, with such a wide choice, it is a matter of picking the machine best suited to your needs; but the question of whether a rotary or cylinder model is chosen will depend on the length of grass you expect the machine to cut (a rotary mower will cut long grass with ease) and the quality of finish desired. A cylinder mower is the winner in this respect, but it can only be used to cut grass which is relatively short.

A variant of the rotary mower is the kind which uses the aircushion principle to cover the ground. Slight movements by the user will cause it to change direction, and it is admirable for cutting steep slopes.

With powered mowers, should they be petrol-engined or electric? Again, this is a matter of personal preference, but there is no doubt that the battery electric type has great appeal, being quiet, of easy maintenance and almost trouble free. Still, against that one is limited by the time it takes for the battery to run down and the machine is then out of action until it is recharged. A mower with an internal combustion engine will go on as long as you want provided it is kept supplied with petrol and oil. This type nowadays is much more reliable than previously, and with regular servicing should give little trouble.

You have limitations of a different kind with mains-powered electric mowers for here the radius of action is decided by the length of the cable and the positioning of the power point. Also, there is always the business of avoiding the cable when manoeuvring the machine. These can also be powered by a generator which gives the owner more scope, but as a type they do not match up for convenience to the other kinds I have mentioned.

If you have a large expanse of grass a fertiliser spreader is a useful acquisition, for not only does it do the job much more quickly than it can be done by hand but, more important still, it is more accurate. These machines have calibrated rollers which will spread the fertiliser at a pre-determined rate, so all that has to be done

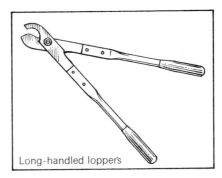
Long-handled loppers

Fertiliser distributor

is to fit the appropriate roller in position.

A wire-tined rake, mentioned earlier, is invaluable for light aeration and clearing the grass of debris – a job which should be done reasonably frequently after the growing season has passed the half way mark. Autumn raking is especially beneficial. Deep aeration should be done with a hollow-tined lawn aerating tool, which ejects small cores of soil, with a spiked roller, or with an ordinary border fork if the area involved is small.

Light aeration can also be done with a stiff broom or besom, and this is especially useful when carried out in early spring, removing dead vegetation and stones which might get caught up in the mower.

Long-handled shears, both the lawn type with horizontally attached blades and the straight-bladed edging type, are invaluable items of lawn equipment, and the battery operated or electric edge trimmers are becoming increasingly popular these days. A scythe or sickle can be extremely useful for coping with rough grass.

A roller is not needed in normal circumstances and over-rolling should always be avoided in any case. With a cylinder-type mower, certainly, the degree of compaction from the mower alone will be perfectly adequate.

I have already referred to garden hoses and the perforated type which send fine

sprays out at angles over a considerable area are ideal for lawn watering. A gentle spray of this kind gives the ground a chance to absorb the water without flooding. Then there are the pulsating sprinklers which water circles or segments of a circle, the simple fountain type which covers a circular area and does not have any moving parts, and the oscillating kind which covers a rectangular area. A variant of this type moves itself along the hose and can be left for a considerable time without attention.

Autumn leaf collection can be quite time consuming if you have a large garden with many trees, and a leaf sweeper can be a very useful aid. It is hardly worth going to such expense, though, for small areas.

THE GREENHOUSE

What kind of greenhouse, and should it be heated or unheated? The choice is wide, from the span-roof type, to the lean-to, the three-quarter span, the Dutch-light house and the space-conserving circular greenhouse; or perhaps, a conservatory or a sun lounge, as its modern derivative is called.

Briefly, a span-roof house allows the widest range of plants to be grown under the best conditions; a Dutch-light house is cheap to buy and allows in the most light; the lean-to type saves money by using an

Budding knife

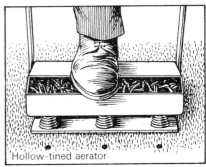
Hollow-tined aerator

Span-roof greenhouse

existing wall as one side; the three-quarter span house is an admirable compromise between a lean-to and a span-roof house; and a circular greenhouse provides more space for plants within a given area than any other type. A conservatory or sun lounge is essentially an 'indoor' garden, usually provided with just enough heat to keep out frost.

An unheated greenhouse has obvious limitations for only those plants which are hardy or which need only slight winter protection can be grown. But it is still very useful for raising seedlings or half-hardy annuals, to flower hardy annuals in during spring, for growing shrubs in pots as well as early-flowering bulbs, and for cropping lettuces, tomatoes and grapes.

A cool greenhouse – minimum temperature 4°C. (40°F.) – gives more scope, and it is easy in such a house to have plants in flower throughout the year. If possible, it should include a small propagating frame. The warm greenhouse – minimum temperature 10 to 13°C. (50 to 55°F.) – is better still and is especially appreciated during winter and early spring. But heat has to be paid for and raising the temperature of a greenhouse from 4°C. (40°F.) to 10°C. (50°F.) by electricity can easily double the heating bill.

Methods of Heating. Electricity is clean and efficient as a method of heating but may be more costly than solid fuel, oil, paraffin or gas heating. An interesting development is the natural gas heater, which is not only cheaper to run than electrical installations but also supplies the plants with additional carbon dioxide, which in turn improves growth. This ques-

tion of heating should be gone into very thoroughly before making a decision.

Insulating Materials. Heat retention can be greatly improved by lining the glass with clear polythene sheeting during the winter months. It can reduce the heating bill by half, but some light is lost, inevitably.

Greenhouse Staging. A solid type of staging made of concrete or asbestos sheeting and covered with gravel to retain moisture is the most satisfactory kind. Slatted staging is all right, but it allows dry air to circulate around the plants and does not usually provide such a good growing atmosphere as the other type.

Propagating Frame. A small electric propagator which can stand on the bench and in which a minimum temperature of 16 to 18°C. (60 to 65°F.) can be maintained is an enormous asset.

Capillary Bench Watering. This automatic watering system, in which the water is fed by gravity into channels in the bench beneath a sand covering, gives the less experienced gardener far more accurate control of this vital function than can be achieved with a watering-can. The plants take up moisture by capillary action, as they need it.

Trickle Watering. This consists of a plastic hose with outlet nozzles along its length corresponding to the average distance between quite closely set pots. It is connected to a storage tank which releases its contents when full, so plants (or greenhouse beds) get set quantities of water at regular intervals. Less precise than the capillary bench, it is, nevertheless, useful.

Mist Propagation Unit. This piece of equipment has made the rooting of cuttings (including some notoriously difficult ones) much easier. A simple but ingenious device ensures that a mist-like spray comes on as soon as the leaves start to dry out, thus preventing the cuttings from flagging. Such a unit is invaluable if you are interested in this kind of propagation.

Soil Sterilisers. Steam sterilisation of loam with a small electric steriliser is very worthwhile if you wish to mix your own composts – but you can do the same job by standing a bucket in a copper of boiling water and raising the temperature of the loam to 93°C. (200°F.) for 20 minutes.

Sprayers. A small hand sprayer is essential for pest and disease control, and for spraying water over the plants in hot weather.

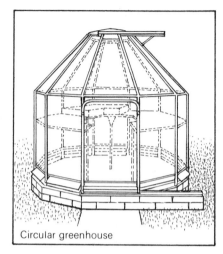
Circular greenhouse

Flower Pots. Light, cheap, durable, easily stored and cleaned, plastic pots have now almost entirely superseded the traditional clay pots. But watering must be watched more carefully with these containers, for the soil dries out much more slowly and it is easy to make it waterlogged.

Seed Boxes. These are invariably made of plastic, too, and the advantages listed for plastic pots also apply. A standard box measures 14 in. by 8½ in. by 2 in.

A Dibber. The greenhouse version of this tool is rather like a thick pencil, and is used to make holes for seedlings and cuttings. The end should be rounded rather than pointed so that no air space is left under the seedlings or cuttings.

Sieves. The sieve most often needed is one with a ⅜-in. mesh, and a finer one is needed to grade compost used to cover seeds. This last can be made by knocking the bottom out of a small wooden box and replacing it with a piece of perforated zinc.

A 'Presser'. This, too, can be home made. It consists of a wooden block with a short handle and it is used to level and firm the compost before sowing seeds.

A Bucket. This is an essential item of equipment, and any domestic model will do.

Labels. Many kinds are available, in plastic, wood and metal, and they should be put to good use. The human memory is only too fallible!

Tying Materials. Raffia and fillis, a specially prepared soft twine, together with green gardening twine, are the materials generally used.

A Measure. A calibrated measure is invaluable when mixing liquid feeds, insecticides and fungicides.

Your
Weekly
Guide

January: first week

Topdress lawns. Read the new catalogues. Renew grease bands. Prune outdoor vines. Dig vegetable garden. Make hot beds. Prepare for chrysanthemum cuttings. Stake pot-grown bulbs.

The wise gardener is always looking ahead, and it is best to start off as you mean to go on. Why not make it a New Year resolution? Such forward thinking certainly makes gardening easier, and invariably leads to better results.

FLOWERS

When the lawn is reasonably dry, take the first opportunity to sweep it with a besom to scatter worm casts and remove dead grass.

If the lawn was not given a topdressing in autumn this should be done now, after the sweeping just suggested. I use a mixture of equal parts peat and loam applied at the rate of 4 lb. to the square yard. If this mixture is pushed backwards and forwards with the back of a rake, it will be worked well down into the turf where it will do most good.

Look carefully at trees, shrubs and roses planted last autumn and re-firm them if they have become loosened by wind or frost. However, it is most important to carry out this task when the surface of the soil is fairly dry or it will become too compacted. It is not always realised just how much plants of this kind can be set back by movement of the roots.

Now that the new season's catalogues are available it is interesting to go through them carefully and note the new plants which are being offered. This is especially so with the seed catalogues, which gener-

If recently planted shrubs and trees have been lifted by frost they should be carefully firmed in again

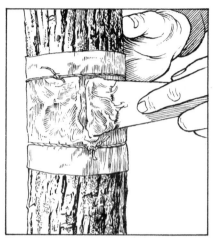

Renewing the grease on fruit tree grease bands. These bands are particularly effective against winter moths and woolly aphids

ally include plenty of novelties of one kind or another. It is always a good thing to get in orders for seeds and plants early so that deliveries can be made on time.

FRUIT

Examine any fruit trees or bushes planted earlier and firm them if they have been loosened by wind or frost. Continue to plant fruit trees and bushes when the conditions are satisfactory.

At this time, too, check all the grease bands put on older trees last autumn and renew the grease where this is necessary. It is also a good thing to make regular inspections of fruit in store for just one rotting fruit left among others can result in further losses very rapidly.

If fruit trees have not already been given their winter spray, take the earliest possible opportunity to complete this important task.

If outdoor vines were not pruned in December do this now. The method of pruning adopted for vines growing freely on walls or on a trellis is similar in principle to the pruning of indoor vines (see p. 123), but it need not be so severe.

Where animal oil is used to repel mice, care must be taken not to put it on or very near the plants. To paint such oil directly on the trunk of a tree could cause much damage and might even be fatal. The correct way is to soak sacking in the animal oil and place it loosely on the soil or grass around the base of the tree. Another way of preventing mouse damage is to rub ordinary carbolic soap on the stem of the tree.

VEGETABLES

Clear away the stems and roots of savoys and other green vegetables which have finished cropping, and get on with winter cultivations whenever this is possible. Heavy clay soil dug over at this time of year benefits from the action of frost and rain, which helps to break down the large clods and makes it that much easier to get a fine tilth when spring arrives and seed beds have to be prepared.

In fact all soils should be prepared now for future crops, and it will be necessary to decide where the root crops are going to be grown this season so that the chosen area can be left free of manure. The best plan is

Sweeping the lawn with a besom to scatter worm casts and remove dead grass, leaves and other debris

Spraying a young apple tree with tar oil wash to kill the overwintering eggs of insects and remove green algae

Regular checking of apples in store is essential if infection is to be prevented, for one bad fruit will soon affect others

used for early sowings of such crops as lettuces, carrots, spring onions and radishes. The fermenting material should be covered with a 6-in. layer of good loam in which the plants will grow, and the frame is set on top of this. After these early crops have been cleared away, the heap can be used for marrows or cucumbers.

Inspect vegetables in store for signs of decay. If root vegetables are beginning to rot, they can often be used if the decayed area is cut away at an early stage.

GREENHOUSE

This is an important time for the chrysanthemum enthusiast, for preparations should be made now to take cuttings of these flowers. The chrysanthemum stools from which the cutting material will be taken should be brought as near to the glass as possible to encourage the development of sturdy growths. All pots or boxes which are to be used should be thoroughly cleaned in readiness, and a suitable cutting compost prepared. I find that a good mixture is 1 part of loam, 2 parts of granulated peat and 3 parts of sharp sand.

Special attention should be paid to watering at this time of year for with the atmosphere likely to be damp and the temperature less high, perhaps, than one would wish it to be, plants can fall prey to all kinds of troubles. This is particularly the case with large-flowered calceolaria hybrids, cinerarias and cyclamen.

If the foliage of cyclamen plants is held back, water can be applied direct to the soil without splashing the leaves

to divide the vegetable garden into thirds, and manure one third of the total area each year. If farmyard manure is not available, use compost or peat as substitutes.

Now is the time to put cloches over ground one intends to make into early seed beds later on. This will dry out the soil and bring the sowing dates forward quite a bit in relation to what would otherwise be possible. Plastic cloches rather than glass ones are the most popular these days.

If leaves or straw are available make up a hotbed on which a frame can be stood to raise early seedlings. To generate the necessary amount of heat, such a hotbed will need to be 2 to 3 ft. deep. It can then be

Bring more bulbs in pots and bowls from the plunge bed into the greenhouse to provide a succession of flowers later on. The cooler the house the better, for their introduction to warm conditions should be gradual to achieve even growth.

Daffodils and hyacinths are liable to flop all over the place if the growths are not supported. Stake the plants neatly so that the support can scarcely be seen, and use green garden twine for the ties so that it merges in with the foliage. Alternatively, use florists' wire, one piece per stem, pushing this down into the compost and bending it into a crook.

Pot on the autumn-sown sweet peas. If these have been raised five or six seeds to a 3-in. pot, the seedlings should be divided up and potted separately now. Place each one in a 3-in. pot of John Innes No. 1 Potting Compost.

If bulbs of *Lilium auratum* and *L. speciosum rubrum* were not potted up in October (see p. 106) do this now.

Freesias which have yet to bloom will benefit from feeding with a little weak liquid manure. Indeed, most plants benefit at this time of year from a feed at 10- to 14-day intervals.

Plants that have been in the home over Christmas and are showing signs of distress can be revived by a short spell in the greenhouse. The fresher atmosphere, better light and more carefully controlled conditions work like a charm on such invalids.

I find, like most gardeners, that this is an excellent time to give the greenhouse a thorough clean, while it is relatively empty.

Potting up autumn-sown sweet peas separately in 3-in. pots using the John Innes No. 1 Potting Compost. Afterwards, twiggy sticks are inserted around the edge of the pots to give the young plants the support they need

23

January: second week

Repair lawns. Lay turf. Prepare ground for outdoor chrysanthemums. Force chicory and rhubarb. Sprout seed potatoes. Sow vegetables in heated frame. Clean greenhouse. Take chrysanthemum cuttings. Remove faded flowers from azaleas.

FLOWERS

In many parts of the country the first snowdrops of the year are reminding us that life is stirring in the garden again. It will not be long before these delightful plants are joined by crocuses and other spring flowers.

If established lawns need renovating in any way, it is a good idea to do this work now. Choose a day when the weather is open and the soil reasonably dry. Bumps and hollows in the lawn can be levelled out by lifting small areas of the turf and either adding or removing soil as appropriate. Where the turf at the edge of a path or flower bed has become worn this, too, can be made good by cutting away the damaged area, and replacing it with new turves. It is often better to cut out a rectangle of the existing turf and move this to the edge, putting the patch behind it, as a narrow strip of new turf might not otherwise stay in position too easily.

New lawns from turf can also be made at this time of year. However, one should remember that it is not always easy to purchase good quality turf nowadays, and very often it is infested with weeds, moss, leatherjackets or wireworms. Another disadvantage of this method of lawn making is the cost, for a lawn made from turf is about 75 per cent. more expensive than one made from seed.

When flower seeds which you have ordered arrive, keep them in a cool and dry place until they are required, and protect them from mice. An old biscuit tin or something similar makes an excellent container for seeds and they will keep in perfect condition for a long time if stored in this way.

Dig over the ground which will be needed later for outdoor chrysanthemums. This job must be done thoroughly, some farmyard manure being incorporated at the same time. Add, too, a dusting of bonemeal and hoof and horn meal if flowers of exhibition quality are required.

Slugs can cause damage to carnations and pinks at this time, and as soon as any trouble is noticed a slug-killing preparation should be put down.

FRUIT

It seems to me that many gardeners do not know how to make good use of north-facing walls. These are excellent for growing Morello cherries trained as fans. Such specimens are both decorative and profitable, and they should be planted now.

If cuttings of currants and gooseberries were taken in the autumn, they may have become loosened by recent frosts. Look them over carefully, and, if necessary, firm them in again with the feet.

Paint outdoor vine rods with one of the proprietary sulphur dressings as a preventive against mildew. The outdoor vine border should also be topdressed with fresh soil to which has been added a little bonemeal, hoof and horn meal and sulphate of potash, say 4 oz. of both bonemeal and hoof and horn meal and 1 oz. of sulphate of potash to each bushel of good soil. Alternatively, sprinkle 4 oz. of general organic fertiliser around each plant.

VEGETABLES

Bring more chicory roots into the greenhouse for forcing (see p. 116). Salads are scarce and expensive at this time of year, and chicory makes a good alternative.

Lift more strong roots of rhubarb for forcing, or cover them where they are growing with an upturned bucket, tub or box, covering this in turn with straw or leaves to keep out the frost. If seakale has has been left in the ground, cover the crowns in the same way to encourage early shoots to form.

Vegetable seeds should be stored until they are needed in exactly the same way as flower seeds. Particular care should be taken with peas which are much liked by mice.

When seed potatoes arrive these must be kept in a place where frost cannot penetrate, and the tubers should be stood, eye end uppermost, in shallow boxes to sprout.

If you have a hotbed or electric soil-warming cables in a frame, then seeds of some early crops can be sown. These include carrots, onions and lettuces with radishes sown between them as these will be pulled before any of the other crops

Repairing the damaged edge of a lawn. Avoid putting too small a patch at the edge as it is unlikely to stay in position

January is a good time of the year to lay turves. Remember, however, that although quick results can be had from this method of lawn making, good quality turf is expensive and hard to find

Firming in currant cuttings. This is an important job to see to after frost, which is likely to loosen the soil

Covering rhubarb shoots with an upturned bucket to keep them in the dark and encourage them to grow more rapidly

As soon as seed potatoes arrive they should be stood in shallow trays, in a frost-proof place, to sprout

require more room. I find the lettuce variety Kordaat particularly suitable for this kind of cultivation.

GREENHOUSE

Wash the outside of the glass of your greenhouse and frames, especially if you live in an industrial area. This can make a tremendous difference to the amount of light the plants receive, which is rarely sufficient in the winter months, even with conditions at their best.

We are all very much preoccupied with heating costs at this time of year, and it is timely, perhaps, to mention the recently introduced natural gas heaters which are now available for these have definite cost benefits and they provide extra carbon dioxide for the plants as well.

Do not be tempted by a few days of fine weather to sow seeds too early, for it is extremely important with seedlings that reasonable temperatures should be maintained throughout their period of growth. We are more than likely to have some very cold weather ahead, so if it is not possible to maintain a temperature of at least 10 to 13°C. (50 to 55°F.) it is unwise to sow anything for the next few weeks.

Take cuttings of chrysanthemums, selecting, where possible, shoots growing directly from the roots rather than the stem. The latter should only be used when stock is really short and the supply of the preferred type of cutting is inadequate. Choose sturdy, short-jointed shoots about 3 in. long, and these will be obtained by keeping the chrysanthemum stools in a really light place.

Trim the cuttings just below a leaf joint with a sharp knife or razor blade and remove the lower leaves to give a clean stem for insertion in the compost. Before inserting them, though, the cuttings should be dipped in water and then in a suitable hormone rooting powder.

Use a compost made up of 1 part loam, 2 parts peat and 3 parts coarse sand, or a soilless compost, and insert the cuttings around the edge of 3-in. pots, four to six in a pot. Then place these in a propagating frame with a temperature of 7°C. (45°F.).

Late batches of cyclamen seedlings should now be potted up into 3- or 3½-in. pots.

Inspect hydrangeas for any sign of botrytis which can affect the terminal buds from which the flower stems will be produced. In such cases reduce the water

supplies, keep the atmosphere dry and spray with thiram.

Remove flowers from plants of *Azalea indica* as soon as they begin to fade and before the seeds begin to form. When flowering has finished, repot the plants into a larger size if they are at present in 3-, 4-, or 5-in. pots and into others of the same size if they are in 6- or 7-in. pots (having first teased away some of the old soil). Use a compost consisting of 2 parts peat and 1 part sand, and feed once every 14 days during spring and summer.

Prepare supplies of John Innes Seed Compost now so that it is ready when required. The ingredients are 2 parts by bulk sterilised loam, 1 part granulated peat and 1 part coarse sand. To each bushel of this mixture add 1½ oz. of superphosphate of lime and ¾ oz. of either ground limestone or chalk.

Inserting chrysanthemum cuttings around the edge of a 3-in. pot of cutting compost with the aid of a dibber

To prolong the flowering period of *Azalea indica*, the dead flowers should be removed as soon as they fade

The well-known Cox's Orange Pippin apple, one of the most popular of all varieties. New fruit trees can be planted between November and March when conditions are favourable

January: third week

Order herbaceous perennials. Tie in raspberry canes. Remove canker wounds. Feed black currants. Prune gooseberries. Sow vegetables under cloches. Start to force pot-grown strawberries. Sow onions under glass. Prune fuchsias. Topdress vine borders.

FLOWERS

If the weather is open during February and the soil in a workable condition, it is a good month to plant many herbaceous perennials. This work should not be done later than March in any case, and plants should therefore be ordered now if they are to arrive in time. Of course, this does not apply to container-grown plants which can be planted at more or less any time of the year.

Useful plants for positions near the front of the border are *Sedum spectabile*, nepeta (both the ordinary form of catmint and the large variety known as Six Hills Giant), *Physostegia* Vivid, the dwarf forms of solidago, *Tradescantia* Leonora, *Veronica incana* and any of the varieties of *Dianthus allwoodii*.

If dahlia sites are prepared now, it will give any manure worked in at this time a chance to become really well incorporated with the soil before planting time in late spring. I know that this is a counsel of perfection, but it is certainly the way to get the best results. Dahlias are gross feeders and they like plenty of humus-forming material in the soil as well as bonemeal and hoof and horn meal.

Viburnum fragrans can be propagated this month or next by layering. Peg suitable low-growing branches down into the ground.

FRUIT

Tie in raspberry canes to the training wires. When this is done properly, they should not be closer together than 9 in. Where the tips of the canes are much higher than the top wire, cut them back to only a few inches above the wire. It is unwise to allow any plant to carry more than 5 ft. of cane.

Examine apple trees for canker wounds, and if any are seen cut out the affected bark and wood until clean tissue is reached. Then paint over with white lead or bitumastic paint. This treatment can only be carried out on fairly thick branches, and any thin stems showing signs of canker should be cut right out.

Black currants will benefit from a feeding of general, organic-based fertiliser used at the rate of 4 to 6 oz. to each established bush. Sprinkle it thinly on the soil and keep well away from the stems of the plants.

Now is a good time to prune goose-

Above: *Eranthis tubergenii*, the Winter Aconite, gives a welcome display from January to March. It likes a shady position

Below: Dwarf conifers, with their interesting shapes and colours, are decorative at all times but particularly in winter

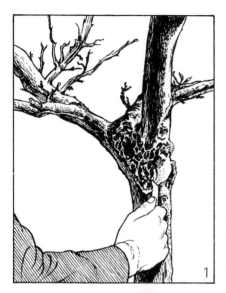

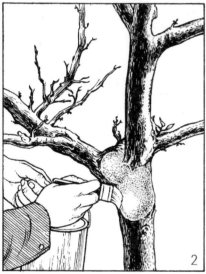

Removing canker from an apple tree. **1.** First, all the diseased bark and wood must be cut away with a sharp knife. **2.** When the wound is absolutely clean, it should be painted over with white lead or bitumastic paint to prevent further infection

berries, unless you live in an area which is subject to bird damage, in which case it would be better to wait until next month. Generally, a moderate thinning is all that is necessary, but further details are given on p. 37.

VEGETABLES
In sheltered districts, especially in the South and West, some seed can now be sown under cloches. Early sowings should include lettuces, carrots, radishes, onions, round-seeded peas and broad beans.

Clean away any dead or decaying leaves from winter lettuce as these, if left, may give the botrytis fungus a chance to start its work of decay. Lettuces in frames should also be picked over.

If you have a frame, sow seed of cauliflower, a quick-maturing variety of cabbage and some lettuces, all for planting out later on. Care should be taken to sow the seed thinly for overcrowding encourages damping off.

If the site of the onion bed has now been chosen, a lot of good can be done by pricking over the surface when it is dry. This will help when the time comes to make a good tilth in March in preparation for seed sowing. Onions appreciate bonfire ash, and if this is available, spread it over the bed now and fork in lightly. Also, a dressing of bonemeal sprinkled over the surface is beneficial.

GREENHOUSE
Strawberries in pots which have been in a cold frame until now should be brought into the greenhouse. Scrape away a little of the surface soil and replace it with a topdressing of John Innes No. 3 Potting Compost. The plants should then be stood on the staging or a shelf close to the glass where they will receive the maximum amount of light.

If onions have not already been sown in boxes for planting out later, do this as soon as possible. If seed was sown in December, the seedlings will probably be ready for pricking out into boxes of John Innes No. 1 Potting Compost. When onions are being grown for exhibition purposes it is better to prick out the seedlings singly at this stage into 3-in. pots for this way they can be transferred with the minimum of disturbance.

Do not sow tomato seed early unless a minimum temperature of 16°C. (60°F.) can be maintained. This may not be easy during late January or early February unless the house is very well heated.

Look over chrysanthemum cuttings and remove any leaves which are decaying. More cuttings can be inserted as suitable material becomes available.

Prune established fuchsias now. All side growths on standards must be cut hard back to within two or three buds of the main stem, and bushes should be cut back fairly severely too.

Tying in raspberry canes to their supporting wires. When properly trained, the canes should be spaced about 9 in. apart

Scraping away the surface soil from a pot-grown strawberry before adding a topdressing of fresh compost

Specimens of *Primula malacoides* can be moved into 5-in. pots if large plants are wanted.

Cuttings of perpetual-flowering carnations taken in December should have rooted by now and can be potted into 3-in. pots of John Innes No. 1 Potting Compost. Keep conditions cool – 7°C. (45°F.) is quite adequate. Ventilate freely to prevent the air becoming damp and stuffy.

Topdress vine borders with well-rotted manure and give each plant 6 oz. of bonemeal.

January: fourth week

Replant herbaceous borders. Protect sweet peas. Prune ornamental trees. Protect primulas from birds. Prune newly-planted fruit bushes. Protect peas and beans from mice. Make first greenhouse sowings. Repot fuchsias. Take cuttings of perpetual-flowering carnations.

FLOWERS

If some replanting is to be done in the herbaceous border, preparations should begin now. Those plants which are to be moved should be lifted and put on one side. If the clumps are placed close together and a little straw or some dead leaves are scattered over them they will keep in good condition for some time. The soil in the border can then be turned over to at least the depth of a spade, and manure, peat or compost worked in as digging proceeds. A good handful of bonemeal should be sprinkled along each yard of trench. This thorough preparation is well worth while because, once replanted, most herbaceous plants remain undisturbed for at least three years. I would make an exception in the case of Michaelmas daisies which I prefer to lift and divide into small pieces annually. I find that I get stronger and larger spikes by doing this and the plants are less susceptible to mildew attack.

If sweet peas were sown out of doors in the autumn, it may be wise to place cloches over them as a precaution against the possibility of severe weather which is often experienced at this time. If cloches are not available, twiggy pieces of stick pushed in along each side of the rows will provide some protection.

Violets in frames need full ventilation whenever this is possible.

Ornamental trees should be looked at carefully to see if any pruning is necessary. If so, this can be done now while they are dormant, but take care not to cut out wood that will bear flowers in spring or early summer.

The flowers of hardy primulas, such as

Primula denticulata and *P.* Wanda, are often damaged by birds and it is a good idea to protect these now while they are still in bud. Black cotton stretched across the plants is a good deterrent or, alternatively, they can be sprayed with a bird repellent. The same applies to polyanthus.

FRUIT

Newly planted black currants and raspberries should be pruned severely, the black currants to within 2 to 3 in. of the ground to encourage the production of strong growths from below ground level. If desired, young shoots removed when pruning can be inserted as hard-wood cuttings. Raspberries should be cut down to a prominent bud 6 to 9 in. above the ground.

In country districts bullfinches do a lot of damage to plums and damsons as the buds begin to swell. Unless something is done to check them the whole season's crop can be lost. It is very difficult to protect large trees, but bullfinches are rather shy birds and I find that they can often be scared away by tinfoil which rattles in the breeze. Foil milk bottle tops will make quite good bird scarers if threaded on black cotton. Alternatively, spray with a bird repellent.

Damsons, incidentally, make a very useful windbreak and can be planted on the east side of the garden. They should be grown as bush specimens or standards. The best variety for this purpose is Merryweather.

The buds on wall-trained peach trees in the South and in sheltered places in the West will soon begin to swell so spraying

Newly planted raspberries should be cut down to within about 9 in of the ground. Make the cut just above a prominent bud

and cleaning of the trees should be completed as quickly as possible. Use a winter spray for this purpose, preferably thiocyanate.

VEGETABLES

As soon as Brussels sprouts have been gathered, the stalks should be cleared from the ground, unless there is a shortage of purple-sprouting broccoli or kale. In this case, a few Brussels sprouts should be left to produce young shoots for gathering later on.

Do not be tempted to make outdoor sowings of vegetables too early. There is probably a good deal of hard weather ahead.

Mice often damage early-sown peas and

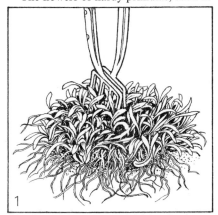

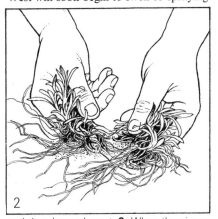

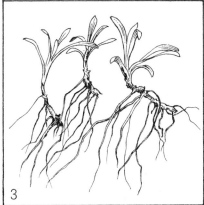

Dividing Michaelmas daisies. **1.** Large crowns should first be split up with the aid of two forks thrust into the clump back to back and then levered apart. **2.** When the pieces are a more manageable size they can be split up further with the hands. **3.** The single shoots can then be replanted, and will grow into strong, healthy plants

Above: *Primula kewensis*, a pretty plant for the cool greenhouse in spring. The flowers are fragrant and long lasting

Below: *Cyclamen persicum*, one of the most popular of greenhouse plants, is also very decorative in the home

beans. Trapping or poisoning now can prevent a lot of damage later on, but if poison is used it must be kept away from children, animals and birds. As a precaution, place the poison in a drainpipe or cover it in some way so that you can be reasonably sure that only the mice can get at it.

GREENHOUSE

Seed sowing of a few half-hardy and tender plants can begin if a seed raiser or small propagating frame is available in the greenhouse, but I, personally, prefer to wait until a little later. Do not be too impatient about seed sowing for if you have a cold house you will not gain anything by early sowing.

Repot fuchsias which were pruned earlier. I do this by shaking away all the old soil and then accommodating the plants in the smallest pots which will contain their roots. The plants are then moved on into larger pots as they make more growth.

Regal pelargoniums which are starting to grow may be potted on into pots which are one size larger than those they are in at the moment, provided their existing pots are well filled with roots. With fairly old plants I remove most of the old compost and repot them in new compost, using pots of the same size.

Take cuttings of perpetual-flowering carnations at any time between November and March, using short, non-flowering sideshoots for this purpose. Those from mid-way up the stems are best. Make the cuttings 3 to 4 in. long and cut cleanly at the base. Root in pure sand in a propagating frame with a temperature of 16°C. (60°F.).

Remove the dead leaves from pelargonium (geranium), fuchsia, heliotrope and coleus cuttings to prevent disease gaining a hold. Ventilate the greenhouse to keep the atmosphere buoyant.

Hydrangeas, which have been overwintering in the coolest part of the greenhouse, can now be moved to a warmer position to encourage the development of early flowers.

Watering should be carried out with particular care at this time of year, especially when plants are grown in plastic pots which hold water considerably longer than clay ones.

February: first week

Prune winter-flowering shrubs. Make and plant rock gardens. Prune cobnuts. Feed fruit trees. Prepare asparagus beds. Sow vegetables under cloches. Sow peas and beans in pots. Start dahlia tubers. Prune and repot pelargoniums.

FLOWERS

Winter-flowering shrubs should be pruned as soon as they finish flowering. The Winter-flowering Jasmine, *Jasminum nudiflorum*, is one shrub that benefits from such pruning, this attention preventing it from becoming straggly. Train in as many of the growths that have just finished flowering as are needed to cover the wall comfortably during the coming spring, and cut the remainder back to three or four buds so that they make strong young growths for flowering next winter. This is a splendid shrub for a north-facing wall, and the flowers can be cut for room decoration at a time of year when cut blooms are scarce.

Trim back winter-flowering heathers as the blooms fade to prevent them becoming too straggly. Shears should be used for this job.

This is a good time of year to make a small rock garden. An interesting home for alpine plants can be made with no more than six to eight stones of moderate size. These should be sited with care and the spaces between them filled with good soil – it is most important that it should be weed free – mixed with plenty of coarse grit and some peat. Never place such a rock garden under trees or in the shade but always in a sunny, open position. Good drainage is another necessity.

Dahlia tubers in store should be examined periodically, and if there is the slightest sign of mould on the stems or tubers they should be dusted with flowers of sulphur. Make sure that they are well protected against frost.

FRUIT

Cobnuts and filberts should be pruned now, the method being to thin out the branches to prevent the bushes becoming overcrowded. Remove all suckers coming up around the bushes also. These plants usually crop better if two or three are planted together for pollination purposes.

Morello cherries growing against walls should be trained in such a way that the growths are not overcrowded.

Fruit trees growing in grass often make little growth because they are starved of nitrogen. This can be remedied by feeding now with sulphate of ammonia or Nitro-

Below left: The graceful, male catkins of *Garrya elliptica*. **Below centre:** *Crocus tomasinianus*, with its delicate flowers in February and March, is especially suitable for the rock garden. **Above:** *Camellia japonica* Adolphe Audusson, an evergreen shrub for the garden or cool greenhouse. **Below right:** *Helleborus corsicus*, the Corsican Hellebore

Preparing the ground for an early sowing of vegetables. **1.** When sowing seeds a fine tilth is essential and this is achieved by

careful raking to break up the surface soil and remove any debris. **2.** When the soil is sufficiently fine, drills should be drawn out

with a hoe using a line as a guide. **3.** Seed should always be sown thinly because overcrowding will lead to weak plants

chalk. This should be applied at the rate of about 4 oz. per tree. In cultivated soil, apples and pears will, in most cases, benefit from a dressing of sulphate of potash applied at the same rate and time, but such trees rarely need any extra nitrogen.

VEGETABLES

Make preparations for planting asparagus. Do not forget that as this is a permanent crop, the ground must be really clean and should be deeply dug and well manured. This means digging to the depth of a spade and incorporating plenty of manure or compost, with a liberal dressing of bonemeal.

I think it is better to plant asparagus in single rows rather than in beds. Three-year-old crowns are usually advised, but I prefer to start with one-year-old crowns even though one has to wait a little longer for a full crop.

In the South and other sheltered areas and on light soils many seeds may now be sown under cloches. These include onions, carrots, peas, lettuces and radishes. The rows can be a little closer than they would be in the open, and in order still further to economise on space, carrots or peas can be sown down the centre with a row of lettuces or radishes on either side. These last will reach maturity and can be cleared well before the carrots or peas need the extra space.

Lift and divide rhubarb clumps.

GREENHOUSE

Now is the time to bring the stools of outdoor chrysanthemums into the greenhouse and give them warmth and all the light possible so that they make sturdy growths from which cuttings can be taken.

In cold areas, particularly in northern districts, where it is not possible to make early sowings out of doors, broad beans and peas can be sown in pots now for planting out later on. Sow three or four peas in each 3½-in. pot, but only sow one broad bean per pot.

Cuttings of heliotrope which were inserted during the autumn should now be in 3½-in. pots on a shelf near the glass and

Boxing up dahlia tubers in moist peat to start them into growth. Cuttings can be made from the shoots that will appear

making fresh growth. These young shoots will, in turn, be put in as cuttings for I find that spring-rooted cuttings make better plants for setting out in beds at the end of May. I like to plant them near a garden seat as they have a delightful scent on summer evenings. When rooted, pot the young plants singly into 3½-in. pots of John Innes No. 1 Potting Compost, and move them on into 5-in. pots as necessary. They are also good pot plants for the cool greenhouse.

If dahlias are to be raised from cuttings the tubers should be boxed up now and covered with moist peat. If they are placed in a warm greenhouse they soon throw up plenty of young shoots.

Spray fuchsias on warm, sunny days to encourage them to produce many young shoots. This, of course, applies to the established plants pruned and repotted a little earlier.

If the weather is mild and your greenhouse is warmed at night, schizanthus can be given a final move to 6- or 8-in. pots.

Cut back old pelargonium (geranium) plants, shortening the growths to a joint or bud 6 to 9 in. above the pot. The plants can then be repotted, shaking all the soil from the roots first and putting them into the smallest pots which will take the roots comfortably. Use John Innes No. 1 Potting Compost. If cuttings of pelargoniums taken last autumn were not potted up in November (see p. 116), these should be put into 3½-in. pots, using John Innes No. 1.

February: second week

Feed herbaceous plants. Plant lilies. Protect gooseberry bushes. Complete the planting of fruit trees and bushes. Topdress asparagus beds. Plant shallots. Feed spring cabbages. Divide herbs. Sow sweet peas and asparagus fern. Pot up indoor chrysanthemums.

FLOWERS

Established herbaceous plants which have not recently been lifted and divided will benefit from feeding. The ideal is to spread rotted manure or compost around the plants and lightly fork it in, but if this is not possible use a good general fertiliser. This last should be applied as the manufacturer directs, and the amount will probably work out at something like a tablespoonful to be sprinkled around each plant. The fertiliser should then be lightly stirred into the soil with a fork.

Scabiosa Clive Greaves and other varieties of Caucasian Scabious are among the best herbaceous plants to give a continuous supply of cut flowers throughout the summer and early autumn. I would certainly advise gardeners who have not tried them to order some now for spring planting. These plants love lime, and ground limestone should be worked into the soil before planting at the rate of 4 oz. to the square yard. The plants do not take too kindly to frequent transplanting, so I grow mine in three batches, lifting and dividing one batch each year.

Another group of herbaceous plants which make impressive cut flowers are the echinops or Globe Thistles. The best known is the 4-ft. *Echinops ritro* which gives a delightful display with its deep blue flowers in summer. The distinctive ball-like, prickly flower heads and the deeply cut foliage make this handsome plant

If manure or compost is not available, herbaceous plants should be fed with a good, general organic-based fertiliser,

immediately recognisable. The variety Taplow Blue is rather taller and with its bright blue flowers, even more garden worthy. All echinops need a deeply dug, well-prepared site for they form tap roots which delve down a long way into the soil. They also need to be left alone as long as possible after planting, like the Caucasian Scabious.

Also excellent for cutting are the perennial rudbeckias or Coneflowers. A striking one is *Rudbeckia speciosa*, which used to be known as *R. newmanii* and is still listed

applied according to the manufacturer's instructions. Afterwards, stir it lightly into the soil with a fork

as such in some catalogues. This is 2 to 3 ft. tall and has deep yellow petals around a purplish-black centre. The splendid *R. sullivantii* Goldsturm, with orange-yellow blooms, is only 1½ ft. tall.

A perennial for which I have a strong regard, and which is excellent as a cut flower is the dainty *Thalictrum dipterocarpum* Hewitt's Double. Its feather-light, violet-amethyst flowers, borne in branching panicles, are a lovely sight for this is a plant which grows 5 to 6 ft. tall.

Flowers for cutting are much in demand these days, and it is not only to the herbaceous plants one should look for suitable material. There are numerous shrubs which are splendid for this purpose, including forsythia, lilac, *Spiraea arguta* (sometimes known as Bridal Wreath) and *Choisya ternata* (the Mexican Orange Blossom). Many hardy annuals sown under cloches now will provide such flowers in early summer. Those I would especially recommend are larkspur, cornflower, godetia, calendula and helichrysum. Sweet pea seeds sown under cloches now will provide plants which will give cut flowers for late summer.

If lily bulbs were not available for planting in late autumn (see p. 109) they should be obtained now and planted when conditions are suitable. Full cultural instructions and a suggested choice of species and varieties are detailed on the page just referred to.

Before herbaceous plants start into growth again, they will benefit from a mulch of well-rotted manure or garden compost. Spread the mulch around the crowns, and then lightly fork it in, taking care not to go too deeply and damage the roots

Birds can play havoc with the buds on fruit bushes and trees and it is essential to protect them if a good crop is required. Small bushes, like gooseberries, can be well protected by completely covering them with netting

FRUIT

As the buds on gooseberry bushes begin to swell, they will become more attractive to bullfinches and other birds. They can be protected in various ways; for example, with a permanent fruit cage, or by covering the fruit bushes temporarily with fish netting, or by straining black thread from branch to branch over the bushes. I find that spraying with bird repellent also helps, but it must be repeated frequently.

The planting of fruit trees and bushes must be completed as soon as possible, before they start into growth.

Tar oil and DNOC winter washes must not be used on fruit once the buds begin to burst, though DNOC washes can be used with safety a little later than tar oil. If, for some reason, the time is missed for either of these sprayings it is still possible to use thiocyanate on the trees until well into March.

VEGETABLES

Asparagus beds should be cleaned ready for the spring growth. Rake the top inch or so of soil from the beds or rows, topdress with well-decayed manure or garden compost and then replace the soil on the surface. This work must be done before the crowns begin to grow, otherwise the brittle asparagus tips will be damaged.

In the South and in other sheltered areas where the soil is not heavy, shallots can be planted. Space the bulbs 6 to 9 in. apart in rows 12 in. apart, and barely cover them with soil. Later, they will work their way to the surface.

After frost, look over the spring cabbages, and firm any that have been loosened by movement in the soil. This is also a good time to feed the plants with a quick-acting nitrogenous fertiliser such as nitrate of soda. It will serve as a tonic and help to increase the rate of growth of the cabbages as the days begin to lengthen.

Herbs such as sage and thyme which have become too large can be divided by pulling the clumps apart to provide small pieces with roots attached for replanting. In some cold districts the tops of sage plants may be damaged or even killed by frost in a hard winter. When this happens the bushes should be cut down to within 9 in. or so of the ground and plenty of young shoots will grow up from the base. In fact, all established sage and thyme bushes will benefit from this treatment which will ensure that there is a continual supply of young shoots.

GREENHOUSE

On bright days the temperature of the greenhouse may rise rapidly, and more attention must now be paid to ventilation. On sunny days most plants which are in growth will benefit from a light overhead spray with clear water during the early part of the day. A hand sprayer should be used for this operation.

A sowing of sweet peas made now in the greenhouse will provide plants for flowering in the late summer.

Other seeds to sow now are *Asparagus sprengeri* and *A. plumosus*. Sow the seeds in a temperature of 18°C. (65°F.) and pot the resulting seedlings singly in 3-in. pots as soon as they can be handled. Move them on later to pots of 5- or 6-in. size. The John Innes No. 1 Potting Compost should be used. Seeds of these asparagus may be sown also in summer and autumn.

Cuttings of indoor chrysanthemums taken last month (see p. 25) should be well rooted and ready for potting up separately. Use 3-in. pots and the John Innes No. 1 Potting Compost. Afterwards, encourage sturdy growth by maintaining a temperature of 7°C. (45°F.).

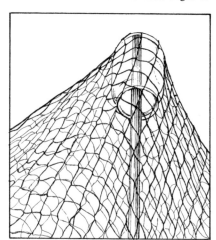

Netting placed over a framework of poles to protect fruit is easily kept in position by placing a jam jar over each pole

Sowing sweet peas for late-summer flowering. About five seeds should be placed in a 3½-in. pot

February: third week

Plant lilies-of-the-valley. Replace old shrubs. Prune buddleias. Protect apricot and peach flowers. Prune autumn-fruiting raspberries. Transplant autumn-sown onions. Sow peas. Lime vegetable garden. Take fuchsia and verbena cuttings. Sow lupins and delphiniums.

FLOWERS

Now is the time to fill any gaps in the wallflower bed before the plants begin to grow more actively. At the same time firm around plants which are already in beds and borders as some may have become loosened by frost.

There is still time to plant lilies-of-the-valley before the crowns start into growth. The roots should be spread out in wide, shallow holes so that they can be covered with about 1 in. of soil. Established beds of this plant can be top-dressed with compost or manure and fed with bonemeal at the rate of 4 oz. to the square yard.

Crocosmias – what we used to call montbretias – are often neglected and left to form such large clumps that they cannot give a good display of flowers. The newer and better varieties deteriorate very quickly under such conditions. Flowers will be of better quality and more numerous if the plants are lifted and divided into small portions every second year. This job should be done now. It should be realised that some of the better crocosmia varieties are not completely hardy in all parts of the country.

At this time of year I often remove old and poor shrubs so that their place can be taken by more worthy species and varieties. I am referring now to deciduous kinds, for evergreens are best planted between late March and May.

Among my choices might well be the 4-ft. *Berberis thunbergii* which bears pale yellow flowers in spring but whose main display is made in autumn when it is a picture with its scarlet berries and brilliant red foliage. Others which would be considered are the red-barked Dogwood, *Cornus alba*, which is such a cheerful sight in winter; a winter-flowering viburnum like the fragrant, white, tinted pale pink *V. fragrans* or the white-flowered *V. tinus*; a forsythia for spring, say the bright yellow *F. intermedia spectabilis*; the superb golden-yellow *Hypericum* Hidcote for July to August flowering; and varieties of *Hibiscus syriacus* for late summer flowering.

Correct planting is especially important with permanent subjects like shrubs which are going to remain in position for a very long time. The soil must be suitable, of course, and the hole should be of the right depth and large enough to accommodate the roots at their full spread. So far as the planting depth is concerned, it is best to be guided by the soil mark on the stem for this will indicate the depth at which the plant was growing previously in the nursery. Try to plant at exactly the same level. It also pays to cut off cleanly with sharp secateurs any broken or damaged roots before actually planting to avoid any chance of later die-back which could give disease a ready entry.

In the South, the purple-flowered *Buddleia davidii* and its numerous varieties in other colours should be pruned at this time. In the Midlands and North, however, it is advisable to wait until the end of March before doing this job. This is a shrub which it pays to prune severely, and the branches can be cut back to within $1\frac{1}{2}$ to 2 ft. of ground level. A feed with a

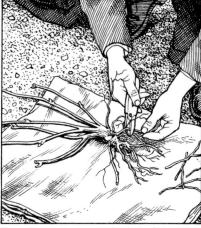

Sometimes when new shrubs arrive one or two of the roots are damaged. These should be cut away cleanly before planting

general, organic-based fertiliser after pruning will be beneficial.

Buddleias of this kind flower from the beginning of July until October and they make large plants up to 12 ft. tall and as much across in many cases. This means that they need to be left plenty of space to develop properly.

FRUIT

In the warmer parts of the country, particularly in the South, the first flowers will now be showing on apricots, peaches and nectarines trained against sheltered walls. These should be given some protection against night frost. Two or three thicknesses of garden netting, or net curtains draped over the trees, will give sufficient protection, but even better is hessian,

When planting shrubs and trees it is particularly important to make sure that the planting hole is sufficiently large to accommodate the roots easily. Notice how they are spread out carefully before filling in with soil

Severe pruning of *Buddleia davidii* will be well repayed in the summer by a beautiful display of fragrant flowers

Lifting and replanting autumn-sown onions. **1.** The seedlings should not be left for too long in the crowded seed rows or they will become drawn and spindly. **2.** When replanting, space the seedlings 9 in. apart in rows 15 in. apart

which must be rolled back by day to admit light and allow the flowers to be pollinated.

Autumn-fruiting raspberries must be pruned now, all canes being cut back practically to ground level. Lloyd George can be treated as an autumn-fruiting variety if so desired, or, of course, it can be grown for a summer crop. If this is the case, the canes made last year should not be cut back but only lightly tipped at a height of about 5 ft.

VEGETABLES

Where early sowings have been made under cloches watch out for slug damage, which can be severe at this time of year, especially if the weather is mild. Slug bait should be put along the rows under the cloches.

Autumn-sown onions should be transplanted carefully to the place in which they will mature. This should be an open position, the ground having previously been well dug and manured or treated with compost. Plant the onions at least 9 in. apart in rows 15 in. apart.

Continue to plant shallots as soil and weather conditions permit. A deeply dug soil with good drainage is essential for this crop, and although the soil needs to contain plenty of plant food it should not have been recently manured. Ideally, one wants soil which has been manured for the previous crop. The site should also be open to the sun. For further details on cultivation see p. 34.

Much the same kind of site is needed by garlic. The soil should be well drained, but need not be quite so rich as for shallots. Plant the bulbs 2 in. deep and 6 in. apart in rows 8 in. apart. This is a useful plant to grow between other crops. Garlic is only used in small quantities, but even so it is well worth growing.

Round-seeded peas can be sown now in a sheltered border. All peas need a rich soil which has been well prepared and well manured.

One third of the vegetable garden should be limed each year and this job should be completed before the end of February. Apply hydrated lime at the rate of 4 to 6 oz. to the square yard – but not when potatoes are to be planted for this encourages scab, the disease which one can recognise immediately by the brown, flaky scabs which form on the tubers.

GREENHOUSE

Early onion seedlings raised under glass should now be pricked out into boxes of John Innes No. 1 Potting Compost. These should be spaced 3 in. apart each way to allow them plenty of room to develop properly.

Cuttings made from the young growths on fuchsias and inserted now will root quickly and make good plants for greenhouse decoration or for planting out of doors at the end of May. Dip the ends of the cuttings in hormone rooting powder and insert them in sandy soil around the edge of a 3-in. pot. Then place them in a warm propagating frame until roots have formed.

There are two verbena varieties which I value greatly for use in hanging baskets and window-boxes, for bedding and for growing as specimen plants in pots. These are the bright scarlet Lawrence Johnston and the pale blue Loveliness. I keep a few plants of each for stock, and hundreds of cuttings can be obtained from the growths on these and rooted during the spring. They will form roots in a matter of three or four weeks and can then be potted up individually.

Lupins and delphiniums can be grown from seed sown in the greenhouse now. Such plants will come into flower in August or September. Plants raised in this way are very vigorous and there are many improved strains to choose from.

Continue to pot up cuttings of indoor chrysanthemums as they become sufficiently well rooted (see p. 34).

Preparing fuchsia cuttings. **1.** A clean cut should be made just below a node or leaf joint using a razor blade or sharp penknife.

2. After dipping the cuttings in hormone rooting powder they should be inserted around the edge of a 3-in. pot

February: fourth week

Prune willows and dogwoods. Spray roses for black spot. Prune fig trees. Spray peach trees against leaf curl. Sow Brussels sprouts, cabbages, leeks, lettuces and radishes. Start achimenes. Sow gloxinias and tuberous begonias. Reduce vine shoots. Feed schizanthus.

FLOWERS

If the weather is mild, the spring flowers will already be opening. How welcome they are. In my Shropshire garden the snowdrops are often out by the middle of January. *Primula* Wanda is another early gem and some of the other primulas, such as *P. rosea* and *P. denticulata* and the common primrose (*P. vulgaris*), show their first flowers at this time.

One of the best late-summer shrubs is the creamy-flowered *Hydrangea paniculata*, and this species is, in fact, much more suitable for exposed gardens than the more commonly grown Hortensia varieties. The reason for this is that, unlike Hortensia hydrangeas, *H. paniculata* carries its flowers on wood made in the current season, so there is no fear of the flower buds being damaged by frost. To encourage strong growth carrying large panicles of bloom, prune hard back now in a similar way to the purple buddleia I referred to last week (see p. 35). Larger bushes with smaller heads of flowers are produced if the plants are left unpruned.

Shrubs such as the Common Dogwood and the red- and yellow-twigged willows which are grown for the colour of their young stems are also best pruned hard back each year to encourage strong young growth and now is the time to do this work. The prunings can be used as hard-wood cuttings, and if inserted outdoors in a sheltered place they will soon form roots and begin to grow.

If roses were attacked by black spot in previous years, remove any dead leaves

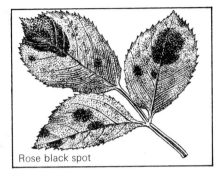
Rose black spot

that may still be lying around on the surface of the beds and then spray thoroughly with a copper fungicide to kill the resting spores. A spray can be made up with copper sulphate (1 oz. of this to 1 gallon of water) and the plants and the soil beneath them duly treated. The affected leaves which have been collected should be burnt to ensure that the fungal spores are destroyed.

Already lawn grass will be showing signs of new growth, and it will not be long before the mowing season is back again. Rake or sweep the lawn to scatter worm casts if this was not done last month.

FRUIT

If gooseberries were not pruned earlier for fear of bird damage to the buds, this should be done now before growth is too advanced. Bushes should be shaped as they are pruned and generally only a light thinning is necessary after dead, diseased and crossing branches have been removed. Trained gooseberries should be spur pruned, in other words all young side growths should be cut back to two or three buds.

Fig trees trained on walls outside can also be pruned. Cut out some branches of the old wood and train in the long, young branches. Make sure that the fan shape is maintained.

Cuttings of black, red and white currants and gooseberries put in during the autumn may need firming if they have been lifted by frost.

Outdoor peaches and nectarines should be sprayed with a copper fungicide as a protection against leaf curl.

VEGETABLES

Established asparagus plants should be fed now with agricultural salt at the rate of 2 oz. to the square yard.

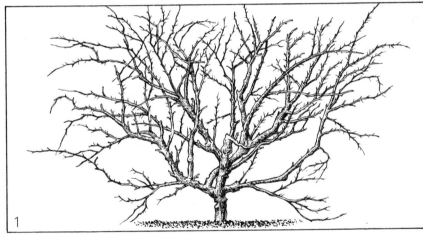

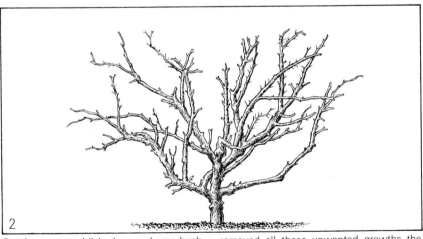

Pruning an established gooseberry bush. **1.** Before pruning, the bush is a mass of growths, with some branches touching the ground, some rubbing against others, and some, possibly, dead or diseased. **2.** Having removed all these unwanted growths the remaining branches can either be lightly tipped, or, as is shown in this illustration, spur pruned. In this case, the side growths are cut back to two or three buds

Chives make a useful substitute for spring onions in the salad bowl and now is a good time to divide and replant them. They will grow well in any ordinary garden soil in a sunny position. If the site chosen is close to the kitchen door, so much the better.

In a sheltered border you can now sow Brussels sprouts and early cabbages as well as making a first sowing of leeks.

Lettuces and radishes can also be sown outside when the weather is favourable and the soil is dry enough to form a good seed bed. Alternatively, cloches may be used to produce these conditions.

It is not easy to obtain pea sticks nowadays, but if you do possess some get these ready for later use. Plastic netting, which is, of course, very long lasting, makes a good alternative.

Radishes are often sown between rows of Brussels sprouts and broad beans as they are quick to mature and a useful catch crop. Make the drills about $\frac{1}{2}$ in. deep and sow thinly, pulling the roots as required. They should not need to be thinned.

GREENHOUSE

Freesias which finished flowering some weeks ago can now be laid on their sides in their pots to dry off.

Small, scaly tubers of achimenes should be removed from the dry soil in which they have overwintered and a few may be potted for early flowering. I like to start them into growth in pots or boxes using a mixture of moist peat and sand. The tubers should be pushed gently into the compost and given a temperature of 13 to 16°C. (55 to 60°F.) to encourage growth to start. When the young shoots appear pot them up into 5- or 6-in. pots, spacing the plants 2 to 3 in. apart. Use the John Innes No. 1 Potting Compost.

The Scarlet Lobelia, *Lobelia cardinalis*,

Two ways of supporting peas. On the left, the traditional method of twiggy pea sticks is used, and on the right a more modern method using netting is shown. As pea sticks become increasingly difficult to obtain, netting makes a good alternative

can be potted now. I prefer to pull away single shoots with roots attached and to pot these separately in 3½-in. pots. Each plant will then produce a strong single spike in the summer with flowers almost throughout its length.

Seeds of antirrhinums, salvias, ageratums, lobelias and petunias should now be sown but I prefer to leave the sowing of the general run of half-hardy annuals—such as French and African Marigolds, annual phlox, stocks and asters – until the end of March or early April.

Sow seed of tuberous begonias and gloxinias if you prefer to increase these plants this way rather than by the easier way from tubers. Seeds sown now will provide flowering plants by mid-summer. Sow these in pots or pans filled with seed compost and cover the very small seeds with sand rather than compost. Germinate the seeds in a propagating frame with a temperature of 18 to 21°C. (65 to 70°F.). Sow seed, too, of *Begonia semperflorens* and germinate in a temperature of 16°C. (60°F.).

Young shoots on Lorraine begonias kept in warm conditions can now be removed and made into cuttings. Trim the base of each cutting just below a leaf joint with a sharp knife or razor blade, and root several cuttings round the edge of a 3-in. pot. A suitable rooting mixture consists of 1 part loam, 2 parts moist peat and 3 parts coarse sand. Water the cuttings well and place in a propagating frame with a temperature of 18°C. (65°F.).

Young shoots on vines should be reduced to one or two per spur. When the shoots are 2 to 3 in. long the rods, which were

lowered in December (see p. 123), should be tied back in position against the side of the greenhouse.

If clivias have not been repotted for several years this can be done now, but over-potting is something to be avoided with this flower and the plants should only be given larger pots when this is essential. Use the John Innes No. 1 Potting Compost when repotting, and if new plants are wanted, the crowns can be divided at this stage.

As schizanthus become well established in their final pots, feed them once a fortnight with weak liquid manure or very small doses of a general fertiliser watered well in. All feeding of pot plants should be done sparingly. Fertiliser should never be given to pot plants when the soil is dry or the roots will be scorched; first water and then apply the fertiliser. Most plants which have begun to make growth can also be fed once a fortnight.

Peach leaf curl

After flowering, freesias should be allowed to die down and rest. This is facilitated if the pots are laid under the staging

March: first week

Divide snowdrops. Plant herbaceous perennials and hardy cyclamen. Pollinate peach and apricot trees. Sow onions, parsnips and broad beans. Stop schizanthus and fuchsias. Take dahlia cuttings. Start begonia and gloxinia tubers. Take outdoor chrysanthemum cuttings.

FLOWERS

Early March is a good time of year to have a pair of secateurs handy in the pocket when one is in the garden for there are a number of shrubs which need pruning now. I have already mentioned the purple buddleia and *Hydrangea paniculata*; another good late-flowering shrub which loses much of its attractiveness unless it is pruned each spring is *Caryopteris clandonensis*. All last year's flowering branches should be pruned back now to within an inch or so of the point from which growth started in the previous year.

Unlike so many other bulbous-rooted plants, snowdrops can be lifted and divided as soon as the flowers fade. There is no advantage in waiting until the foliage has died down. It is advisable to lift and re-plant in this way every few years for if the bulbs are too close together many may fail to flower.

Oil and grease the lawn mower ready for

If snowdrops have become overcrowded, they should be lifted and divided as soon as flowering has finished

the mowing season which will soon be starting. Make sure that the blades are really sharp and correctly adjusted. A good test for both is to place a piece of paper between the blades and the bottom plate. When the blades are revolved, the paper should be cut through cleanly.

Herbaceous perennials may be planted now. Always plan your borders before you begin planting, and plant in groups so that you obtain the maximum colour effect.

If Brompton stocks have been over-wintered in a cold frame they should be bedded out now.

This is a good time to plant the corms of such lovely autumn-flowering cyclamen as *Cyclamen neapolitanum*. These grow particularly well under a beech or oak tree for they like cool, shady conditions.

FRUIT

Peach, nectarine and apricot trees growing on walls will now be in flower in many parts of the country. If the weather is cold and windy, there will be few insects air-borne to pollinate the flowers. In former years gardeners usually pollinated the flowers by hand with the aid of a rabbit's tail tied to the end of a cane, but rabbit tails have become rather scarce and it may now be necessary to do the work with a camel-hair brush.

There is still time to spray apple and pear trees with thiocyanate winter wash if tar oil or DNOC washes were not used during January or February.

If fruit trees have been ordered make quite sure that the site for each one has been prepared for planting. Nothing is more harmful to trees and bushes at this

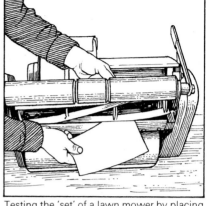
Testing the 'set' of a lawn mower by placing a piece of paper between the blades and the bottom plate

time of year than getting their roots dry, so even if you cannot plant them take off the straw wrappings, soak the roots and cover these with soil or wet sacks until planting can be carried out.

VEGETABLES

In the southern counties and in many parts of the Midlands sowing in the vegetable garden can now begin in earnest, particularly on the lighter soils which dry and warm up so much more quickly than heavy soils. It is all a question of watching the soil and the weather carefully and seizing the first opportunity to do this when conditions are right. The soil must be sufficiently dry to work easily with a rake and it must not stick to the boots.

First sowings of onions, parsnips and broad beans may now be made.

The preparation of the seed bed itself is an important job, particularly for onions. If the soil was dug over during the winter

Planting up an herbaceous border. Young plants or divisions from older plants are put into well-prepared ground with a trowel. For the best effect, they should be planted in groups rather than individually

Hand pollinating peach blossom with the aid of a camel-hair brush to ensure a good crop of fruit

and left rough to expose as much of the area as possible to frost, it should crumble down easily and there should be little difficulty in obtaining the fine tilth which is the hallmark of a good seed bed. It is important to tread the bed well and to make certain that it is firm all over. Finish off by raking to provide a fine tilth and level surface. Every good gardener takes a pride in the preparation of seed beds and looks with real pleasure at one which has been well made. Sow the onion seed in drills 1 ft. apart. Later the plants will be thinned to about 6 in. apart in the rows.

In the case of parsnips it is most economical and saves time in thinning later on if three or four seeds are dropped into the drill at intervals of 9 to 12 in. If parsnips are being grown for exhibition it is better to bore holes 2 ft. or more deep. Each hole is filled with a mixture of well-riddled soil, sand and peat and two or three seeds are then sown at each prepared point. Sow broad beans in drills 3 in. deep and 2 ft. apart and set the seeds 4 to 6 in. apart in the rows.

Horseradish is grown from 6-in. lengths of root dropped into 9-in. deep holes so that the tops are 3 in. below the surface. These holes should be 1 ft. apart each way. Be careful, though, to put the horseradish in a place where it can be easily kept under control for it is very vigorous.

Jerusalem artichokes are useful plants for screening the compost heap or garden

Preparing a seed bed before sowing vegetables. After breaking down the large lumps of soil, the ground should be firmed evenly by treading. Fertiliser is then applied and raked in until a fine, level tilth is obtained

shed and their 6-ft. tall stems will also make a good windbreak in an exposed garden. Sometimes they produce large, yellow, sunflower-like blooms which are an added attraction. Plant the tubers 15 in. apart and 3 in. deep in rows 3 ft. apart. They will grow almost anywhere, and are especially suitable in soil that is not rich enough for potatoes.

GREENHOUSE
Schizanthus plants will need stopping again to encourage a branching habit.

Fuchsias which were pruned earlier should now be making several growths. To ensure that you obtain bushy plants, or, if you have standard specimens, that they have fine heads, pinch the tip out of each shoot when it has produced four to six pairs of leaves. If standard fuchsias are required for planting out later on, this tipping also enables them to stand up to wind much better than if the shoots were allowed to grow long without being stopped.

The sun will be gaining warmth and on bright days it will be necessary to damp the pots and staging and to spray growing plants overhead. This will provide the moist atmospheric conditions that plants need if they are to grow well.

If coleus plants are to be grown from seed, this can be sown now. Germinate in a propagating frame with a temperature of 16 to 18°C. (60 to 65°F.).

Dahlia cuttings can be prepared, as well as soft-wood cuttings of many other plants including coleus, heliotrope and verbena. All will root readily in a sandy compost in a warm propagating frame.

A few tubers of begonias and gloxinias should now be started into growth. Press them into boxes filled with moist peat and sand well mixed together, and grow them on in a moist atmosphere.

Young plants of indoor chrysanthemums in 3-in. pots may now be moved to a frame if space is at a premium. It is certainly an advantage if the frame is heated, but if not it must be covered on cold nights with some kind of protective material such as straw or sacking. Watch the watering carefully, and if the weather turns cold keep the soil rather dry.

It is best to raise new plants of *Solanum capsicastrum* from seed annually and this is a good time to make a sowing. Sow the seeds as evenly as possible in small pots of seed compost. Cover the seeds with a very thin layer of fine compost and then place a sheet of glass over the pots. A temperature of 16 to 18°C. (60 to 65°F.) is needed for germination and when this has taken place the glass should be removed.

Sow seed of Brussels sprouts in a frame or cool greenhouse.

Now is the time to take cuttings of outdoor chrysanthemums. They should be rooted in exactly the same way as those of indoor varieties.

Removing the straw packing from fruit trees. If conditions are unsuitable for planting they should be heeled in temporarily

March: second week

Sow hardy annuals. Prune large-flowered clematis. Feed lawns. Feed raspberries, loganberries, blackberries and strawberries. Prepare celery trenches. Sow summer and autumn cabbages. Feed pot-grown hydrangeas. Stop mid-season chrysanthemums. Sow tomatoes.

FLOWERS

During the next few weeks hardy annuals of all kinds should be sown where they are to flower. Later on the seedlings will have to be thinned out according to their type. The soil must be in ideal condition for sowing, that is, it should be drying on the surface and sufficiently crumbly to allow it to be raked down to a fine tilth. There will, of course, be small differences in sowing times depending on the district and the kind of soil which has to be coped with.

When sowing annuals in a border I first mark off irregular-sized patches with a cane and place a label in each patch with the name of the plant which is to occupy it. I then sprinkle the seed thinly over the allotted area and lightly rake it in.

Nasturtiums are one of the many hardy annuals which give such a colourful display during the summer months. Sow the seed now, and remember that the double varieties are best as they do not seed themselves and become a nuisance. Dwarf Double Gleam is one to consider.

The new shoots of some of the earlier-flowering herbaceous plants are now ready for thinning. In most cases they can be reduced to between five and eight shoots per clump, but common sense must be used here for much will depend on the size and age of the plants as well as on their precise nature.

Bulbs which have finished flowering indoors may either be tipped out of their pots and bowls and heeled in or they can be planted out between shrubs or in other positions where they can grow permanently.

Large-flowered clematis, such as *Clematis jackmanii* and the many hybrids derived from it, should be pruned at this time, and all are better for being cut back quite severely. I shorten mine to within 2 to 2½ ft. of the ground each year, cutting back to good, well-developed buds.

Lawns should now be fed with a general, organic-based fertiliser applied at the rate of about 2 oz. to the square yard. Follow the manufacturer's instructions and spread evenly over the surface.

FRUIT

Where fruit trees have recently been planted in grass, be careful to keep a clean, cultivated area of 2 to 3 ft. around the trunks. If this precaution is not taken the trees will suffer from lack of nitrogen and will make little new growth.

Plums and damsons will now be coming into flower in many gardens. When these and the blackthorn in the hedges show their first white flowers, country folk take it as a sign of a cold spell which they call blackthorn winter. Gardeners, however, hope to escape this as it may make all the difference between a good and a poor damson and plum crop.

Feed raspberries, loganberries and blackberries now with a general, organic-

Applying lawn fertiliser with a distributor. Such a tool makes the even application of fertilisers a relatively easy job

based garden fertiliser at the rate of 4 oz. to each plant. Keep the fertiliser away from the stems of the plants or they may be scorched.

A good general fertiliser can also be sprinkled between the rows of strawberries and around the plants, but again be careful to keep it off the leaves and crowns. While doing this, clean up the bed by picking off any dead leaves and then prick over the surface lightly with a fork.

VEGETABLES

In the South and in sheltered places elsewhere it is worth the risk of planting a few early potatoes. It is possible that later on their first shoots may be cut by late spring frosts, but that is a chance one is prepared to take. I am particularly fond of the old variety Sharpe's Express which may not be as heavy a cropper as some other varieties but which does have an excellent flavour. I do not think that it pays to plant a lot of potatoes in a small garden, but it is certainly worth while growing a few earlies so that they come in when new potatoes are expensive.

Prepare celery trenches making them 1½ ft. wide with 3 ft. between the trenches. Do not make them so deep that the celery has to be planted in the cold subsoil. Break up the soil deeply by all means, but leave the finished trench 6 to 8 in. below the surface of the ground. Work in plenty of well-rotted manure or compost, for celery

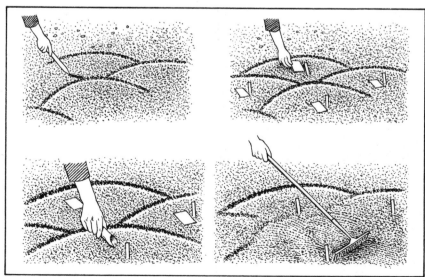

When sowing an annual border it is best to mark out the design first with a pointed stick. Seeds can then be allocated to each area, and, after sprinkling them lightly over the surface, they should be raked in

is a plant which likes plenty of humus to hold moisture.

The root cuttings of seakale which were prepared in October can now be planted. Drop the cuttings, slanting end first, into dibber holes and cover them with about $\frac{1}{2}$ in. of soil. Space the cuttings 1 ft. apart in rows 18 in. apart.

Broad beans and peas started in pots or boxes indoors should now be hardened off for planting out in a week or two's time.

Sow seeds now of summer and autumn cabbages such as Winningstadt and Primo.

GREENHOUSE

Pot on young cyclamen plants sown last June into 4-in. pots. Afterwards, they should be housed in a cool greenhouse.

If onions have been raised in boxes for planting out a little later on, keep the soil stirred between the plants with a pointed stick or label. Onions, perhaps more than any other plant, appreciate this treatment.

Sweet peas which have been raised in the greenhouse should now be hardened off.

Hydrangeas growing in pots should be fed from now on with weak liquid manure. Give them this at intervals of ten days to a fortnight instead of water, but of course, continue normal watering at other times.

As soon as fuchsia cuttings have rooted pot them up separately into 3-in. pots. Use either the John Innes No. 1 Potting Compost or a soilless compost for this purpose. When the plants are about 6 in. tall, pinch out the growing tips to encourage the plants to make bushy growth.

Seeds of pansies, violas and polyanthus may be sown now under glass.

Some cuttings of indoor chrysanthemums, already well rooted and potted, will be in need of their first stopping. For general decorative purposes, I stop all the mid-season varieties during the middle of March and again in the middle of June.

Bring pot-grown lilies which have been overwintered in a garden frame into the greenhouse. These will have had their pots only half filled with compost originally, and they should now be topdressed with fresh compost to within $\frac{1}{2}$ in. of the rims. Start to feed these plants in a week or so with a liquid fertiliser and continue once a week until they are showing flower buds.

Tomato seed should be sown now. A minimum temperature of 16°C. (60°F.) is essential for good germination.

Above: The pretty, star-like flowers of *Anemone blanda* appear in March and April. These plants are ideal for the rock garden

Below: *Chaenomeles speciosa* Knap Hill Scarlet, with its waxy flowers, is especially attractive when trained on a sunny wall

March: third week

Prune, spray and feed roses. Plant gladiolus corms. Remove protection from alpines. Mulch wall-trained fruit. Spray black currants. Sow leeks and carrots. Feed winter lettuces. Feed annuals in pots. Divide ferns. Pot up outdoor chrysanthemum cuttings.

FLOWERS

I am sufficiently old-fashioned to believe that late March is the proper time to prune hybrid tea roses, despite what others may say about the advantages of winter pruning. In fact, it is around this date that I begin my own pruning. If fine exhibition flowers are needed, prune severely, cutting all strong young growths back to three or four buds from the position where growth started last spring. For general garden purposes it is not necessary to prune so hard as this and good shoots may be left with five or six buds, only the weaker ones being cut back to two or three.

The floribundas can be pruned fairly lightly in a similar manner to hybrid teas being grown for garden display. Climbing roses on walls should have their side branches or laterals cut back to within two buds of the main stems, but these may have been pruned already.

All newly planted bushes being pruned for the first time should be cut back to within 6 or 8 in. of the ground. This is important both with hybrid teas and floribundas as an initial hard pruning

encourages strong growth the first year. In fact, ultimate success depends upon it.

Where rose bushes have been neglected for several years or even lightly pruned for so long that they have acquired a lot of hard old wood, some drastic thinning out may be needed, but do not expect to get good new growth from stumps of this old, hard wood. The best of the young growth should be retained and shortened, but a little more severely than formerly.

After pruning the rose bushes, spray them immediately with one of the fungicides especially recommended for dealing with black spot. If this disease has been troublesome it is best to scrape off the top $\frac{1}{2}$ in. or so of soil and replace this either with fresh soil or with peat. It is also a good time to feed roses with bonemeal applied at the rate of a handful per bush or with a fertiliser having a fairly high phosphate content. Alternatively, one of the special rose fertilisers containing magnesium may be used, or just a general fertiliser.

Plant some gladiolus corms for early flowering. Spread the planting period over the next six weeks or so to provide con-

tinuity. The corms should be planted 3 to 4 in. deep. On heavy soils put a layer of sand at the bottom of each planting hole. This will improve drainage and greatly lessen the possibility of the corms rotting.

Remove the panes of glass which were placed over choice alpines for protection last autumn.

FRUIT

This is the time to mulch wall-trained fruit trees and all newly planted fruit trees with compost, very strawy manure or even straw. On no account use wet, sticky manure for this purpose.

Where trees are planted against a wall, it is wise to remember that the soil in which they are growing often becomes drier than one imagines – even in rainy weather. Watch this situation carefully all through the summer and water freely when necessary.

Black currants should be sprayed with malathion when the most forward of the young leaves are about an inch across. The purpose of this spraying is to kill big bud mites.

One of the loveliest of spring-time flowers for the rock garden is *Pulsatilla vulgaris*, the Pasque Flower. The foliage, too, is particularly attractive with its silvery, down-like hairs and rather feathery appearance

The brightly coloured flowers of *Abutilon* Fireball which hang like bells from slender branches, are produced throughout the year

VEGETABLES

As soon as soil conditions allow sow maincrop leeks, if necessary using cloches to assist in getting the seed bed into a sufficiently dry condition.

In sheltered borders or where the soil is light, stump-rooted carrots can be sown now. Continue to do so at intervals throughout the season as a catch crop.

Pelleted seeds are becoming more and more widely available and their great advantage is that they make accurate placement very easy, thus cutting down or eliminating altogether the need for thinning the resulting seedlings. Particularly useful in pelleted form are carrots and lettuces.

Give winter lettuces a little general garden fertiliser to hurry their growth along, but be very careful to keep this off the leaves. Do not use more than 2 oz. to each yard of row and hoe it in afterwards.

GREENHOUSE

Annuals sown during the autumn for flowering in pots are now growing rapidly and will benefit from weekly feeding.

Staking and tying needs attention, in particular with salpiglossis, clarkias, schizanthus, calceolarias and godetias.

Gloriosas may now be repotted and started into growth. I grow three or four bulbs in each 8- or 9-in. pot. The John Innes No. 2 Potting Compost is very satisfactory for this purpose and the bulbs

should be set 2 in. deep. These plants really need a temperature of 21°C. (70°F.) to grow well and freely but can be grown at 16°C. (60°F.). I train them up strings or wires.

If a temperature of 16°C. (60°F.) is available at night, sow seeds of verbena, nicotiana and thunbergia. Freesias, too, can be sown but they need a temperature of 18°C. (65°F.).

Pelargonium (geranium) cuttings which were potted into 3½-in. pots last September should be moved on now into 5- or 6-in. pots. When the plants are 6 to 8 in. tall pinch out the tips of the shoots to encourage a bushy habit.

Young plants of perpetual-flowering carnations should be potted on into 5-in. pots, using the John Innes No. 1 Potting Compost, as soon as the small pots in which they are growing are well filled with roots. Keep the plants in a light, airy and cool place for they do not relish a lot of heat. When the plants have produced about eight pairs of leaves, their tips should be pulled out to encourage sideshoots to develop, giving a well-shaped plant.

Ferns such as the popular pteris and the Maidenhair Fern can be repotted now and started into growth by placing them at the warm end of the greenhouse. If the plants are becoming quite large they can be divided before repotting.

Asparagus ferns, *Asparagus plumosus*

Supporting the flowering stems of a calceolaria. The canes should slope outwards to open up the growth of the plant

and *A. sprengeri*, can also be divided by cutting the growths apart with a sharp knife. Pot each piece separately in a 5-in. pot using the John Innes No. 1 Potting Compost. Remember that although these plants are called ferns, they do not in fact belong to the same family.

As the cuttings of outdoor chrysanthemums develop a good root system, they should be potted up singly in 3-in. pots of John Innes No. 1 Potting Compost. Give them cool, light conditions so that growth is sturdy.

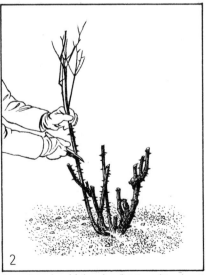

Pruning an old hybrid tea rose. **1.** Before pruning, there are a lot of thin, weak shoots which should be removed. **2.** The main branches should then be shortened to about a third of their length. In each case, the cut should be made just above an outward pointing bud. **3.** Pruning completed. Note that the old woody stumps from the centre of the plant have been removed

March: fourth week

Sow pansies and violas. Prune early-flowering shrubs. Sow sweet peas. Graft fruit trees. Spray pears against scab. Plant potatoes and mint. Sow peas and parsnips. Plant onion sets. Sow greenhouse primulas. Take coleus cuttings. Sow half-hardy annuals.

FLOWERS

Pansies or violas can now be sown out of doors in a nursery bed. They will be sufficiently mature to flower during the late summer and again next year and are excellent as an edging to rose beds.

The popular Japonica (*Chaenomeles speciosa*) is one of those shrubs which should be pruned when flowering has finished. When grown as a bush in the open it requires little or no pruning, but if it is planted as a wall shrub it is necessary to keep it in shape.

The fragrant *Daphne mezereum* is a spring flowering shrub which should not be pruned as it dislikes cutting of any kind. This shrub has a life span of about eight to ten years and then has to be replaced. It does not like root disturbance, so young, pot-grown specimens should be bought. Plants are raised from seed rather than cuttings.

Penstemons overwintering in frames should be given full ventilation now.

Autumn-sown annuals may need thinning and after this twiggy sticks can be put round them or along each side of the rows for support.

In the South and in other mild places sweet peas can be sown out of doors.

Violets may now be increased by division. It is best to divide the plants into pieces with two or three crowns, but do not use small, weak pieces for replanting. Plant the divisions in a shaded nursery bed. When carrying out this division it is a good idea to dip the plants into a solution of insecticide to kill greenfly. Watch carefully for aphids throughout the summer and spray whenever necessary.

FRUIT

Young fruit stocks or old fruit trees that are to be top grafted with a new variety should be grafted as soon as the sap is rising freely, so watch now for the swelling and bursting of the buds. Many old trees can be given a renewed period of usefulness by top grafting with a better variety. Cut the main branches back to stumps and insert the new scions.

Pears are already coming into flower in some districts, and in other more backward places they should be given their pre-blossom spraying with lime sulphur or captan as a preventive for scab. Derris or BHC may be given with either of these sprays if there is any suspicion that caterpillars or aphids are active.

I know that there are people who feel that the hygiene so much talked about is not absolutely vital to the good health of the trees, but there is no doubt that one can be far more certain of a cleaner and better crop if this routine spraying is carried out.

VEGETABLES

Plant more potatoes, still giving preference to the early varieties.

This is a good time to start new mint beds or to replant old ones. Such beds are best remade once every two years, as this reduces the possibility of rust being troublesome to a minimum. Mint is very vigorous, so restrict the roots within the confines of an old bucket or sink.

Make the first outdoor sowing of wrinkled or marrowfat peas. I make a drill the full width of a spade and 1½ in. deep and space three rows of peas in this, one along each side of the drill and one down the centre. The seeds themselves are spaced 2 to 3 in. apart, and the rows should not be crowded. Varieties which will grow 18 in. to 2 ft. tall should be grown in rows at least 2 ft. apart. Varieties which will grow 3 to 4 ft. tall should have that distance left between the rows. While the pea plants are still young, the space between can be used to grow a catch crop of radishes, lettuces or spinach.

Make a sowing of turnips on fairly rich, but not newly manured, ground.

Where rhubarb is being forced, take the covers off now as if they are left too long the plants become very weak.

The cultivation of onions from sets has become increasingly popular, particularly in districts where onions do not succeed too well from seed. The sets can be planted now. I prefer to plant them just below the surface using a trowel rather than a dibber. I find that there is then less likelihood of the sets pushing themselves out of the ground as they grow.

GREENHOUSE

Seedlings must be pricked out before they become too crowded in their pots or boxes. This is work that requires regular attention now and it is often difficult to find space for all the boxes containing the seedlings. A shelf near the glass can prove very useful.

Sow seeds of *Primula obconica* and *P. sinensis* and provide these with a temperature of 16°C. (60°F.). (*Primula kewensis*, a nearly hardy plant that produces its whorls of yellow flowers in winter and early spring, is usually sown a week or two earlier to give it a longer growing season.)

Put in cuttings of coleus made from growths taken off plants which have overwintered successfully. Select sturdy sideshoots for this purpose and insert them in small pots filled with sandy compost. Place them in a propagating frame with a

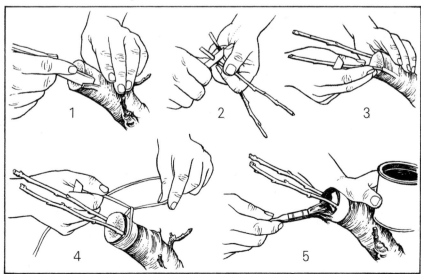

Top grafting an old fruit tree. **1.** An incision is made in the bark, which is then carefully lifted. **2** and **3.** Scions of the new variety are prepared and inserted under the bark. **4** and **5.** After securing, the area is treated with sealing compound

Above: Primulas and *Scilla sibirica* growing informally together. Such a grouping would suit many gardens

Below: This dwarf narcissus Beryl shows the characteristically reflexed perianth of the Cyclamineus group

temperature of 16°C. (60°F.). It is best that the cuttings should be taken in batches so that there is a continuity of young plants, for these have the best colour.

Young coleus plants raised from seed sown in the first week of March should be ready for pricking out singly into 3-in. pots filled with John Innes No. 1 Potting Compost.

Half-hardy annuals to sow now in seed trays or pans include French and African Marigolds, annual phlox, asters, celosias, nemesias, salpiglossis, ten-week stocks and zinnias. This applies particularly to northern districts.

Start tubers of pendulous begonias in a mixture of peat and sand. These plants are particularly attractive when grown in a hanging basket.

Prick out seedlings of *Begonia semperflorens* into boxes of John Innes No. 1 Potting Compost.

Start a few more begonia and gloxinia tubers in a mixture of peat and sand in a warm greenhouse. The begonias will be suitable for bedding out in the garden later, when all fear of frost has passed.

Tuberous begonias and gloxinias started earlier should now be ready for potting. Put the begonias into 5-in. pots and use John Innes No. 2 Potting Compost. Place the tubers halfway down the pots and cover them with about $\frac{1}{2}$ in. of compost. When the plants are established, topdress them with more compost so that eventually they are 2 in. below the surface.

Gloxinias are treated in a similar way except that no space is left for topdressing and the tubers are covered with about 1 in. of soil.

Cuttings of winter-flowering begonias taken in February (see p. 38) should be potted into 3-in. pots of John Innes No. 1 Potting Compost and provided with a temperature of 16 to 18°C. (60 to 65°F.).

When the sun comes out the temperature inside the greenhouse rises rapidly and unless action is taken, plant growth will be speeded up too much. As the temperature increases, open the ventilators, a little at a time at first and always on the sheltered side of the house. They should be closed again before the sun goes down to conserve the sun's heat.

Late-flowering chrysanthemums should be given their first stopping. The second one will be towards the end of June.

April: first week

Take cuttings of herbaceous perennials. Mow lawns. Spray peaches against aphids. Mulch raspberries, blackberries and loganberries. Plant asparagus. Plant maincrop potatoes. Sow parsley. Complete sowing of half-hardy annuals. Sow tomatoes, celery and celeriac.

FLOWERS

Some choice herbaceous plants can be propagated from cuttings taken now. This is true of delphiniums, herbaceous phlox, lupins and heleniums, among others. All will grow well from young shoots cut off below ground level, close to the crown of the plant. With delphiniums and lupins it is particularly important to get well down, because higher up the growth is hollow or pipey and will not root easily. Dip the ends of the cuttings in a rooting powder and insert them in a cold frame. A perfectly satisfactory frame can be improvised by using a fairly deep, bottomless, wooden box placed directly on the soil in the garden. Mix peat and sharp sand with the soil, put a covering of the sand on top and dibble the cuttings in 3 or 4 in. apart.

Water them well, cover the frame with a sheet of glass and shade from bright sunshine.

Lawns now need regular mowing, and the edges must be kept neatly trimmed. If this job is done fairly frequently before the grass gets too long there will be no need to pick up the clippings as they will soon wither and mix with the soil.

The South African chincherinchee, *Ornithogalum thyrsoides*, has become a very popular plant in the past ten years or so, and in addition to its value as a garden plant it is also a first-class cut flower. The white blooms, marked brownish-green at the centre, are borne on 2-ft. stems and the narrow leaves are about half this length. It is not hardy in this country except in the most favoured gardens, and the bulbs

should be lifted in October, stored in a cool, dry place and replanted at this time of year. I make a trench for the bulbs some 4 to 5 in. deep and sprinkle sand along its base. The bulbs are then spaced 2 to 3 in. apart and covered with soil. The site chosen must be sunny and the soil well drained if they are to do really well. The flowers are borne in late July, August and September.

FRUIT

It is always worth while pollinating wall-grown fruit trees by hand as they come into full flower. This can be done by jarring the trees or by dusting the open flowers with a rabbit's tail or camel-hair brush.

Watch peaches and nectarines for any sign of aphids on the young leaves, and spray, if they do appear, before the leaves curl and give the insects protection. BHC is a good insecticide to use for this purpose, and, if necessary, a fungicide, such as lime sulphur or dispersible sulphur, can be added to it to protect against mildew and leaf curl.

If black currants have not already been sprayed, this should be done now with malathion as, except in the coldest localities, this is the latest time for it to be effective against the big bud mite.

Mulch between the rows of raspberries, blackberries and loganberries with well-rotted manure, compost or peat. The purpose of the mulch is not only to feed the plants but also to protect the roots and keep them moist.

VEGETABLES

Now is the time to plant asparagus crowns. As already described on p. 32, the old method of planting in beds is giving way to the cultivation of asparagus in single rows, the plants later being earthed up like potatoes. But whatever method is employed, the ground must be well prepared by deep digging and generous manuring. It is best to plant one-year-old crowns and the new plants should not be cropped until they have been in the garden for two years.

Brussels sprouts sown earlier in a frame or greenhouse should now be pricked out in the open ground. Space them 4 to 6 in. apart so that they have room to develop sturdily. Early plants such as these are the ones which produce the finest crops.

Preparing lupin cuttings. **1.** Young shoots are cut off below soil level. It is particularly important to sever them close to the crown, otherwise the stems will be hollow and will not root easily. **2.** The base of the cutting is trimmed neatly with a razor blade or sharp knife, making the cut directly below a leaf joint. **3** and **4.** After moistening the base of the cutting in water, it is dipped in hormone rooting powder and then inserted in a propagating box of sandy compost

Trimming the edges of a lawn—an easy job, but one which can make all the difference to the apperance of the garden. Long-handled shears save unnecessary bending and are a great help in a large garden

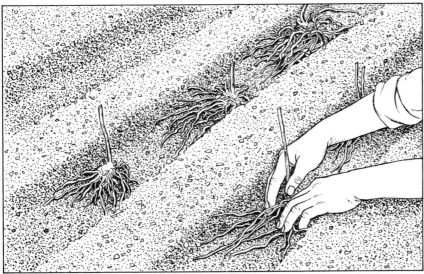

Planting asparagus crowns in well-prepared ground. One-year-old plants should be selected, if possible, and the roots should be well spread out before covering them with soil. Later, the rows will be earthed up in the same way as potatoes

It is at this time of the year that we appreciate to the full the value of sprouting broccoli. This may serve as a reminder to purchase a little seed for next year's crop, although this need not be sown for a few weeks.

Complete the planting of early potatoes and start on the maincrop varieties, particularly if you live in the South or West. Good varieties include Pentland Crown, Majestic and Arran Banner.

Spring cabbages should be given a light topdressing with a general fertiliser to hurry along growth. Such a dressing should always be hoed in.

Early sowings of many vegetables under cloches may need thinning, otherwise the plants will be weak and spindly.

Seedlings of broad beans and peas which have been gradually hardened off during the last few weeks (see p. 42) should now be in a suitable condition to plant out.

Parsley seed can be sown now for summer use. This is often very slow to germinate, so do not be surprised if several weeks elapse before the seedlings appear.

GREENHOUSE

The sowing of half-hardy annuals should be completed this week. Many seedlings from earlier sowings will be in need of pricking out and some of the most forward may even need to be potted individually.

It is also a good time to sow seeds of tomatoes for outdoor planting in early June. The bush tomatoes, like Amateur, are particularly useful for this purpose. Tomato plants to be grown in a moderately heated greenhouse should be ready for pricking out now into 3½-in. pots filled with John Innes No. 1 Potting Compost. They must be given a temperature of 16°C. (60°F.) if they are to maintain satisfactory growth.

Sow seeds of *Mimosa pudica*, the Sensitive Plant. This plant is quite a novelty with its sensitive leaves which close up at the slightest touch. The resulting plants will be ready for potting up in late May.

Grevillea and jacaranda are two other plants grown in the greenhouse for their foliage effects, and seeds should be sown now.

Prick out seedlings of tuberous begonias and gloxinias into boxes filled with John Innes No. 1 Potting Compost, and provide them with shady conditions and a temperature of 18°C. (65°F.).

Sow seed of celery and celeriac in the greenhouse now to provide plants for planting out in prepared trenches in June. Celeriac is a useful vegetable for flavouring soups and stews. It forms turnip-like roots which are lifted in the autumn and stored until required.

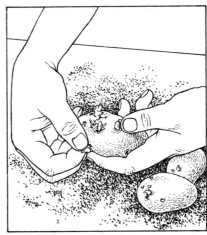

Before planting potato tubers the surplus shoots should be rubbed away, leaving only the two or three strongest

Improved Ailsa Craig, a particularly fine
strain of onion if really large bulbs are
required. Plants raised from a sowing in
December should be planted out in April

April: second week

Sow new lawns. Plant sweet peas and biennials. Prune forsythias. Plant clematis. Disbud peaches and apricots. Spray gooseberries and pears. Sow asparagus and carrots. Earth up peas and broad beans. Sow melons and cucumbers. Tie in vine rods.

Fritillaria meleagris, with its beautifully marked flowers from which it derives its common name of Snake's-head Fritillary. These plants like moist but well-drained soil in partial shade, and are ideal for naturalising in grass

Doronicum plantagineum Harpur Crewe, one of the earliest plants to flower in the herbaceous border

FLOWERS

This is a good time of year to make a new lawn from seed (see also my remarks on p. 13). Watch the weather now and sow the grass seed as soon as the soil is in a reasonably dry, crumbly condition. A really good seed bed must be prepared, and time spent on levelling, firming and raking is well worth the effort. The grass seed should be broadcast as evenly as possible over the surface and then raked in. If black cotton can be stretched over the ground it will help to keep the birds away.

It is most important to purchase good grass seed which does not contain too much rye grass. Nowadays, mixtures are available for special purposes (to provide top-quality lawns, hard-wearing lawns, lawns which will put up with shady conditions, and so on), which makes things easier than they used to be. A suitable rate of sowing is 1½ oz. to the square yard. Some seed is treated with a bird repellent dressing, which is also helpful.

This is the time to plant sweet pea seedlings. They can be planted either in single rows or in double rows 9 in. apart with 9 in. also allowed between the plants For production of really good cut flowers it is best to grow the plants on single stems, selecting the strongest shoot from the base of each plant and removing all sideshoots from time to time throughout the growing season. Long canes should be used to support the plants and a sturdy framework should be made to resist the wind.

There is still time to sow all kinds of hardy annuals, but the sooner this is done the better.

If biennials, such as Sweet Williams, Canterbury Bells and foxgloves, were not planted in the autumn or in March they can still be planted where they are to flower; but again with no delay.

As forsythias finish flowering they should be pruned. The way to do this is to cut out the stems which have just flowered but to keep all young stems as it is these which will bear the best flowers next year. Shape the bushes as you prune.

Clematis should be planted now, and, if possible, obtain pot-grown plants.

Continue to plant gladiolus corms throughout this month (see p. 43).

FRUIT

Disbudding of peaches, nectarines and apricots can begin now. With fan-trained trees all shoots should be rubbed out which are growing on the backs of the branches—towards the wall – and those growing on the front of the branches–away from the wall. The best shoots to retain are those growing along the tops of the branches.

Put cloches over strawberries to encourage the ripening of a few early fruits.

Spray gooseberries against mildew with lime sulphur or with a washing soda spray on sulphur-shy varieties such as Leveller.

Pears will benefit from spraying with a combined BHC and lime sulphur spray just before they come into flower, but if the trees are already in bloom leave this spraying until petal fall.

VEGETABLES

If asparagus is to be grown from seed, now is the time to make a sowing out of doors. Choose a well-drained, open position where the soil is fairly rich. The seedlings will make roots large enough for planting in their permanent beds in a year's time.

When making a new lawn from seed it is important to use the correct amount and to broadcast it evenly. This is most easily done if the site is divided up into yard-wide strips and the seed measured out accurately for each piece

Sowing cucumber seeds. If two seeds are placed in a 3-in. pot they can be reduced to one plant if both should germinate

Sowings of such vegetables as lettuces, carrots, radishes and peas should continue to be made to keep up a succession. This is the time, for instance, when maincrop carrots should be sown, and a good variety is James's Scarlet Intermediate. Among lettuces, the cos type are much to be valued; a favourite variety is Little Gem. Continue to sow for succession until August. French Breakfast and Cherry Belle are good varieties of radish, and Kelvedon Wonder and Onward are popular peas.

Early-sown peas which have already germinated will be helped if the soil is drawn up a little on either side of each row. Similarly with broad beans.

It is too early to sow French beans without any protection except in the mildest localities, but in most places they can be sown with safety under cloches.

In the South sow a little round beetroot seed for an early crop. Do not sow too much as the beet soon becomes coarse; it is much better to make successional sowings from early April until July to give a continuous supply of young beets.

Winter greens such as the ordinary winter cabbage January King, which is a very hardy variety, savoy cabbage and broccoli (both the heading and sprouting kinds) should all be sown now.

GREENHOUSE

Remember that a slightly humid atmosphere is essential in houses where nectarines and peaches are growing. This is achieved mainly by early-morning syringing and damping down the floors, and if the latter can be done again at mid-day when the weather is sunny, so much the better. Dry air would encourage the development of both thrips and red spider.

Sow seeds of both melons and cucumbers. The best method is to place two seeds in each 3-in. pot, and later on, if both seeds germinate, reduce them to one seedling per pot. Germinate them in a temperature of 18 to 21°C. (65 to 70°F.). Cantaloupe melons are a good type to choose, for they have a fine flavour and are excellent for greenhouse, frame or cloche.

As pot-grown camellias finish flowering, they should be repotted into larger pots if those in which they are at present growing are well filled with roots. There is a proviso, though, in that once the plants are in 8- or 9-in. pots it is better to tease away some of the old compost and return them to the same size pots with new compost added. For all such repotting use a special camellia compost consisting of 2 parts peat, 1 part lime-free loam and 1 part coarse sand.

Greenhouse chrysanthemums, now housed in frames, will need potting on into 5-in. pots (from the 3-in. pots in which they are growing at present), using John Innes No. 2 Potting Compost. As the plants become established in their 5-in. pots, leave the lights off during the day.

Vine rods growing in unheated greenhouses should be tied up to their supporting wires as growth should be sufficiently well advanced all along the rods.

Young plants of outdoor chrysanthemums should be moved to a cold frame and hardened off gradually.

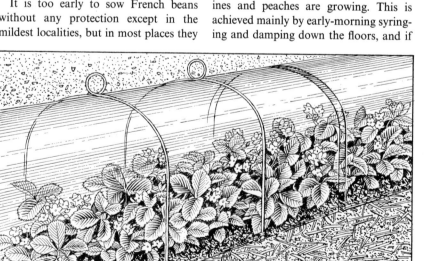

For an early crop of strawberries, cloches can be placed over the plants to bring them forward. Nowadays, cloches tend to be made of plastic rather than glass, which is an obvious advantage for they are lighter to handle and less likely to break

April: third week

Prepare ground for outdoor chrysanthemums. Remove dead heads from daffodils, pansies and violas. Layer rhododendrons and azaleas. Spray raspberries and apples. Plant maincrop potatoes. Make up hanging baskets. Stake pot-grown lilies. Side-shoot tomatoes.

FLOWERS

It will soon be time to plant border chrysanthemums outside and it is most important that the soil should be well prepared. Space the plants at least 1½ ft. apart and allow 2 ft. between the rows so that there is sufficient room to work between them when weeding, stopping, disbudding and so on. I always put the canes or stakes in position first and plant to these, tying the plants in immediately.

As daffodils and other early bulbous flowers finish blooming, remove the dead flowers. This is done not only for the sake of tidiness but also to prevent seed formation and so encourage the growth of the bulbs.

It is also wise to pick dead flowers off pansies and violas regularly before they produce any seed pods. I find that greenfly often make a first appearance on these plants and on polyanthus at this time of year and quickly spoil their beauty. Watch for this pest and as soon as it is seen spray with a BHC insecticide.

Take advantage of any fine, mild weather to harden off the more tender summer bedding plants that cannot, with safety, be planted out until well on in May. A frame is the best place for these now and on really good spring-like days the lights can be removed altogether for a few hours.

Young penstemon plants overwintering in frames should be stopped by pinching out their growing tips. This will encourage them to form bushy plants.

Cuttings of rhododendrons and azaleas are not easy to root, at least by the

Dusting brassica seedlings with BHC powder as a protection against flea beetle, an insect which eats holes in the leaves

amateur, but these plants can be readily increased by layers pegged down at this time of year. Choose branches of last year's growth which can be bent down easily to soil level and make a slit halfway through the stem on the lower side where it touches the soil. Dust this wounded portion with hormone rooting powder and peg it firmly to the ground. A mixture of peat and sand added to the soil at this point will facilitate rooting.

If hebes (which used to be known as veronicas at one time) have been damaged by severe frost during the winter, they can be cut back hard now.

FRUIT

Straw can be obtained now ready for the strawberry beds, but there is no need to put it on for a week or two yet. Alternatives to this are special strawberry mats or black polythene sheeting.

Raspberries should be sprayed for the first time with derris as a precaution against the raspberry beetle. If mildew has been troublesome in previous years, add a colloidal copper fungicide to the insecticide.

If the weather should turn dry, make sure that newly planted fruit trees and bushes are not short of water while they are becoming established.

When apple blossom reaches the pink bud stage, which is just before the buds open fully, spray with lime sulphur or captan as a precaution against scab and add to this BHC to kill any caterpillars or greenfly that may be about.

Propagating a rhododendron by layering. **1.** An incision is made on the underside of a branch that can be easily lowered to the ground. **2.** After dusting the wound with rooting powder the branch is pegged down into the soil with a piece of bent wire. If

some sand and peat are added to the soil in this area it will facilitate rooting. **3.** The end of the branch can be made additionally secure by tying to a bamboo cane. **4.** Finally, compost is placed over the wounded portion from which roots will form

VEGETABLES

Parsnips raised from seed sown last month will now be ready for thinning, if the weather has been favourable. Thin the seedlings to at least 9 in. apart in the rows.

As soon as the rows of earlier-sown onions and carrots can be seen clearly hoe between them, both to aerate the soil and destroy any weeds there may be. As it is after hoeing that these plants are most likely to be attacked by onion fly and carrot fly, dust along the rows with a BHC preparation. Brassica seedlings should be dusted occasionally with BHC to kill flea beetles.

Maincrop potatoes should be planted now. Give them plenty of room and plant in narrow trenches chopped out with a spade. If the seed potatoes have been sprouting, reduce the growths to the three best on each tuber. The surplus shoots are quite easily removed by rubbing them away with the thumb.

Prepare trenches for runner beans to be sown or planted next month by digging the soil thoroughly and incorporating plenty of well-rotted manure or garden compost. I sometimes recommend sowing the seed in

pots, one seed to each 3-in. pot. They can then be germinated in a greenhouse, frame or even under cloches and the resulting seedlings transplanted to their growing positions at the end of May. This is safer than running the risk of sowing in what may be cold, wet soil and perhaps finding that a lot of seeds fail to germinate.

Onion plants which were raised from seeds sown in the greenhouse last December (see p. 121) can now be planted out.

GREENHOUSE

Further batches of achimenes can be started into growth for succession. Tubers of begonias and gloxinias, started into growth a few weeks ago, should be ready for potting up.

All the young shoots on established standard fuchsias should be stopped for the last time. Young fuchsias that are being grown on from autumn cuttings to form new standards should now have reached the required height for the head of branches to be developed. This is done by pinching out the central growing tip to encourage sideshoots to form.

Make up hanging baskets with pelargoniums (geraniums), lobelia, verbena and other suitable trailing plants. I particularly like pendulous fuchsias for this purpose. The baskets should be lined with moss and John Innes No. 3 Potting Compost is placed around the roots of the plants.

Stake pot-grown lilies, taking care not to damage the bulbs when inserting the canes.

Solanum seedlings should be pricked out into 3-in. pots filled with John Innes No. 1 Potting Compost.

Large-flowered calceolarias are now coming into flower and will continue in bloom until June.

Early-planted tomatoes will be in need of side-shooting. This means that all the side growths forming in the axils of the leaves are removed. Water carefully until the first fruits have formed, and from then onwards feed the plants weekly with a good tomato fertiliser.

As vine growths lengthen, gradually tie these down to the training wires to keep them under control.

Pieris formosa forrestii is particularly attractive in spring with its fragrant flowers and young, bright red leaves

The graceful flowers of *Erythronium revolutum* White Beauty have brown markings at the base of the petals, and contrast well with the dark, shiny, mottled foliage. These plants flourish when left undisturbed in semi-shade

April: fourth week

Plant dahlia tubers, penstemons and half-hardy calceolarias. Spot treat lawns. Plant water lilies. Protect strawberries. Spray plums. Disbud peaches. Earth up early potatoes. Sow sweet corn and marrows. Prick out half-hardy annuals and tomatoes. Stop vines.

FLOWERS

Dahlia tubers can be planted now with safety, but plant them reasonably deeply so that the young shoots will not appear until all danger of frost has passed. The tubers can be divided up at this time, provided there is a piece of stem attached to each tuber. If new shoots have started to develop, do not plant until the end of May or the beginning of June as frost could damage the young growths.

Penstemons and half-hardy calceolarias which have been overwintering in a frame may also be planted out now.

When the seedlings of hardy annuals have germinated, choose a showery day to look over the border for any gaps. Many hardy annuals can be lifted and transplanted so that the gaps can be filled from places where the seedlings are too thick. There are some kinds, however, such as eschscholzias and annual poppies, which form long tap roots and do not transplant satisfactorily. Put twiggy sticks around the most forward plants to support them.

Spot treatment of weeds in lawns can begin. This method of treatment of such perennial weeds as Mare's Tail and convolvulus can even be carried out between shrubs and other plants as long as the selective weedkiller is not allowed to blow on to them.

Water lilies and all other kinds of hardy aquatics can be planted during the next few weeks. If it is not possible to plant water lilies at the time when they are received from the nurseryman, place them in water or damp moss until such time as they can be dealt with.

In sheltered areas, sow seeds of statice, helichrysum and acroclinium. These can be cut and dried in August for use in flower arrangements. In cold districts they are better sown under glass in March.

FRUIT

If some strawberry plants are to be used to give early runners for propagation purposes, they should not be allowed to flower. Pick off the blossom buds as soon as these are seen. Make certain that any plants reserved for this purpose look really healthy with no yellow mottling or rolling of the leaves which might indicate virus.

Strawberries which are to be allowed to flower and fruit should be protected from late frost. Newspapers placed over them on cold nights will make quite a difference, or straw may be kept at hand to be sprinkled lightly over the plants on any evening when there appears to be a threat of frost.

It is most important to watch plum trees at this time of year for the first sign of aphid attack, spraying at once if these pests are seen.

Complete the disbudding of wall-trained peaches, nectarines and apricots in the manner I have already described. Again, keep a look out for insect attack and use an insecticide immediately if this becomes evident.

VEGETABLES

Seeds which can be sown now include those of salsify and scorzonera.

Complete the planting of maincrop potatoes and earth up any early ones which are showing through the soil, even if they have already been earthed up once. This protects the growths against night frosts.

Put up the supports for runner beans,

The numerous species and varieties of clematis ensure that there is something to please everyone. Illustrated here is *C.* Lasurstern, which flowers in May and June and again later in the summer. Others will extend the display into the autumn

Weigela Abel Carrière, one of several hybrids of this easily grown and attractive shrub for early-summer flowering

Spot treatment of a lawn weed by painting herbicide directly onto the plant. This is most effective with persistent weeds

Water lilies and other aquatics are usually planted in special baskets which are then sunk in position in the pond

Unwanted shoots on wall-trained peaches and apricots must be removed regularly if the trees are to be kept under control

using either sticks or string. A seedling can then be planted against each support or the seed sown direct in the ground.

If celery trenches have not already been prepared (see p. 41), complete this work as soon as possible. The manure should then have time to become incorporated with the soil before the celery is planted.

Keep the hoe going between all crops where the rows can be seen clearly. This frequent aeration of the soil and checking of weeds does a great deal of good.

Sow sweet corn and marrow seeds in 3-in. pots and place these in a garden frame or under cloches. The bush type of marrow is best for the average garden as these are less spreading than the trailing kind. Varieties include Green Bush, White Bush and Superlative. Courgettes are also very good and can be treated in the same way.

GREENHOUSE

Many half-hardy annuals will now be ready for pricking out. Some are better if they are pricked out straight into pots rather than into trays in which they are apt to get starved. Flower pots are an expensive item, and pots of bituminous paper, black polythene or pressed peat are quite suitable for many of these plants.

This is the time to prick out tomato seedlings which will be planted out of doors after hardening off.

On bright, sunny days begonias, gloxinias and some other plants will need shade.

Young growths of vines should be pinched back to two leaves beyond the fruit trusses, and if two bunches of fruit form on one lateral, one should be removed. Secondary growths which develop should have their tips taken out at one leaf, and tendrils should be removed.

Fuchsias must now be moved on into larger pots. Use the 5-in. size and John Innes No. 2 Potting Compost.

Seedlings of *Begonia semperflorens* should now be potted into 3-in. pots. They will later be hardened off for planting out of doors in early June. Alternatively, they can be potted on and used to decorate the greenhouse, sun lounge or conservatory.

Pendulous begonias which were started into growth at the end of March should now be planted into the hanging baskets in which they are to flower. These flowers are ideal for the sun lounge or conservatory, but remember that they do not like strong

sunshine and should be given some shade at the height of the summer.

Pansies and violas raised from a sowing made in March (see p. 42) should now be big enough to prick out into boxes. They will be ready for bedding out in June.

Pot coleus cuttings into 3-in. pots filled with John Innes No. 1 Potting Compost.

Dracaenas, codiaeums and Rubber Plants (*Ficus elastica*) which have grown too much for convenience or have even become rather unsightly may be reduced in size by air layering. An inch-long cut is made half way through the stem at a convenient point, and this wounded area is treated with a hormone rooting powder, covered with damp moss and, finally, wrapped around closely with polythene film. A tie is then made above and below the wound with raffia or twine so that the covering is held firmly in place and moisture retained in the moss. Roots will form into the moss, and when these are seen to be plentiful the stem can be severed just below the point of layering. The polythene is carefully removed and the new plant potted into the smallest size of pot which will hold its roots conveniently. Do not remove the moss from around the stem or the roots may be damaged for they are very brittle. Use the John Innes No. 1 Potting Compost for this initial potting, and when the plants need to be moved into 5- or 6-in. pots, use the John Innes No. 2 Potting Compost.

Earthing up early potatoes. This is done as a protection against late frosts, and to exclude light from developing tubers

May: first week

Stake herbaceous perennials. Trains sweet peas. Plant outdoor chrysanthemums. Tie in peach shoots. Examine fruit-tree grafts. Plant out Brussels sprouts. Sow sweet corn, endive and chicory. Harden off bedding plants. Plant tomatoes in greenhouse border.

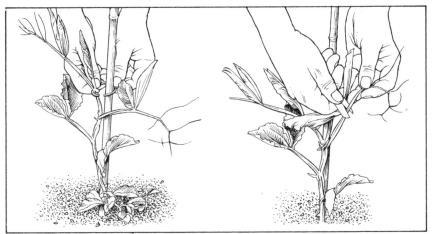

Training cordon-grown sweet peas. The main stems are supported by tall canes, and are secured with special split rings or raffia.

All tendrils which develop should be cut off so that the strength of the plant goes into the production of flowers

Planting and staking outdoor-flowering chrysanthemums. **1.** The young plants are knocked from their pots by tapping the rim

FLOWERS

If April was a busy month, then I can only promise that May will be an even busier one for all good gardeners.

As usual, many half-hardy bedding plants will be offered for sale now though it is not safe to plant them out of doors except in the mildest parts of the country. Even if plants such as pelargoniums (geraniums), salvias, lobelias, nemesias, fuchsias, zinnias and French and African Marigolds are not actually killed by frost, they may receive such a severe check from cold May nights that they never completely recover to give a proper display. I think it is far better to delay the bedding out of

such plants as these until at least the last week in May. This, of course, is particularly true in the Midlands and the North.

Stake the flower spikes of herbaceous plants as they develop, and pay particular attention to delphiniums and lupins. These last deserve one cane to each spike. Where the shoots of delphiniums are overcrowded they should be thinned out.

Growers of exhibition sweet peas will be kept busy from now on removing the sideshoots and tying in the main stems. Exhibition plants are always grown on the single stem system and the tendrils at the ends of the leaves, as well as the sideshoots, should be removed. Thus tying becomes absolutely essential as the plants have lost their natural means of support. Sweet peas can be fed but do not use a fertiliser with too high a nitrogen content at this time of year as this may aggravate bud dropping. In the North, this is about the right time to plant sweet peas, but the weather must be watched as this is quite as important as the calendar date.

Plant outdoor-flowering chrysanthemums. I have already described how to prepare the ground and suggested that a cane should be placed to mark the position of each plant. All that now remains is to drop one plant into the trowel hole made beside each cane. Be sure to plant firmly and to make certain that the ball of soil rests on the bottom of the hole.

of the pot with the handle of a trowel. **2.** The plants are inserted close to the canes which were put in a week or two ago when

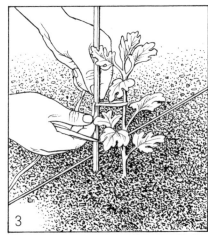

the ground was prepared. **3.** After firming the soil, the plants are secured to the canes with raffia

Staking the flower spikes of a delphinium. If possible it is best to put one cane to each spike to give maximum support

FRUIT

The tying in of the young growth of peaches and nectarines should begin. Professional

Dipping the roots of brassica seedlings in a paste made with calomel dust and water as a preventive for club root

gardeners call this job 'heeling in' and it is a matter of looping the young shoots to the branch from which they are growing to encourage them to grow in the direction in which they are required. This is necessary for the perfect formation of a fan-trained tree.

Watch gooseberry bushes closely for any sign of attack by aphids or caterpillars and spray at once with derris should either of these pests be seen.

If any fruit trees were grafted last month, examine the grafts carefully now as it may be necessary to loosen the raffia or string to prevent it cutting into the swelling branches. In any case, shoots growing below the grafts should be rubbed off.

Newly planted fruit trees appreciate an early evening spraying with clear water to speed up their development.

VEGETABLES

The earliest Brussels sprout plants may now be planted out and it is these first plants which usually produce the best sprouts. There is frequently a tendency among amateur gardeners to plant them too closely, and if they are planted 3 ft. apart each way the result will be far better sprouts and a heavier crop. The space need not be wasted as early-hearting cabbage or early cauliflowers can be planted between the sprouts and will be off the ground before the sprouts need more space.

If club root has been troublesome, dip the roots of the Brussels sprouts, cabbages and cauliflowers in a paste made with

4 per cent. calomel dust and water before they are planted.

Sow more peas for succession and between the pea rows sow more lettuce – another way of using the ground most economically. Alternatively, grow spinach instead of lettuce, a good variety being Longstanding Round.

Again, it is important not to stint on space for peas. Leave plenty of room between the rows so that the plants get the benefit of full light. Peas which grow 3 ft. tall should be given at least 3 ft. of space between the rows.

Sow seeds of heading broccoli (autumn-, winter- and spring-heading) and kale.

Seed of sweet corn can be sown out of doors now where the plants are to mature.

Seed of endive and chicory can also be sown out of doors. It should be sown very thinly and at a depth of $\frac{1}{2}$ in.

GREENHOUSE

Bedding plants must be properly hardened off in readiness for planting out at the end of the month or in early June. They should, if possible, be in a frame now, and air must be given increasingly as the weather becomes warmer.

Topdress tuberous begonias which were potted a few weeks ago with a little John Innes No. 2 Potting Compost. Space was allowed for this at the time of potting, but now the compost can be brought up to within about half an inch of the rim.

Attend to watering regularly. It is surprising how quickly pot plants can dry out when the weather is really bright. Except when watering young plants, seeds and cuttings, when an appropriately fine or coarse rose should be fitted to the can, all watering should be done from the spout. This must be held close to the soil, so that it is not disturbed or washed away. It cannot be too frequently said that when plants are considered to need water, it should be given in generous quantities. Sufficient, in other words, to soak right through the pot.

One learns from experience when plants need water, and both the aural method (tapping the pots with a wooden 'hammer' made by fixing a cotton reel to a bamboo cane) and the lifting method, where one tests the weight of the plant and pot, are equally good. But the first cannot be used with plastic pots, which are becoming more and more predominant, as these do

not 'ring' like a dry clay pot. You can tell quite a lot, too, from the colour of the compost on the surface, although this is not an infallible guide to what is going on underneath the surface.

Of course, much watering can be done automatically nowadays with the excellent capillary bench watering system, or by trickle watering with a special perforated hose (see p. 20).

Specimen pelargonium (geranium) plants for winter flowering should be potted this month. Use the John Innes No. 2 Potting Compost.

When the first flower buds can be seen in the tip of each tomato plant (which should be about now) they will be ready to plant out in the border or for moving on into 9-in. pots or large boxes – or bottomless rings if the admirable ring-culture method of growing them is to be adopted. John Innes No. 3 Potting Compost should be used in the containers for this move, and if planting in the border make sure that it consists of a good loamy mixture. I, personally, like to dig well-rotted manure or peat into the border soil when preparing for planting, giving a sprinkling of bonemeal at the same time as well as a dressing of a well-balanced organic-based fertiliser, applied at the rate of 2 oz. to the square yard.

When the first truss of fruit has set, feed the plants once a week with liquid or soluble fertiliser.

Celery and celeriac seedlings raised from seeds sown at the beginning of April should be ready for pricking out into boxes.

Planting brassica seedlings with a dibber. Note the line which is used to ensure that the plants are inserted in straight rows

May: second week

Sow half-hardy annuals. Stop outdoor chrysanthemums. Train rambler roses. Water newly planted trees and shrubs. Spray black currants. Straw strawberries. Thin apricots. Plant melons. Hoe onions. Sow French and runner beans. Shade greenhouse.

FLOWERS

In sheltered gardens and on light, well-drained soils half-hardy annuals can be sown out of doors in the next week or so. Many gardeners without a greenhouse can grow these colourful plants in this way. Those to sow include ageratums, nemesias, *Mesembryanthemum criniflorum*, tagetes (French and African Marigolds) and zinnias. Look over hardy annuals which were sown earlier and as the young seedlings develop thin them out so that they have room to develop.

As soon as *Prunus triloba* has finished flowering it pays to cut back the shoots that have flowered to encourage strong, new growths on which next year's flowers will appear. Flowering currants, too, can be pruned as soon as flowering has finished by cutting out some of the older wood. Remove any weak growth at the same time.

Stop outdoor-flowering chrysanthemums by pinching out the young centre tip of each plant.

As rambler roses begin to make strong shoots from the base, these should be carefully tied in, for if they are left unsupported they are liable to be damaged.

If the weather is dry keep a careful watch on newly planted trees and shrubs to make sure that they do not suffer from lack of water. It is a very good plan to spray newly planted trees and shrubs in the evenings when the weather is dry. Then, after a heavy shower of rain, mulch around them with several inches of well-rotted manure, compost or moist peat to conserve mois-

ture in the soil. It is important that such mulches should be drawn back occasionally, though, and the ground be given a good soaking if this is necessary, for while such materials do a splendid job it must be realised that their bulk also stops rain-water percolating into the ground as it would do normally.

FRUIT

Greenfly (aphids) can cause serious blistering of black currant foliage, and spraying should be carried out against these pests before the leaves have curled. Derris or malathion can be used for this purpose, and, as always when using sprays, the manufacturer's instructions should be followed strictly. Morello and dessert cherries should also be sprayed against black fly to prevent serious trouble later. If apple trees were not sprayed earlier, this, too, can be done now.

Put clean straw around strawberries to protect the fruit from mud splashing, making sure that it is tucked well underneath the plants. Instead of using straw from a bale, straw mats can be purchased from most garden shops. Black polythene is another alternative.

Apricots will need thinning, especially where small fruits are clustered very closely together. A few should be removed but this job should not be completed until the stones have formed (see p. 71).

If peach leaf curl disease begins to show on peaches and nectarines, pick off affected leaves immediately and burn them.

Plant out melons from their 3-in. pots.

Hoeing between rows of onions to keep down the weeds. A hand or onion hoe is the best tool for this job

These can be grown in frames, under cloches or in the greenhouse.

VEGETABLES

Keep onion rows clear of weeds, and thin the plants where necessary. Regular hoeing between the rows will keep down the weeds and after thinning or weeding dust along the rows with BHC dust to keep onion fly away.

Both runner and French beans can be sown with safety out of doors now. These vegetables appreciate a well-drained soil into which rotted manure or compost has been dug beforehand (see p. 54). Prior to sowing, dust the soil with a general fertiliser at the rate of 2 oz. to the square yard.

With runner beans, I like to sow one seed at each string or cane and put in a few surplus ones at the end of the row which can be transplanted to fill any gaps which may occur. The seeds are sown in a double row, allowing a space of 12 in. between the rows and 9 to 12 in. between the seeds in the rows. The seeds should be covered with 2 in. of soil. If more than one double row is grown, leave a space of 6 ft. at least between them.

Sow French beans in drills 1 in. deep and space them 9 in. apart in a double row with 6 in. being allowed between the rows. The seeds should be planted alternately in adjoining rows to give each plant the maximum amount of space in which to develop.

Tucking clean straw under the leaves of strawberry plants to prevent the fruits from being splashed by rain and mud. Black polythene sheeting or special strawberry mats can be used as alternatives

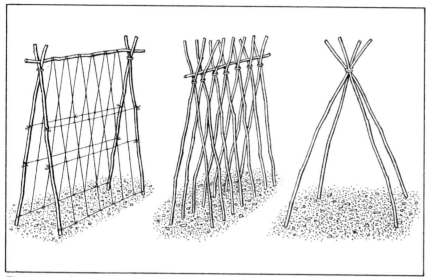

Three ways of supporting runner beans. On the left, strings attached at top and bottom to wires or poles. In the centre, poles or bamboo canes tied at the top to a horizontal pole. On the right, four poles tied together to form a wigwam

Thin beetroot seedlings to 9 in. apart as soon as the leaves begin to touch. Continue to do this throughout the summer with all successive sowings.

Thin carrots to 9 in. apart. Continue to make sowings to provide a continuity of supply, and thin the resulting plants as necessary.

The ground can now be prepared for the planting of outdoor tomatoes later this month. The best position for them is against a wall or fence which faces south. Tomatoes like a good, rich soil containing plenty of rotted manure, compost or peat.

GREENHOUSE

In many districts it should now be safe to stand bedding plants outside, under the shelter of a wall, to harden them off prior to planting out.

It will be necessary to shade the greenhouse now for begonias, gloxinias and many other plants need some protection from the sun. The most inexpensive way of doing this is to coat the glass with whitewash or one of the proprietary shading compounds. Such shading, however, does not have the refinement of blinds as it is in position permanently until it is washed off at the end of the season. Still, within its limitations, it does an excellent job. The alternative is to have fabric or polythene blinds fitted inside the house or wooden lath or split-cane blinds fitted outside. The ultimate refinement is to go the whole way and have automatic blinds fitted, but this, naturally, means quite a bit of expense.

Stake and tie perpetual-flowering carnations, or use the split rings especially designed for this purpose. Many plants will be ready for their final move into 8-in. pots using the John Innes No. 1 Potting Compost.

Tuberous-rooted begonias can be fed as the plants fill their pots with roots. Once they begin to show flower buds, I like to feed them once a week with a liquid or soluble feed. It is important to remember that feeding should not be carried out if the compost in the pot is dry or the roots may be damaged.

This is the latest time for taking cuttings of hydrangeas to produce good flowering plants for next year. If the cuttings are treated with a hormone rooting powder, they should form roots within two or three weeks.

Hydrangea cuttings are made from strong, non-flowering shoots. They should be 4 to 5 in. long and trimmed cleanly just below a joint. Root them round the edge of $3\frac{1}{2}$-in. pots in a mixture of equal parts peat and sand, these being placed in a propagating frame with a temperature of 16°C. (60°F.). If a propagator is not available, a good alternative is to enclose each pot in a polythene bag and seal it with a rubber band.

Make a sowing of *Primula malacoides* to provide plants for flowering during the winter.

Coleus plants raised from seed should now be large enough to pot on into 5-in. pots from their present 3-in. size. Use the John Innes No. 1 Potting Compost.

Potting on a young coleus plant. **1.** Crocking the new 5-in. pot with pieces of broken flower pot. (This job is not necessary if plastic pots are used.) **2.** Removing the plant from its outgrown pot. Care must be taken to keep the soil ball intact. **3.** When the plant is in its new pot, fresh compost is added and gently firmed into place around the roots

May: third week

Remove dead heads from bulbs. Spray roses. Apply weedkiller to lawns. Prick out polyanthus. Bark ring apple trees. Water wall-trained fruit. Prepare frames for cucumbers. Sow cinerarias and calceolarias. Rest cyclamen corms. Pot on begonias and gloxinias.

FLOWERS

Chelsea Flower Show is held in the latter part of May and is one of the big events of the gardening year. It is a happy meeting place for gardeners from all over this country and indeed from many other parts of the world. I always look out, not only for old friends, but also for new plants, equipment and novel gardening aids.

Many of the bulbous plants will have finished flowering by now, and quite apart from the desirability of keeping the garden tidy, it is wise to pinch off the dead flower heads to prevent seeds forming. The foliage, however, must be left to die down naturally for the stems and leaves help to build up the bulbs and so ensure that they flower well next year.

Watch for signs of aphids on roses. They can do a lot of damage to young shoots, particularly after continual cold winds, when roses and other plants are not able to grow freely. A spray can be used containing BHC insecticide, and it is worth while to add a fungicide, such as captan, to control black spot at the same time.

Grass, and weeds growing in the grass on lawns, will be growing freely at this time of year, and it is an ideal time to use a selective weedkiller. This will control most troublesome lawn weeds, but every care should be taken to prevent the chemical from blowing on to the plants and shrubs near the lawn. Treatment should only be carried out on a very still day.

Many lawn fertilisers now contain selective weedkillers, and if these are used, feeding and weeding can be done in one operation.

Two weeds which have become troublesome in lawns over recent years are the blue-flowered speedwell and yellow suckling clover. Most selective weedkillers have little effect on these but there is now a weedkiller based on morfamquat which will eradicate even these difficult weeds.

Polyanthus seedlings raised from a sowing made in the greenhouse in March, can now be pricked out into a nursery bed in the garden. If they are rather small it is wise to shade them with a few leafy branches and spray them with water when the weather is hot.

Seeds of wallflowers, Sweet Williams, Canterbury Bells and other biennials should be sown in the North now, a couple of weeks earlier than in the South. This gives the plants the longer growing season they need in such climatic conditions.

FRUIT

Apple trees sometimes grow very strongly and produce few flowers. This means that crops will be poor and one way to curb the growth is to bark ring the trees. If the whole tree is growing too vigorously the ring of bark can be taken out from around the main stem, but if one branch has a tendency to grow strongly it is only necessary

Removing the faded flowers from daffodils. Not only does this make the garden look tidier, but is also prevents the formation of seeds which is important if the bulbs are to build up a store of food for the following year

Applying selective weedkiller to a lawn with the aid of a dribble bar attachment on a watering-can. It is important to choose a calm day for this job so that the weedkiller does not drift onto other plants

Rose buds infected with greenfly. Regular spraying is essential if this pest is to be kept under control

Watering a wall-trained peach tree. The soil at the base of a wall tends to dry out very quickly, and all wall-trained plants are likely to suffer from drought unless careful attention is given to watering

to ring the branch concerned. The ring must be no more than $\frac{1}{2}$ in. wide, and should go down as far as the wood. Afterwards, seal the cut with adhesive tape.

Wall-trained fruit trees may need watering as the soil at the base of walls tends to dry out quickly. To prevent this happening examine the soil regularly and when it begins to dry out flood the ground with water so that it penetrates deeply.

VEGETABLES
The latest Brussels sprouts should be planted now. They need a really long season in which to grow to maturity so it is important that they should be planted out as early as possible. Give them ample space – at least 3 ft. apart each way. (For further details on spacing, inter-cropping and the prevention of club root, see p. 58.) It is worth noting here that the newer F_1 hybrids are more compact plants than other kinds and so need less space. They produce very good, solid sprouts, too, which are uniformly sized.

The cold frames can now be cleared and prepared for planting cucumbers. I find it best to put a mound of soil, in which some rotted manure or peat has been incorporated, in the centre of each frame and to plant one cucumber in the centre of each mound.

GREENHOUSE
A hanging basket of pelargoniums, fuchsias, ferns or pendulous begonias adds beauty and interest to a greenhouse or conservatory. They do, however, need regular watering and more baskets are spoilt by underwatering than by over-watering. From now on I feed the baskets at least once a week, but if there are fuchsias making strong growth I feed these twice a week, having first made sure that the soil is moist.

Seeds of cinerarias and large-flowered calceolarias may be sown now in pots and placed in a cold frame. Cinerarias can be sown at intervals between April and late June to give a succession of plants, the first of which will flower at the turn of the year. Calceolarias are sown between May and July and these will flower from April until early June of the following year.

Old cyclamen corms will now have finished their growth and water should be gradually reduced so that the corms can be given a short rest. Do not, however, allow them to dry off completely.

Tuberous begonias and gloxinias raised from seed sown in February will need potting up into 3- or $3\frac{1}{2}$-in. pots filled with John Innes No. 1 Potting Compost. How these plants respond after potting depends very much on the prevailing atmospheric conditions. Aim to provide warm, humid and shady surroundings.

Seedlings of *Primula obconica* and *P. sinensis* should be pricked out before they become overcrowded in the seed boxes. Use John Innes No. 1 Potting Compost.

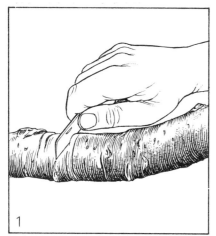

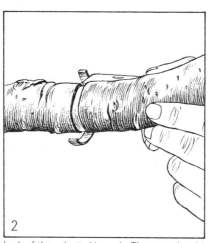

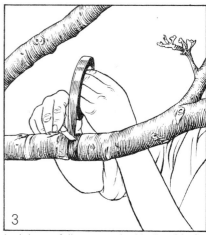

Bark ringing a vigorous apple tree to encourage the production of fruit rather than leaves. **1.** Two cuts are made encircling the bark of the selected branch. The cuts should be no more than $\frac{1}{2}$-in. apart and should go down as deep as the wood. **2.** The ring of bark is carefully removed with the aid of a knife. **3.** Finally, the wound is sealed with insulation tape

May: fourth week

Prepare for summer bedding. Lift and divide primulas. Prepare ground for dahlia cuttings. Thin raspberry canes. Spray apple trees. Net strawberries. Plant runner beans and cucumbers. Prepare ground for marrows. Stake and feed verbenas. Take pelargonium cuttings.

Planting out summer bedding plants. These will soon grow and give an attractive display of flowers. A board placed on the bed to work from prevents the soil from becoming too compacted

FLOWERS

Now is the time to plant summer bedding plants. Wallflowers and other spring-flowering plants may still look attractive and it is tempting to leave them a little longer, but as soon as the flowers begin to fade the plants should be pulled out to make way for the summer bedding subjects. The beds and borders must be dug over and some peat or good garden compost dug in to help to retain moisture.

The lovely early-flowering *Clematis montana* and its pink-flowered form, *rubens*, can be pruned as soon as flowering has finished.

It is a good idea to put a small stick against the best polyanthus so that after flowering has finished they may be lifted and divided. This splitting up is usually done in about the middle of June, but, of course, the plants must be marked when they are at their best. As I lift the plants I divide them into separate crowns, pulling them apart with roots attached to each crown. To make sure that they are free from aphids and red spider each one is dipped into a good insecticide before planting. It is best to plant in positions where the soil is fairly moist and there is partial shade.

As auriculas finish flowering, they can be lifted and divided for planting out in a similar manner to polyanthus. This is also a good time for lifting and dividing *Primula* Wanda, *P. rosea* and *P. denticulata*.

Persistent weeds such as bindweed and ground elder growing between shrubs and other plants can be spot treated with selective weedkiller. This may be brushed on to the weeds or applied with a small sprayer, though I would emphasise the importance of choosing a still day.

It is now time to prepare for planting rooted dahlia cuttings. Dahlias like a good, well-worked soil to which rotted manure, compost or moist peat has been added, as well as a dressing of a general, organic-based fertiliser applied at the rate of 2 oz. to the square yard. The stakes for the dahlias can also be put in place, ready for planting in early June.

Sow seed out of doors of *Alyssum saxatile* and aubrieta.

Lobelia cardinalis and *L. fulgens* can be planted out now.

FRUIT

Raspberries are producing an abundance of young shoots from the base of the plants, and if these are thinned now the

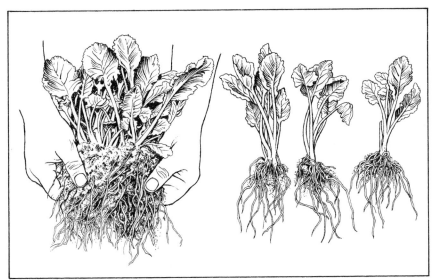

Dividing a polyanthus plant. One large crown can be split up into several small plants, each with roots attached. This job is usually done in mid-June, but suitable plants should be selected now while they are in flower

Tying in a replacement growth on a wall-trained peach. This young shoot will replace the fruiting growth next year

63

Covering strawberry plants with netting, supported by a framework of posts and wires. If this job is not seen to it is quite likely that many of the fruits will be eaten or damaged by birds

new canes required for next year's fruiting will be stronger and better. Sucker growths which appear well out of the rows can be cut off with a hoe.

Spray apple trees at petal fall as a further protection against scab. Use lime sulphur or captan, and add BHC to kill maggots which damage the fruits.

Continue to tie in young growths on peaches and nectarines as they develop, and pinch out the young side growths on wall-trained plums when they have made about six leaves. Where growths are needed to fill a bare space on the wall these should be trained into position without pinching.

Netting used to cover strawberries should be examined and any holes repaired. The sooner these nets are in position the better. Stakes will be necessary to carry the supporting wires, and these can be cut and pointed now.

VEGETABLES

It should now be safe to plant out runner beans which have been raised in pots or boxes. Where French beans are growing under cloches keep them well supplied with water. This applies equally to other vegetables under cloches.

More peas can be sown for succession. Sticks can be placed in position for peas from sowings made earlier.

Cucumbers can now be planted in cold frames but do not plant too deeply. If the base of the stem is buried, water is likely to collect and cause rotting of the stem, known as foot rot.

Potatoes should be earthed up regularly, and if the ground is hard lightly fork over the soil in the rows to make earthing up easier. A little fertiliser sprinkled between the rows before earthing up will also help.

Prepare the ground for planting out frame-raised vegetable marrow plants. The actual planting should be done next week. Dig a hole 2 ft. wide and 1½ ft. deep, put a 9-in. layer of well-rotted manure or garden compost in the bottom and return the soil.

GREENHOUSE

I often grow those two excellent verbenas Loveliness and Lawrence Johnston in pots. They make fine specimen plants and add colour and variety to the greenhouse. They need regular staking and tying and a feed once a week throughout the summer will keep them healthy.

Schizanthus have now almost come to the end of their flowering period, and a few of the plants with good colours and large flowers can be set on one side to produce seed, if so desired. I sometimes do this if I have one or two particularly good plants, but it must not be forgotten that some of the flowers will, no doubt, have been cross-pollinated and the seedlings which result from the saved seed will not necessarily be true to type. Generally, I prefer to buy new seed each year, in small packets of selected strains and varieties.

Pelargonium (geranium) cuttings may be taken now and these will make good plants for winter flowering.

Any shrubs grown in pots should be plunged out of doors by now, and it is essential to keep them well watered, now and throughout the summer.

Plants of *Begonia semperflorens* can be bedded out now or next week. Alternatively, they can be grown as pot plants in 6-in. pots. They are excellent for display in the sun lounge or conservatory.

Planting out pot-raised runner beans, putting one plant to each stake. This method ensures that there are no gaps in the row, which is sometimes the case if seeds are sown direct in the ground

June: first week

Water bedding plants. Stake herbaceous plants and lilies. Spray roses. Sow biennials. Spray raspberries. Pick gooseberries. Spray cherries. Plant marrows, celery and celeriac. Sow turnips. Plant outdoor tomatoes. Rest arum lilies. Start poinsettias.

Above: The simple blooms of *Rosa* Nevada are carried in profusion during June, sometimes with a second flush in August

Below: *Ceanothus thyrsiflorus*, the Californian Lilac, one of the hardiest of the evergreen species of ceanothus

FLOWERS

The weather should be getting warmer now and possibly drier, so remember that bedding plants put out last month may need watering. They have not yet anchored themselves to the soil and if allowed to become dry they could soon deteriorate.

Although the grass where daffodils have been flowering may look untidy it must on no account be cut until the bulb foliage has turned yellow and died down. If the clumps of bulbs in the grass have been growing there for several years and are not flowering well, the reason is probably that they have become overcrowded and could do with lifting and dividing.

Herbaceous plants and lilies should be watched carefully and the stems tied in as they develop, otherwise they may be damaged by the wind.

This is a good time to sow seeds of *Primula denticulata*, *P. rosea* and *P. Wanda* for it should be ripe now.

Aphids or greenfly can be very troublesome and regular spraying is necessary, particularly on roses, to prevent damage. The insects are usually found feeding on the young growths.

In the Midlands and South, wallflowers, forget-me-nots, Canterbury Bells, Sweet Williams, foxgloves and many other biennials can be raised from seed sown now. Remember, though, that if the weather turns dry it will be necessary to water them.

Take care never to allow sweet pea plants to become dry, and feed them regularly with a good general fertiliser.

FRUIT

The small white maggots so often found in raspberries are the grubs of the raspberry beetle and they can be controlled by spraying with derris. Where this pest has been troublesome in the past, it is usually advisable to give a second spraying about 10 days after the first application.

Suckers which sprout up from the base of plum, damson and other fruit trees are often troublesome and should be dug out.

As soon as gooseberries are large enough for bottling or cooking some of them can be picked. The rest of the berries should remain on the bushes to attain their full size, but they must be protected with netting otherwise they will be damaged by birds. Mildew is often troublesome with this crop, attacking the tips of the shoots.

Potting on a greenhouse chrysanthemum into its final pot. **1.** The plant is placed in the centre of the pot and held steady with one hand, while compost is added with the other. **2.** To help firm the new compost, a wooden rammer can be used. **3.** Staking is very important as the plant develops, and three large canes are inserted around the edge of the pot for later use

If infection is seen, in spite of an earlier spraying with lime sulphur (see p. 51), the affected shoots should be nipped out and burnt and the bushes sprayed again with a solution of dinocap.

Blackfly can be a nuisance on dessert cherries and it is wise to spray regularly with malathion to prevent damage to the young shoots and leaves. Alternatively, use a systemic insecticide which will be effective for a much longer period. Remember that the manufacturer's instructions must always be followed, and particular care must be taken in relation to the time gap between spraying and harvesting.

VEGETABLES
Marrows and courgettes can be planted out in positions already prepared, or in hot beds which should be cleared by now. Sweet corn can also be planted now, if seeds were sown in 3-in. pots towards the end of April.

Continue to thin carrots and beetroots, as well as endive and chicory. After thinning carrots dust along the rows with BHC.

Celery should be planted in prepared trenches (see p. 41), spacing the plants 10 to 12 in. apart. Water well after planting.

Celeriac, too, can be planted out now. The soil does not need to be so rich for this crop as for celery and the planting is not done in trenches. Space the plants 1 ft. apart with $1\frac{1}{2}$ ft. between the rows. No earthing up is necessary.

A sowing of white turnips can be made between pea rows or along the sides of runner bean rows.

It should now be quite safe to plant tomatoes out of doors.

GREENHOUSE
The final potting of chrysanthemums must be completed without further delay, and afterwards the plants should be stood out of doors in rows. Pot the plants on into 8-in. pots using the John Innes No. 3 Potting Compost and leave a space at the top for topdressing later on. When the plants are taken out of doors they should be stood on an ash base. Support the plants with bamboo canes tied to wires stretched between posts at a height of about 4 ft.

Cyclamen should now be potted on into their final 6-in. pots using the John Innes No. 2 Potting Compost with a little extra coarse sand added. These plants need cool, moist, shady conditions in the summer and they will be quite happy in a cold frame.

Hydrangea cuttings should be potted individually in 3-in. pots as soon as they are well rooted. If blue flowers are wanted, use John Innes No. 1 Potting Compost but omit the lime and add hydrangea colourant instead.

Arum lilies may now be stood out of doors to give them a rest; or, better still, the pots can be laid on their sides under a west- or south-facing wall.

Pot solanums up into their final 5- or 6-in. pots, using John Innes No. 1 Potting Compost.

Begin watering poinsettias which have been resting. This will encourage the production of new growths from which cuttings can be made by the end of the month.

Planting out celery in prepared trenches. The plants are spaced out at 10- to 12-in. intervals using a measuring rod for a guide.

As the plants grow, the trench will be filled in to blanch the stems

June: second week

Cut grass edges. Trim alpines. Lift tulips. Tie in blackberries and loganberries. Train cordon gooseberries. Stop and topdress cucumbers. Stop broad beans. Lift early potatoes. Thin grapes. Stop mid-season chrysanthemums. Stake tuberous begonias and achimenes.

FLOWERS

A job which I like to see done regularly is the edging of grass verges. If this can be done at frequent intervals, the trimmings need not be swept up; but if lawns are made with the creeping bent type of grass the trimmings should be collected and burnt, otherwise they will root.

As alpine plants in the rock garden finish flowering I trim them back to keep the plants neat and compact. This also encourages them to make good growth for flowering next spring. Any gaps or vacant spots in the rock garden can be planted with late-summer-flowering annuals and bedding plants. Those I like particularly to see are portulaca, *Mesembryanthemum criniflorum*, *Begonia semperflorens* and silene. Remember that the mesembryanthemums must be in a sunny position or the flowers will not open.

Flea beetle can damage wallflower seedlings badly and it is wise to dust along the rows frequently with derris powder or BHC.

Stakes should now be put in position for gladioli, and bamboo canes are ideal for the purpose. If this is done now, the flower spikes can be tied to the canes with soft string as they develop.

As tulips finish flowering, lift the bulbs and, if they are still growing strongly, heel them in elsewhere. Otherwise, dry them off and store them until replanting time comes round again.

FRUIT

As the young shoots of blackberries and loganberries grow, keep them tied to the supporting wires. They are very brittle and easily broken if not adequately supported.

I like to see cordon gooseberries trained against the wall of a house. This is a good way of growing this fruit when space is limited and where dessert fruits of good size are desired. Young side growths are produced in abundance and it is important to keep these pinched back regularly. It is also wise to give an occasional spray with derris to prevent caterpillars eating the foliage, and if this is done the results are usually excellent.

Continue the training of peaches and nectarines by tying in the young shoots regularly so that they grow in the desired manner. As the fruits form, feed the trees with a general fertiliser (applied at the rate of 4 oz. per tree) and afterwards water the fertiliser into the ground. This means giving the area round the tree a good soaking. A thick mulch of garden compost or manure to follow will also help. The fruits must be thinned to about 9 in. apart. This can be done now or it can be left until after the stones have formed.

VEGETABLES

Seakale should now be growing actively and the young shoots should be thinned to leave the best one on each plant so that a good crown develops.

Cucumbers growing in frames must be stopped regularly, and as soon as the soil shows signs of drying out, water it thoroughly. Topdress the mounds of soil with fresh compost before they are completely covered with growths. Cucumbers are stopped by pinching out the growing tip. Four laterals will develop, and these are trained to the four corners of the frame. They should be stopped at the fourth leaf.

Early broad beans will have set about three clusters of flowers by now and can be stopped to encourage pods to form by pinching out the growing tip. This will also help to prevent blackfly damage as this pest likes young shoots to feed on.

Spinach seedlings raised from a sowing made in May should be thinned to 9 in. apart.

Early potatoes should be lifted, and when the site is clear it can be prepared for planting leeks.

To keep onions growing sturdily, water when the soil is dry and give the plants a weekly feed of a general, organic-based

Staking the young shoots of a gladiolus. Each plant will need a separate cane, as the flower spikes are very heavy

fertiliser, applied at the rate of 1 oz. to each yard of row.

Shallots, too, will benefit from the application of a general fertiliser, applied in this case at the rate of 2 oz. to each yard of row. Note, however, that this is a single dressing, unlike that recommended for onions.

Scorzonera and salsify sown at the end of May will now need to be thinned. The seedlings should be spaced about 9 in. apart in the rows.

GREENHOUSE

Cineraria and large-flowered calceolaria seedlings should be pricked out as soon as possible into boxes filled with John Innes No. 1 Potting Compost. Give them a light position with shade from strong sunshine.

Cutting back aubrieta after flowering. This will encourage a mass of new shoots to develop from the base of the plant

If tulips are still growing strongly when the time comes for lifting, they should be heeled in elsewhere until growth has finished

Above: The Excelsior Hybrids are especially attractive foxgloves, for they bear their flowers all round the stems

Below: *Campanula medium*, or Canterbury Bells, are delightful biennials for early-summer flowering

Cyclamen should be moved into cold frames. The lights must be shaded as these plants do not like strong sunshine. Spray the plants over each morning and evening. At this time of year I like to give the later spray just after teatime, closing the lights then to conserve sun heat.

The yellow-flowered *Genista fragrans* can be propagated from cuttings taken now. These should be rooted in a warm propagating frame. This is a useful plant for pot cultivation, and it adds brightness to the greenhouse with its beautiful, fragrant flowers. Plants which have now finished flowering can be trimmed back and repotted.

Grape thinning is a task requiring frequent attention at this time of year. Surplus berries should be removed with long, pointed scissors. Start at the bottom of the bunch and work gradually upwards, removing small, seedless berries first. Use a small forked stick to isolate berries which are to be removed with the scissors as in this way it is possible to avoid touching the berries which remain and perhaps spoiling their bloom.

Mid-season chrysanthemums, such as Loveliness, can be stopped for the second time.

Tuberous begonias need careful attention to staking and in some cases it may be necessary to provide support for the large flowers. Feed them each week to keep the plants growing sturdily.

Achimenes also need supporting and I find that twiggy sticks are best. Insert them around the edge of the pots.

As the flowers fade on established hydrangeas, cut back the stems and repot the plants. Afterwards, they can be stood out of doors for the summer.

Spray chrysanthemums with an insecticide at regular intervals to keep down aphids, capsid bugs and leaf miner. A suitable fungicide (it must be compatible) could be incorporated with the insecticide to give the plants protection against mildew.

Pot on coleus plants raised from cuttings into their final 5-in. pots, using John Innes No. 1 Potting Compost.

The appearance of hanging baskets can often be improved if some of the more flexible stems are pinned back to the side of the basket with pieces of wire bent like hairpins.

June: third week

Dead-head lupins and delphiniums. Disbud roses. Prick out aubrietas and alyssums. Sow winter-flowering pansies. Stop outdoor vines. Thin apricots. Protect cherries from birds. Plant leeks and cabbages. Pick tomatoes regularly. Spray carnations.

FLOWERS

I sometimes wonder if it is fully realised that there are nowadays insecticides which embrace chemicals of various kinds to effect a control over many pests. This is an important time saver for there are few gardeners who want to spend more time than they must on this kind of work.

At times when the weather is dry for long periods, watering is one of the most important tasks in the garden. I cannot impress on you too much how important it is to give the plants a good soaking. To do less than this will do more harm than good for if the surface soil only is moistened it will encourage the plants to make surface roots which are more likely to suffer from drought. So, water the soil well, and when the water has soaked in, water again so that the moisture penetrates deeply.

Shrubs and other plants growing under trees often suffer from a shortage of water, partly because the trees keep off the rain but also because they are competing with the trees for whatever moisture there is in the soil. Again, close attention to watering is necessary or plants growing in such conditions will not remain healthy.

I always cut the seed pods from lupins and delphiniums as soon as the flowers fade and I find that this encourages them to give a second display in July or August.

If you want rose blooms of especially good quality then the clusters of buds should be reduced to one each, but if quantity rather than quality is the aim then disbudding is not necessary. It is best to retain the centre bud if possible as this will

be most advanced. This task should be carried out at an early stage of bud development, and it is usually only done to hybrid tea roses.

If last winter happened to be severe and hydrangeas had their flower buds killed, it would be wise to cut back the stems which would have carried flowers so that any buds emerging from near the base will have the benefit of extra light. It is at the tip of such growths that the buds for next year's flowers will form, so it is wise to let them have all the benefits. Any thin or poor shoots are best removed altogether.

Aubrieta and *Alyssum saxatile* are extremely useful garden plants and seedlings raised from sowings made earlier can now be pricked out in a nursery bed. I mix a little peat and sand with the soil before doing this and afterwards shade the young plants from strong sunshine for a few days.

Low-growing bedding plants such as verbenas and Ivy-leaved geraniums can be pegged down so that they cover the soil with a continuous carpet of growth and flowers. Use pieces of galvanised wire bent like hairpins.

A place should be found in every garden for some winter-flowering pansies. Their cheery flowers are doubly welcome at that time of year. Sow the seed in boxes and put these in a cold frame. When the resulting seedlings are large enough to handle, prick them out into boxes of John Innes No. 1 Potting Compost. When well established in the boxes they can be planted out in the garden.

Now that the rose season is getting into

Removing the seed pods from a lupin. If this is done promptly, a second display of flowers will appear in July or August

full swing, it is a good idea to start taking notes on roses which especially interest one when they are seen in other people's gardens, in public parks and so on. Such notes are extremely helpful when the time comes to order new roses in the autumn – and however good we think our memories are we are all fallible. The things to watch for are performance after prolonged rain (what has happened to the blooms), for some varieties show up very badly under such conditions while others do well; resistance to disease; the way the blooms age; degree of fragrance; and the habit of the variety – lax, compact and so on. It is things like these, and the all-important

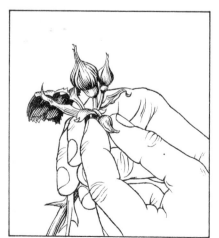
Disbudding a hybrid tea rose to give large flowers. The small, side buds are removed as soon as they are big enough to handle

Pegging down the shoots of verbena with pieces of bent wire so that eventually the ground will be covered with a carpet of flowers. This can only be done with plants that have a tendency to trail

colour balance of a variety which should interest us all.

FRUIT

Vines growing out of doors can be stopped now. New side growths should have their growing points pinched out at two leaves beyond the embryo bunches of fruit. Secondary growths should be stopped after the first leaf, and tendrils should also be pinched out. Do not allow any side growths to carry more than one bunch of fruit.

Apricot fruits should be thinned now, if the stones have formed. It is not always essential to do this, especially if the flowers failed to set well. Apples and pears can also be given an initial thinning. This task must not be carried out drastically though, as there may well be some fruits which will fall before they have grown fully.

This is about the right time in the north of the country to spray or dust raspberries with derris as a protection against raspberry beetle.

As dessert cherries begin to ripen, protect them from birds. There will be little fruit left to harvest if this is not done.

VEGETABLES

Leeks can now be planted, and for general purposes I think the best way to set about this is to make planting holes 6 to 8 in. deep with a large dibber. One leek can be dropped into each planting hole which is then well watered. Sufficient soil should be carried into the hole with the water to cover the roots and no more filling in is necessary.

Savoy cabbages and January King cabbages can also be planted out at this time.

More peas can be sown for succession, but the drills must be well watered before sowing. While on this subject of watering, if the weather is dry it is advisable to drench all vegetable plants thoroughly but especially peas, runner beans and celery.

Sow more lettuce seeds now. I would also suggest having a row of parsley for winter and spring use.

Asparagus cutting should cease at about this time so that the crowns have a reasonable period in which to build up their strength for next year's cropping. If the soil is poor it is advisable to apply a dressing of a general, organic-based fertiliser at the rate of about 2 oz. to the square yard.

GREENHOUSE

Tomatoes should be ripening fast now, and the fruit must be picked regularly. If some of the fruits are showing signs of greenback (the symptom is hard green skin forming around the top of the fruit), water the plants with a solution of 1 oz. of sulphate of potash in a gallon of water, for this complaint is connected with a shortage of potash in the soil.

One of the most valuable winter- and spring-flowering plants for the amateur gardener is *Primula malacoides*. It bears its numerous, small flowers in elegant sprays, one whorl of flowers above another, and colours include pink, rose, lilac and salmon-scarlet. Sow the seed in pots or boxes of seed compost and germinate in a temperature of 13 to 16°C. (55 to 60°F.).

Young hydrangea plants raised earlier from cuttings will probably now be in need of stopping. In any case, this task must not be carried out later than mid-July, otherwise the side growths would be made too late to flower well the next spring.

Many plants in the greenhouse need staking and tying at about this time. Do this job neatly or the whole reason for doing it is defeated. Use thin canes and narrow strips of raffia for the purpose. Always be careful not to inhibit growth when making the ties. The best way is usually to wrap the raffia around the cane, then loop it around the stem to be supported and make the tie behind the cane. If this is done there will be no constriction of growth.

Perpetual-flowering carnations should be potted on into 8-in. pots using John Innes No. 1 Potting Compost if this has not already been done.

It is at this time of year that carnations can be spoilt by aphids, thrips and red spider mites, and it is vital that the appropriate insecticide should be used immediately trouble is noticed. If this is not done, there is every chance that the whole crop will be lost or spoilt to a lesser degree. Use a BHC fumigant or a malathion spray against aphids. Fumigate with azobenzene against red spider mite, or spray with water, for this pest thrives in dry conditions. Fumigate or spray with BHC against thrips.

Pot winter-flowering begonias on into 4- or 5-in. pots using the John Innes No. 2 Potting Compost. Do not pot too firmly.

Planting out seedling leeks. **1.** If the plants are dipped in water to start with, the roots will cling together. **2.** This makes it much

easier to drop the plants straight into the ready-prepared dibber holes. **3.** Firming is not necessary, for when the plants are

watered in, sufficient soil is washed down the hole on top of the roots to hold the plants securely in position

June: fourth week

Divide irises. Take cuttings of alpines. Feed lawns. Prune early-flowering shrubs. Thin overcrowded fruit trees. Pick raspberries. Reduce strawberry runners. Protect cauliflower curds. Spray French and runner beans. Plunge azaleas outside. Fumigate against whitefly.

FLOWERS

Roses are now at their best, and it does no harm if the flowers are cut regularly. When cutting make sure that sharp secateurs or a good knife are used, and cut immediately above a strong bud at a leaf joint. This will encourage the bud into early growth, which will mean more flowers later on. Watch out for suckers which appear from below ground level and cut them away as near to the rootstock as possible to prevent further growth.

The tall bearded irises (which used, in the old days, to be called flag irises) have now finished flowering, and where the rhizomes are crowded together they should be lifted, divided and replanted. Select firm young pieces of rhizome and discard the old parts from the centre. Cut back the leaves to about 9 in. in length so that the plants will not be loosened in the ground by the wind. Irises like a rich soil containing plenty of humus-forming material and a light, sunny, open position. With planting completed, the top of the rhizome should show just above the soil.

It is always as well to have a few surplus alpines to fill bare spaces in the rock garden, and cuttings of many of these plants can be taken now. For example, alpine dianthus cuttings should root well in a sandy compost in a cold frame. Plant them out in the garden in the autumn when they have rooted.

If lawns are fed now with a good lawn fertiliser there is every reason to expect the grass to keep a good colour for the rest of the summer and autumn.

Gardens with large trees are often troubled with capsid bugs. These insects can do a lot of damage to fuchsias, dahlias and chrysanthemums. They can also spoil the late-summer flowers of the pretty blue-flowered shrub caryopteris, so I like to spray every 10 to 14 days with BHC. Rock roses (cistus) and sun roses (helianthemum) can also be badly damaged by capsid bugs and it is a good idea to spray these as well.

I have mentioned chrysanthemums in connection with capsid bugs. Watch out also for leaf miner, aphids and earwigs on this plant. All can be kept down with BHC.

I prune weigelas, philadelphuses, deutzias and escallonias as soon as their flowers fade to encourage new growth to form.

FRUIT

It is never possible to say what sort of a fruit crop each year will bring, but if the fruits have formed very generously, some thinning must take place if one wants quality, and I certainly do.

Raspberry picking is now in full swing, and as the fruits ripen quickly in warm weather the canes should be looked over every two or three days. If you do not possess a fruit cage for your soft fruits, protect the canes against birds with netting. Keep the plants mulched with straw or strawy manure, spreading this between the rows.

Strawberry plants which have been de-blossomed and earmarked for the production of runners should have these thinned out to leave no more than six strong runners to each plant. Pots and compost can be prepared as they will soon be needed. I prefer to peg the runners into pots to avoid disturbing the roots later.

Melons must be stopped by pinching

The richly coloured *Calendula* Geisha Girl is fully double with incurved petals like a chrysanthemum

Delphiniums are always popular plants for the herbaceous or mixed border. The tall flower spikes must be carefully staked at an early stage if they are to be grown to perfection. The variety illustrated here is Blue Jade

The author tidying up pelargoniums in his greenhouse. It is important to remove dead flowers and leaves at regular intervals to prevent fungal infection and to prolong the flowering display

Removing a rose sucker by drawing away the soil from the plant and cutting off the sucker at its point of origin

out the tips of the shoots one or two leaves beyond the point where the young melon fruits are forming. Secondary growths which arise should be stopped beyond the second leaf.

VEGETABLES

Carrots and beetroot raised from sowings made in late May and early June will now be ready for thinning.

Cucumbers growing in frames must be stopped regularly. As young cucumbers begin to form, place a slate or a piece of glass underneath each one to keep them off the soil.

To help rhubarb plants to build up good crowns for next year, any flower spikes which appear should be removed and the plants well watered and fed. They will appreciate a topdressing with garden compost or well-rotted manure.

Curds are beginning to form in the early cauliflowers, and to protect these from the sun and to keep them clean and white turn the leaves over them now. As cauliflowers and summer cabbages are cut, the stems and roots should be pulled up and burnt. This will help prevent the spread of club root and cabbage root fly.

In dry weather thrips can play havoc with peas and it is wise to spray at the first signs of attack with malathion or BHC.

Runner and French beans are likely to be badly affected by blackfly and it is best to spray with a systemic insecticide, such as one based on menazon, at the beginning of the season to keep the plants free of these pests.

GREENHOUSE

At this time of the year watering of pot plants is a job which needs regular attention. When the weather is hot, plants which have filled their pots with roots may need watering twice a day. If tuberous begonias are allowed to become dry the buds will drop quickly; a dry atmosphere will also cause the same trouble.

Plants of *Azalea indica* benefit from being plunged outside from the end of June to September. Choose a site in partial shade and bury the pots up to their rims. Continue to feed the plants at 14-day intervals throughout the summer.

Late-flowering chrysanthemums must be stopped for the last time now. Overhead spraying will be helpful to the plants.

Solanum capsicastrum, the Winter Cherry, does not always set its fruits freely.

Bending the inner leaves of a cauliflower over the curd to protect it from sun and rain and keep it clean and white

At this time of year the plants should be out of doors and they should be sprayed daily with clear water to encourage the flowers to set fruit. Feed once a week with liquid fertiliser until November, and water freely.

The foliage of freesias which finished flowering some time ago should have died down by now. The corms can be left in the pots until they are started into growth again in August or they can be cleaned, by removing the compost from around them, and afterwards stored in a dry place until the time for repotting comes around.

Freesias which were raised from seed sown earlier can now be stood out of doors in a sheltered place, or they can be grown in a cold frame during the summer.

Tuberous begonias and gloxinias grown from seed sown early in the year should be ready for potting into their final 5- or 6-in. pots. Use the John Innes No. 2 Potting Compost. These plants will be in flower from late July until October.

Tuberous begonias raised from tubers can be potted on into 7-in. pots if really large specimens are wanted. Again, use the John Innes No. 2 Potting Compost.

Sow cyclamen seed in boxes or pots filled with seed compost, and provide them with a temperature of 16°C. (60°F.).

White flies can be a nuisance in the greenhouse as they reproduce so rapidly. They are particularly troublesome where tomatoes are being grown and it is wise to fumigate the house regularly with BHC smoke pellets or cones. The fumigation will kill only the adult white flies and the treatment should be repeated at 10- to 14-day intervals to kill newly hatched adults.

Dividing bearded irises which have become overcrowded. **1.** The rhizomes are lifted and split up into small pieces. **2.** Firm, young portions are chosen for replanting, and the tall leaves should be cut back to prevent wind rocking

July: first week

Feed roses and chrysanthemums. Clip privet hedges. Take pink pipings. Divide hardy primulas. Peg down strawberry runners. Water celery. Spray potatoes. Prune hydrangeas. Tie in chrysanthemums. Disbud tuberous begonias. Take leaf cuttings of begonias.

FLOWERS

I find it a good policy as roses approach the end of their first flush of flowering to feed them with a special rose fertiliser or a general organic fertiliser, as this helps the second batch of flowers.

Outdoor chrysanthemums will also be in need of feeding, and it is a fertiliser fairly rich in potash which is needed. Scatter it lightly around the plants, hoe it in and, if the weather is dry, give a good watering afterwards.

Privet hedges must be clipped fairly frequently if they are to be kept neat and tidy, and this is even more important in the case of young hedges to ensure that the plants make dense, well-branched growth.

Garden pinks of all kinds can be increased by cuttings or pipings taken now, and the same is true of all perennial species of dianthus. The only difference between cuttings and pipings is that the former are severed with a knife or razor blade just beneath a joint, whereas pipings are carefully pulled out at a joint.

From now onwards, dead flowers should be removed regularly from plants as one walks around the garden for this encourages them to go on flowering and, of course, it keeps the garden neat and tidy.

If the weather is dry, I water my standard fuchsias at least once a week as I find that they need a lot of moisture. I also feed them regularly with a compound fertiliser to keep them growing and flowering. Alternatively, add a liquid or soluble fertiliser to the water.

Hardy primulas such as *Primula japonica*

Standard fuchsias need plenty of water if they are to flourish. A liquid fertiliser applied regularly is also very beneficial

and *P. pulverulenta* can be lifted and divided when they have finished flowering. The clumps can be split into several crowns and they should be transplanted into a moist shady position. The old flower heads of primulas can be removed unless they are needed for seed, in which case I tie the flower stems to a thin cane to prevent them being broken before the seed has ripened.

FRUIT

In view of the prevalence of various strawberry diseases, it is probably not very wise to raise any plants at home. It is far better to buy certified stock from a nursery. However, if you do wish to take your own runners be sure to pick the parent plants carefully, choosing only those which appear to be in perfect health. Any plants which show signs of yellowing or rolling and crinkling of the leaves should be pulled up and burnt.

I always prefer to peg the runners into pots filled with potting soil and sink these into the ground around the parent plants rather than peg the layers into the open ground. The main advantage of this is that there is less disturbance to the roots later on. Keep the layers well watered, and when they have rooted well, sever them from the parent plants.

I consider that strawberry beds which are three years or more old have outlived their usefulness and should be discarded.

VEGETABLES

Some of the earlier crops such as potatoes, early peas and broad beans have finished or will soon be finishing. They should be cleared away as quickly as possible to make room for various catchcrops such as shorthorn carrots and globe beetroot. For instance, beetroot sown now will provide roots for pulling in September and October. It is also worth taking the risk of making a further sowing of a dwarf, early-maturing pea such as Meteor or Kelvedon Wonder.

A late savoy cabbage such as Ormskirk can be sown now where the plants can be left to mature. Sow the seed thinly and then reduce the seedlings to 15 or 18 in. apart. The winter cabbage, January King, should be planted now without delay, and this is also the latest time for planting out autumn-heading cauliflower and broccoli. Plant broccoli 2½ ft. apart for it needs

Taking pink pipings. This is done by carefully pulling out non-flowering shoots from the joints of the plants

plenty of room for expansion as the plants are big and leafy. All brassicas like firm ground.

Celery must be watered freely whenever the weather is dry, for it is a moisture-loving plant. If it is allowed to become dry or to receive a check from any other cause at this time of year it is likely to run to seed. Dusting with BHC will help to keep off the celery fly.

Potatoes should be sprayed now, as a matter of routine, with Bordeaux mixture or a copper fungicide as a precaution against potato blight.

GREENHOUSE

This is the latest time for cutting back established hydrangeas after flowering. If this were done later the plants would not have sufficient time to make new growth for next year's flowering.

Greenhouse chrysanthemums, which are now standing outside for the summer, should be fed regularly to encourage growth

Above: The water lily Mrs Richmond has especially large flowers which darken to a deep rose colour as they mature

Below: *Hebe* Midsummer Beauty, a slightly tender evergreen shrub which is particularly suitable for seaside gardens

Young hydrangea plants in 3-in. pots should be repotted into 5-in. pots. Use the John Innes No. 2 Potting Compost but again substitute hydrangea colourant for the lime content. By mid-July they should have their growing tips removed so that they make bushy plants. After stopping, the plants can be moved to a cold frame if this is available. Remember to keep them well watered throughout the summer.

Chrysanthemums, which should be standing outdoors now in their pots, will need regular tying, in addition to watering and feeding. Make sure that the stakes are strong enough to do their job properly.

Tuberous begonias should be disbudded. It is the small side buds of the female flowers that must be removed. It should be remembered, too, that these plants do not like an over-dry atmosphere as this will cause bud dropping.

Young plants of perpetual-flowering carnations are now better accommodated in a frame than in the greenhouse itself. This is the time to give the plants their final stopping to encourage a succession of flowers later on. The sideshoots should be stopped at four pairs of leaves. Once the plants have filled their final pots with roots, feed them once a week using a liquid or soluble fertiliser with a high potash content.

This is the ideal time to propagate *Begonia rex* from leaf cuttings. Slit the veins on well-developed leaves and lay these, with the stem in the soil, on a mixture of sand and peat in a seed pan or box. Small stones placed on the leaves will keep the veins in contact with the rooting medium. Place the leaf cuttings in a temperature of 16 to 18°C. (60 to 65°F.) and shade them if necessary. The young plants which develop should be potted individually into 2-, 3½- and then 5-in. pots, using John Innes No. 1 Potting Compost.

The Rex begonias are grown mainly for their very handsome leaves, and one of the best known is the showy *B. masoniana* whose leaves are marked with a prominent pattern like an Iron Cross. These begonias should never be dried off and they need a minimum winter temperature of 10°C. (50°F.) and shade from strong sunshine in summer. They are very happy when grown on the greenhouse floor, just under the staging, where they will be in partial shade.

July: second week

Layer border carnations. Take begonia cuttings. Feed and mulch dahlias. Thin overcrowded fruit trees. Thin outdoor grapes and spray against mildew. Pollinate melons. Sow endive, spinach beet and seakale beet. Take cuttings of regal pelargoniums. Pot up cinerarias.

The bicolor floribunda rose Daily Sketch, used here as a hedging plant. Such a hedge could be an extremely attractive feature in the garden with its beautiful blooms lasting throughout the summer and well into autumn if the weather is mild

FLOWERS

The many flower shows held up and down the country each summer provide a splendid opportunity to see the new roses. It is a good idea to make a note of these straightaway so that you can order them while stocks are still available. Usually such roses are in very limited supply and the really good ones are soon snapped up.

It is wise to spray all roses now against greenfly and mildew. I find that a combined insecticide and fungicide containing BHC and dinocap control most troubles.

This is the time of year when I layer border carnations and pinks (dianthus). Only good, healthy plants should be selected, and sturdy, non-flowering shoots are the ones which are actually layered. It is well worth while to replace some of the soil around each plant to be layered with potting compost so that the layers, pegged into this, have a good rooting medium.

Cuttings can be taken between now and the end of August from *Begonia semperflorens* used in bedding displays. These are made from young shoots taken from the base of the plants and should be rooted in the greenhouse in a temperature of 18°C. (65°F.). They will flower as pot plants in the greenhouse during the winter.

Outdoor chrysanthemums need good support as their stems are brittle and easily broken by wind and rain. If the stakes were not put in at planting time, this should be done immediately. Take care to make them firm.

Yet another flower that will need staking and tying now is the gladiolus. If the stakes were not put in last month (see p. 67) allow one cane to each spike.

The feeding of dahlias should begin now, but be careful to keep the fertiliser away from the stems. A mulch of lawn mowings or garden compost will help a lot as dahlias like moisture. The taller varieties must be securely staked as heavy and brittle shoots are easily snapped off. This is a job which must be attended to regularly, as the plants develop.

FRUIT

Strawberry runners which have been layered in pots should be watered regularly for the soil in the pots can get very dry.

Pears, plums and even dessert cherries will all repay careful thinning if there has been a heavy set of fruit.

Now is the time, also, to complete the thinning of outdoor grapes and to spray the vines with dispersible sulphur or Bordeaux mixture against mildew and other fungi.

Melons grown under cloches or in frames and greenhouses should now be ready for pollinating. It is essential to hand pollinate the flowers and not to leave it to nature. The female flowers can be recognised by the small embryo fruit behind the flower. All the female flowers on a plant should be fertilised at the same time with pollen from the male flowers. At this time, also, all shoots should be pinched out at one or two leaves beyond the point at which the fruit is forming.

VEGETABLES

Continue to sprinkle fertiliser between the onion rows to produce large bulbs. Apply the fertiliser at the rate of 1 oz. to a yard of row and hoe it in carefully.

If flower stems appear on shallots these should be removed.

More endive should be sown for autumn and winter use. Sow the seeds ½ in. deep and provide them with rich, well-dug soil and an open situation. Late-sown endive – sowings can be made up to mid-August – should be protected with a frame or cloches in the autumn and during the last few weeks the glass can be covered with black polythene to ensure a sufficient degree of blanching.

Spinach beet and seakale beet (Swiss chard) are two vegetables not sufficiently grown in gardens. These are profitable crops which give a supply of edible leaves over a long period. Seeds of both these vegetables can be sown now.

Mulch along the sides of the rows of runner beans with lawn mowings, garden compost or even straw. The object is not so much to feed the beans as to retain the moisture in the soil. But do not forget to water the soil thoroughly before applying the mulch, and pull the mulch back at intervals to make sure that the soil is still moist.

Any flower stems which appear on seakale plants should be removed at once. If they are picked while still young and tender they make a good vegetable.

Propagating border carnations by layering. Sturdy, non-flowering shoots are selected, and an upward cut is made in the stem to form a 'tongue'. The wounded portion, from which roots will grow, is then pegged down into the soil using a piece of bent wire

Hand pollinating the female flowers of a melon with a male flower that has been stripped of its petals

Cucumbers in frames will need regular watering and feeding, and the laterals should be stopped also at regular intervals.

More round-seeded spinach can be sown to provide a continuity of supply. Make the sowings in drills 1 in. deep and 1 ft. apart in ground which has been well dug and well manured. The resulting seedlings should be thinned to 9 in. apart towards the end of August.

More lettuce and salad onions can also be sown for succession.

GREENHOUSE
Grapes growing in unheated greenhouses will now probably be in need of their final

Inserting the stakes for dahlias. Good support is necessary especially for the large-flowered varieties

thinning. Pay particular attention to the shoulders of each bunch where overcrowding is likely to occur. Use the narrow, pointed scissors needed for this job with great care and, if possible, also have a small forked stick with which to lift the individual berries. In this way the bloom on the grapes will remain unmarked.

Regal pelargoniums will prefer to be moved out of doors for the next few weeks. They can be stood in their pots in any convenient place and will need no protection. Cuttings may be taken from these plants throughout the summer and autumn but July is usually the most convenient time as the plants have finished flowering.

Make the cuttings from firm, young, non-flowering growths, 3 to 5 in. in length. Trim them cleanly at the base just below a leaf joint. Remove the lower leaves and dip the cuttings in hormone rooting powder before placing round the edge of 3½-in. pots filled with a mixture of 1 part loam, 2 parts peat and 3 parts coarse sand. If extra sand is spread over the compost, a little of this will trickle down into the bottom of each hole as the cuttings are inserted and will assist rooting.

The cuttings are now placed on the greenhouse bench and well watered in. If they are shaded from direct sunshine and are syringed once or twice a day they should root without any trouble.

Cinerarias should be potted singly before they become overcrowded. Put them into 3½-in. pots of John Innes No. 1 Potting Compost and keep them in a cool

place. They can be moved to a cold frame during the summer.

Flowering plants like tuberous begonias, gloxinias and fuchsias will need to be fed regularly to ensure that they continue to bloom well.

Pick off the flower buds of coleus plants as they appear to prevent them from flowering, and pinch out the growing tip of each plant to encourage bushy growth and the production of more colourful leaves.

The main batch of cyclamen, which should now be growing in frames, will benefit from an overhead spraying with clear water in the morning and evening in warm weather.

Feeding onions with a general organic-based fertiliser at the rate of 1 oz. to the yard of row will produce large bulbs

July: third week

Prick out biennials. Thin dahlias. Bud roses. Spray gooseberries. Prune and feed black currants. Prune trained apple trees. Protect morello cherries from birds. Destroy eggs of cabbage white butterflies. Spray celery against leaf spot and celery fly. Stop outdoor tomatoes.

Thinning apples. The king fruit, which is found in the centre of each cluster, is the best one to remove

FLOWERS

If the season has been kind, seedling wallflowers, Sweet Williams, Canterbury Bells and other biennials should be ready for transplanting. The seedlings must be pricked out into a nursery bed 9 in. apart in rows 9 to 12 in. apart. They need good soil and an open situation so that they will develop into strong plants for moving to their flowering positions in the autumn. If the soil is dry, draw out drills as for seed sowing and prick out the seedlings into these so that a little trench remains into which water can be poured.

Dahlias will almost certainly need some thinning, and even more so where old tubers have been planted rather than dahlias grown from rooted cuttings. It is impossible to be precise, but the number of stems which should be left on a particular plant will depend on the size of the plant and the amount of space available. Common sense should be used to prevent overcrowding.

Floribunda roses do not need disbudding but faded flowers should be removed regularly. When the whole truss has finished the stem should be cut back to a prominent bud.

This is the time to bud roses, both bushes and standards. *Rosa canina, R. laxa* and *R. rugosa* are the stocks most frequently used. The latter is easy to work and is often used for standards. It is, however, very prone to produce suckers.

Buds of the kind needed can only come from half-ripened rose shoots of the current season's growth. The aim is to end up with a small, shield-shaped portion of green rind with a dormant bud and a leaf stalk by which it can be held. The thin sliver of wood at the back of the shield should be removed by lifting it carefully with the point of a knife blade and pulling it away from the rind.

The bud is now ready for insertion in the T-shaped incision made in the bark of the stock. It is slipped under the flaps of the incision and firmly fixed in position with raffia, which should cover the incision entirely so that only the bud itself is

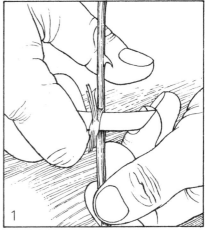

Budding a rose bush. **1.** A bud of the selected variety is prepared by cutting a shield-shaped portion of the rind and including

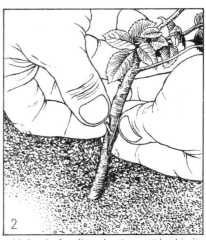

with it a leaf stalk and a dormant bud in its axil. **2.** The prepared bud is inserted in a T-shaped incision which has been made

Dahlia shoots should be thinned to prevent overcrowding, particularly if the plants have been grown from tubers rather than rooted cuttings. This should be done before the plants get too big

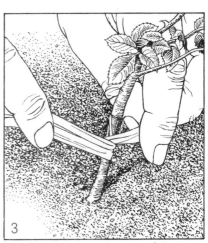

low down on the main stem of the rootstock. **3.** The bud is then firmly tied in position with raffia

exposed to the air. Bush roses are budded just below ground level for preference or as low as possible on the main stem. Standards are budded on the main stem at the height at which it is desired to form a head.

I wait three or four weeks before inspecting shields of rind. If the buds are fresh and plump it probably means that they have taken. Conversely, dry, shrivelled buds will have failed and re-working will be necessary.

Roses are often attacked by mildew if the weather is damp. Watch out for this and spray as soon as it is noticed with a fungicide based on copper, dinocap or thiram.

FRUIT
Now is the time to give the apples their final thinning. If the king fruit has not already been removed and there are other fruits to take its place, this is the one which should go. The king fruit is in the centre of each cluster, and it is seldom of such good shape as the others.

Gooseberries should be sprayed to keep down caterpillars, greenfly and other pests,

but as the fruit has not yet been picked (except for some unripe berries removed in early June for bottling) it is very important to make sure that the spray used is a safe one as harvesting will be in a week or two from now. Derris is a good choice.

As soon as the black currant crop has been gathered the bushes should be pruned. Black currants fruit best on new wood and hardly at all on older wood, so shoots which have fruited should be cut right out. This will encourage the production of new shoots next year. At least one third of the old wood will have to be removed, this being cut back to its point of origin. Some varieties produce strong new shoots on older wood and when this happens the older shoots must be cut back to this point.

After the bushes have been pruned they should be fed with a general organic fertiliser at the rate of 4 oz. to each plant. This will help to ripen the young wood.

Cordon, espalier and dwarf pyramid apples should be summer pruned, both to keep them in shape and to check their vigour. The new sideshoots should be shortened to four or five leaves each, not

counting the basal rosette of small leaves. Do not prune the main stems which are extending the height of cordons or the length of the branches of trained trees.

Cover Morello cherries with nets to protect the ripening fruits from birds.

VEGETABLES
Cabbage white butterflies are often present at this time of year, and caterpillars can be seen on cabbages and other members of the brassica family. Where possible, squash the eggs on the undersides of the leaves before any damage is done, and, in any case, spray with derris.

It is wise to spray celery with a combined fungicide and insecticide now as a protection against leaf spot disease and the maggots of the celery fly.

Runner beans will benefit from daily syringing with water to assist the setting of their flowers. They should be watered freely in dry weather.

Other plants which need similar attention are outdoor tomatoes. Their water needs must be watched carefully in dry weather. Feed outdoor tomatoes once a week with a good tomato fertiliser, as directed by the manufacturer, or a general fertiliser applied at the rate of 1 oz. per plant. Each plant should be stopped at one leaf above the fourth truss.

Make further sowings of parsley and turnips for succession. Remember that with turnips if the plants are left in the ground over winter, the tops can be used as a green vegetable in March and April.

GREENHOUSE
Seedlings of *Primula obconica* and *P. sinensis* should now be large enough for potting singly. Use the John Innes No. 1 Potting Compost. The plants can be put outside in a cold frame for the summer.

Rooted cuttings of Zonal pelargoniums required for winter flowering should be potted on now. When new roots have been made into the fresh soil, the tips of the plants should be pinched out.

Spray tomato plants overhead with water each day to encourage the flowers to set. The ventilators should be closed while doing this and kept shut for half an hour so that the atmosphere becomes really humid. Afterwards, open the ventilators gradually to give the plants the buoyant atmosphere they require.

Two hydrangeas of differing form. In the foreground is *Hydrangea macrophylla* Blue Wave, which takes on a rich blue colouring in acid soil. Behind this is *H. paniculata grandiflora*, which bears large panicles of sterile flowers

July: fourth week

Take half-ripe cuttings of shrubs. Bud fruit trees. Prepare ground for strawberries. Remove plum branches infected with silver leaf. Feed and water cucumbers and melons. Lift shallots and garlic. Gather herbs for drying. Start cyclamen into growth.

Above: The unusual flowers and bracts of *Leycesteria formosa* appear in the summer and are followed by dark purple berries

Below: A pretty annual for a sunny border is dimorphotheca. Those shown here are *aurantiaca* hybrids

FLOWERS

Now is the time to begin to propagate many shrubs. Cuttings of half-ripened wood of such popular shrubs as forsythia, flowering currant, escallonia, weigela, deutzia and *Viburnum tinus* will all root easily. Pull off the shoots with a heel of older wood attached, trim this neatly with a sharp knife or razor blade, dip in hormone rooting powder and then insert the cuttings in sandy soil in a cold frame with a close-fitting light. Shade from bright sun.

The scarlet *Lobelia cardinalis* and *L. fulgens* must be staked and tied to prevent the spikes from falling over as they become very heavy with flowers at this time of year.

Michaelmas daisies also need secure staking for, again, the flower sprays can become very heavy. The canes or sticks should be positioned in such a way that they do not interfere with the natural habit of the plants.

Sow seed of *Primula pulverulenta* and *P. japonica* as soon as this is ripe.

FRUIT

Continue to train wall-trained fruit trees, tying in the shoots which are to be retained as evenly as possible over the space available. This routine work is essential with peaches, nectarines and apricots.

This is the time to bud fruit tree stocks. Peaches, plums and other stone fruits are almost always increased by budding, and it is also a good method of increasing apples and pears; but it does mean that the necessary young rootstocks must be obtained during the autumn and winter.

It is now time to prepare the ground for new strawberry beds. As the plants will probably remain for two to three years (but no longer, see p. 75), the ground should be well dug and cleaned and thoroughly manured, both with well-rotted manure and bonemeal.

Any plum branches which show signs of silver leaf disease should be cut out at once and burnt. This disease, which causes a metallic silvering of the leaf, is not to be confused with mildew which produces a powdery white outgrowth on the leaves.

Melons in frames will need regular watering and feeding to swell the fruits.

When dessert cherries have finished fruiting spray the trees against black fly if this is still troublesome. Derris, malathion

After lifting shallots, they must be dried thoroughly in the sun so that they will store well during the winter. A good method of

doing this is to spread them out on the ground, and cover them with cloches

Applying a topdressing of rich compost to greenhouse chrysanthemums. Space was left for this when the plants were potted

or menazon (a systemic insecticide) can be used for this purpose.

VEGETABLES

Brussels sprouts will benefit if a little soil is pulled up around the stems from each side of the row, much as one would earth up potatoes.

The planting of sprouting broccoli, kale and so on should be completed as soon as possible now and this is certainly the latest time to plant broccoli which are to head by spring. The plants should be spaced 2½ ft. apart each way. Kale is extremely hardy, and the young shoots are eaten in late winter and early spring.

Drying herbs for winter use by tying them together in bunches and hanging them upside down in a cool, airy place

Cucumbers in frames will need a lot of water at this time of year and will also benefit from a weekly feed with a compound fertiliser. Remove the male flowers to prevent fertilisation of the female flowers. If this is not done the fruits will have a bitter taste.

Onions should also be fed for the last time. Sprinkle the fertiliser very thinly between the rows and then hoe it in.

Shallots and garlic have now finished making their growth and should be lifted carefully and laid out in the sun to dry. Often, it is a good idea to cover them with cloches, or if an empty frame is available they can be put in this with a light over the top of them to protect the bulbs from rain – but keep the frame ventilated.

Any flower heads which appear on spring-sown parsley should be removed as soon as they are noticed.

Now is the time to gather herbs of all kinds for drying. Tie the shoots or leaves up in small bundles and suspend them head down in a cool, airy shed or room, not, for preference, in strong sunlight.

GREENHOUSE

Chrysanthemums which are now growing in pots standing out of doors will benefit from topdressing with a good, rich compost. A space was left for this topdressing and I would recommend using the John Innes No. 3 Potting Compost.

Camellias growing in pots should be fed once a week throughout the summer.

Tomatoes which are carrying heavy crops may also need feeding with extra

nitrogen to help the top trusses. Dried blood can be used for this purpose, or sulphate of ammonia, but be careful not to give an overdose as this could easily cause severe leaf scorching. A teaspoonful of the fertiliser per gallon of water would be ample.

Sow seeds of Brompton stocks in seed boxes or pans and place in a cold frame.

At about this time of the year, old cyclamen corms can be started into growth again by watering them lightly. As new leaves appear, the plants should be re-potted in fresh John Innes No. 2 Potting Compost, keeping the corms slightly above the surface of the compost.

Feeding ring-culture tomatoes with a liquid fertiliser to encourage the top trusses of fruit to develop

August: first week

Disbud dahlias and outdoor chrysanthemums. Trim laurel hedges. Plant colchicums and Madonna lilies. Train wisterias. Water celery and runner beans. Bend onion tops over. Spray peas. Spray cyclamen in frames. Spray cinerarias. Remove lower leaves from tomatoes.

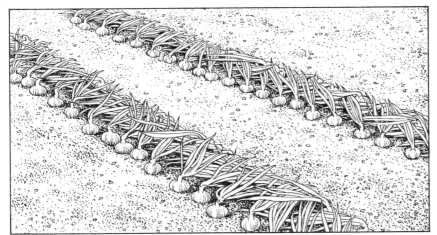

Hastening the ripening of onions by bending over the tops. Partially lifting the bulbs with a fork will also help this process. Later, they will be lifted properly, and thoroughly dried off in the sun

FLOWERS

In addition to thinning the growths of dahlias, which I mentioned earlier, they should be disbudded, only one flower being retained on each stem. There is, however, no point in doing this with small-flowered varieties grown primarily for garden decoration, and it certainly should not be done with small pompons in which to have too large a flower is a fault. The plants will also need regular tying as their stems become very heavy with foliage and bloom and are easily broken by the wind.

Unless outdoor-flowering chrysanthemums are being grown specifically for spray flowers I disbud them to one flower bud per stem. All the remaining buds should be rubbed away, and all sideshoots should be removed.

This is a good time to trim laurel hedges. For this, secateurs should be used and not hedge shears which would disfigure the foliage. It is distressing to see a good hedge spoilt by careless trimming.

This is the latest time to plant colchicums (the Meadow Saffron), autumn-flowering crocuses and hardy, spring-flowering cyclamen. Colchicums produce their lovely lavender flowers before the leaves and the bulbs should be planted with a covering of 2 in. of soil. Where several bulbs are being planted, space them 12 in. apart and make sure that you choose a well-drained site. It is possible to buy dry tubers of hardy cyclamen but results are not always satisfactory as the tubers often fail to grow. To obtain the best results, purchase pot-grown plants.

Most lilies should be planted in November or in early spring, but the lovely Madonna Lily, *Lilium candidum*, is an exception and it must be planted during August. Do not bury the bulbs deeply – an inch of soil above them is ample.

Pinch back the unwanted growths on wisterias to keep the plants under control.

There is still time to take cuttings or pipings of pinks (see p. 75).

FRUIT

If black currants were not pruned and fed last month (see p. 80), this job should be attended to straightaway to encourage strong, young fruiting growths for the following year. Take care when applying the fertiliser to keep it away from the young shoots as they are easily scorched.

VEGETABLES

Both runner beans and celery are crops which need a lot of moisture, and if the weather continues hot and dry they should be watered freely. Both will also benefit from feeding during early August. I like to use a solution of nitrate of soda mixed at the rate of $\frac{1}{2}$ oz. to a gallon of water, this to be given after normal watering.

During dry spells the flowers of runner beans will often wither and fall without setting. A fine spray of water each day over the whole of the plants will help to encourage a good set of beans.

By this time autumn-sown onions and those grown from sets should be making good bulbs and the tops are best turned over to hasten ripening. If the bulbs are partially lifted with a fork, this will also encourage them to ripen. This ripening process is important if the bulbs are to keep right through the winter.

Spray or dust the later peas with BHC as a preventive against thrips, and add a fungicide to this to control mildew which can be troublesome at this time of year. BHC should not be put on food crops which are to be used within two weeks.

Spring cabbage seed may be sown in the Midlands and the North. Make a further sowing of lettuce for late autumn use.

It large flowers are wanted on dahlia plants, it is a good idea to disbud them, leaving only one bud to each stem

To enable light to reach the lower trusses of tomatoes and assist with ripening, some of the nearby leaves may be removed

Above: Kniphofias or Red Hot Pokers are striking plants for the herbaceous border and great favourites with many people

Below: An ideal plant for later summer colour in the border and for use as a cut flower is *Scabiosa caucasica* Clive Greaves

Cucumbers growing in frames will need feeding as well as watering and I like to topdress over the roots with John Innes No. 3 Potting Compost. Cut the fruits regularly as they mature.

GREENHOUSE

Seedling calceolarias should be potted before they become overcrowded into 3-in. pots of John Innes No. 1 Potting Compost. They need cool, shady conditions.

At this time of year cyclamen which are passing the summer in frames need to be sprayed overhead both in the morning and the evening. I close the frame immediately after the evening spraying but open it again just before it becomes dark. From August onwards, when the weather is warm, I like to take the lights off the frames completely in the evening to allow dew to get on the leaves.

Keep a careful watch on cinerarias for aphids and the leaf miner maggots which make white streaks in the leaves. If taken early the maggots can easily be killed with the point of a penknife or between the finger and thumb, but if the attack is severe, spray with malathion.

There is a delightful, fragrant, white-flowered jasmine, *Jasminum polyanthum*, which blooms in winter and is ideal for training up one end of the greenhouse. It needs this protection as it is not quite hardy. The flowers are pink at bud stage. Cuttings of this species can be rooted now in sandy compost in a propagating frame with a temperature of 18 to 21°C. (65 to 70°F.). Make the cuttings 4 in. long.

Some of the leaves must be removed from the lower part of tomatoes grown under glass to allow the sun to ripen the fruits, but do not remove too many leaves at any one time or the swelling of the fruits will be checked.

Prick out cyclamen seedlings raised from a sowing made at the end of June when these are large enough to handle. Some seeds take several weeks longer than others to germinate, so do not discard the seed pan straightaway. Prick the seedlings out into boxes filled with John Innes No. 1 Potting Compost.

This is also the time to prick out seedlings of *Primula malacoides* before they become overcrowded. Put them into seed boxes of John Innes No. 1 Potting Compost and house them in a cold frame.

August: second week

Collect and sow seeds of hardy primulas and meconopsis. Retrain cordon sweet peas. Plant Brompton stocks. Prune raspberries. Sow spring cabbages and onions. Earth up celery. Pot up pelargonium cuttings. Sow schizanthus. Feed ferns.

FLOWERS

To keep the garden neat and tidy cut off the dead flower heads and seed pods on herbaceous border plants regularly. The same applies to annuals, for by preventing seed formation the plants are encouraged to go on flowering into the autumn.

Seed pods of hardy primulas and *Meconopsis betonicifolia* (*M. baileyi*), the lovely Himalayan Blue Poppy, are now ripening. The seeds will germinate better and more quickly if they are sown immediately. The seeds of hardy primulas can be sown out of doors in good, well-drained soil in a shady border. Meconopsis seed can also be sown out of doors in sheltered areas, but in my part of the country (Shropshire) I prefer to sow the seed in boxes. If they are germinated in this way use a light compost containing a good proportion of peat (one of the soilless seed composts would be ideal), and stand the boxes in a shady cold frame or a cool greenhouse.

As cordon-trained sweet peas reach the top of the canes, the stems should be un-

The large, fragrant blooms of *Lilium auratum*, The Golden-rayed Lily of Japan, are borne on stems which may be up to 8 ft. in height,

tied and lowered. Lay them along the ground and retrain them up canes five or six feet further along the row.

Winter-flowering pansies, raised from seed sown in a cold frame in June, will now need pricking out. The young seedlings should be spaced 3 to 4 in. apart in a nursery bed. They should grow rapidly and make good specimens for planting in their flowering positions in October.

If they have not already been pricked out, the same advice applies to wallflowers, forget-me-nots, Sweet Williams and other biennials.

FRUIT

If strawberries are planted within the next few weeks the plants should carry a good crop next year. It is a common fault to plant too closely, and a distance of 2 ft. should be left between the plants and 2½ ft. between the rows. It is most important to make sure that you obtain certified virus-free stock as strawberries are so prone to virus disease.

To assist the ripening of peach and nectarine fruits, move the leaves back to making it an impressive plant by any standards. It likes a lime-free soil, and good drainage is essential

expose the fruits to the sun. A label tucked behind each fruit will help to bring them forward to the sun. Keep the lateral growths pinched back.

Start to prune raspberries as they finish fruiting. The old canes which have fruited should be cut out to ground level and only six or seven of the strongest new canes retained on each plant for fruiting next year. To prevent overcrowding, remove any young growths from the base of the stools.

With raspberry pruning completed, tie the selected new canes to the wires, and then apply a dressing of general fertiliser at the rate of 2 oz. per yard of row. Keep the fertiliser away from the canes, otherwise scorching is likely to occur.

I sometimes think gardeners are not nearly so thorough as they should be when carrying out summer pruning of this kind, and it is as well to remember that reducing growth as much as possible will result in a crop of high quality being obtained next season.

VEGETABLES

Seed of spring cabbages can be sown now. This crop needs to be grown in good, well-worked but firm soil. Good varieties are Flower of Spring and Harbinger. The plants should be ready for setting out by the end of September or the beginning of October. Space them 18 in. apart in rows 2 ft. apart.

A sowing of onion seed to provide plants for spring planting should be made now in a sheltered nursery bed. They need a deep, well-worked soil containing plenty of plant food. Suitable varieties are Ailsa Craig and Autumn Queen.

Make a sowing of the onion White Lisbon, too, this month if you want a supply of spring onions.

Potato blight must not be allowed to develop for if it does, not only will it spoil the potato crop, but it will also attack outdoor tomatoes. Spraying regularly with a copper fungicide will help to prevent serious damage to both these crops.

Start to blanch celery by earthing up the plants. Any small offsets should be removed first, and then newspaper is wrapped around the stalks and tied loosely with raffia to prevent soil getting to the heart. The earthing up should be done in easy stages, drawing up a little soil at a time

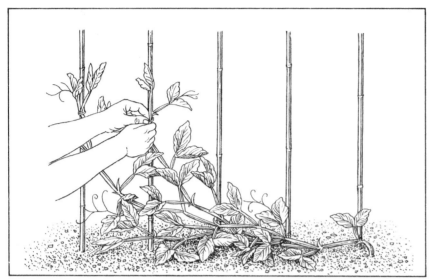

When cordon-trained sweet peas reach the top of their canes they can be untied, laid on the ground, and then retrained up another cane further along the row. This will ensure the continued production of flowers throughout the summer

over the next six or eight weeks until only the tuft of leaves at the top of the plants is exposed.

GREENHOUSE

Pelargonium (geranium) cuttings which have now rooted should be potted without delay into 3- or 3½-in. pots using the John Innes No. 1 Potting Compost. Cuttings of *Genista fragrans* which have rooted need the same attention.

Pelargoniums needed for flowering in the winter are best stood out of doors for a few weeks so that the growths become well ripened. Small attentions like this make all the difference.

Seeds of schizanthus – the Poor Man's Orchid or Butterfly Flower as it is often called – can be sown at this time. This is a lovely flower for a spring display and it is not difficult to grow. The types I would recommend growing are the Pansy-flowered and Dwarf Bouquet.

It is important that schizanthus should be grown without undue heat. Sow the seed in pots or boxes of seed compost and cover them over with sheets of glass and paper until germination takes place. The containers should be stood in a cold frame or greenhouse, and, when the seedlings appear, remove the coverings and give them full light. When they are large enough to handle, the seedlings should be pricked out into boxes or pots of John Innes No. 1 Potting Compost.

As old cyclamen corms begin to make new growth they will need watering more often as the plants will be filling their pots with roots. Cyclamen strongly dislike draughts so ventilate the greenhouse carefully.

Arum Lilies – *Zantedeschia aethiopica* is their correct name although in the past they have been called everything from arum, to calla and richardia – will now be making new growth. Leave them outside in a shady position until the end of the month when they will need dividing and repotting.

Shake the old soil from the roots and then carefully divide them. Put three roots or crowns in each 8-in. pot and use the John Innes No. 2 Potting Compost. Water the pots well and then stand them in a sheltered position out of doors. The plants must, however, be brought into a cool greenhouse before there is any chance of autumn frosts occuring.

Some gardeners seem to think that ferns need no feeding. This assumption is quite incorrect and they should be fed regularly just like other plants during the spring and summer. And into the autumn as well if the fern is not of a type which needs a resting period. Weak liquid manure or soluble fertiliser should be used for this purpose.

Ferns are very valuable in the greenhouse for they are superb foliage plants and make a splendid foil for the many flowering plants which can be grown around them.

Earthing up celery to blanch the stems. **1.** small offsets should first be carefully removed. **2.** Newspaper collars are then wrapped around the plants and tied loosely with raffia. These collars will help to keep the sticks of celery clean. **3.** Soil is then pulled up around the plants, a little at a time over the next six or eight weeks

August: third week

Take cuttings of zonal pelargoniums. Protect dahlias from earwigs. Remove rose suckers. Cut and dry 'everlasting' flowers. Select strawberry plants for forcing next year. Pick early apples. Sow green manure crop. Order Christmas bulbs. Sow cyclamen.

FLOWERS

Zonal pelargoniums are splendid summer bedding plants but one should not overlook their value as pot plants for frost-free greenhouses, sun lounges and conservatories. I am particularly fond of the salmon King of Denmark, the vermilion Paul Crampel and the bright red Irene, but there are, of course, a great many more to choose from.

Cuttings of these plants can be rooted in two ways, either out of doors in a border, or in pots in a cool greenhouse.

First, out of doors. A partially shaded border is preferable and the soil should contain plenty of coarse sand to assist with the formation of roots.

Under glass, place several cuttings around the edge of 3½-in. pots or insert them singly in small pots in a sandy compost. They should soon form roots and can then be potted singly in 3½-in. pots, using the John Innes No. 1 Potting Compost. They will remain in these, in a light position, for the winter, being repotted into 5- or 6-in. pots the following spring. A temperature of between 7 and 13°C. (45 and 55°F.) should be maintained throughout the winter. The cuttings raised out of doors will, after rooting, be treated in exactly the same way.

Growths from which cuttings are made can be taken from plants at this time of the year without greatly disfiguring them or in any way spoiling the appearance of the bedding display. Firm shoots must be chosen and when preparing the cuttings make a clean cut immediately below a node

Earwigs often do a lot of damage to dahlias. A simple trap can be made by inverting a straw-filled flower pot on a stake

Vegetable marrows should be cut while they are still young, otherwise the skin hardens and sets

or leaf joint. It is necessary to use a really sharp knife or a razor blade to get this kind of cut.

Earwigs can be a great nuisance on dahlia plants as they eat the flower buds, thus damaging the petals. It is wise to take all possible precautions to keep their numbers down. Hollow bamboo canes are often a favourite hiding place, and it is a good idea to seal up the tops of the canes used to support the dahlias with putty. Flower pots filled with hay and inverted on stakes amongst the plants make very effective earwig traps. They must be inspected each day, and any insects they contain disposed of. An alternative method to trap-

ping is to spray or dust the plants with an insecticide containing BHC.

Suckers which appear around roses should be cut off close to the rootstocks to prevent further growth. If necessary, draw back the soil so that this job can be done properly. Faded blooms should also be removed to prevent rose hips from forming, except in the case of species roses where these are a decorative feature during autumn and winter.

New growths which appear on climbing roses should be tied into place as they develop to prevent them from being damaged by wind or rain.

It is now time to cut 'everlasting'

Removing the faded flowers of a rose. The stem should be cut back with a sharp pair of secateurs to an outward-pointing bud

French beans must be gathered regularly if they are to be eaten at their best. If left on the plants, the pods become stringy and the beans inside will swell. Also, regular picking will increase the size of the crop

Autumnal shades in the herbaceous border. Often, subdued tones of green and grey with just a touch of brightness here and there can be much more effective than a riot of colour

flowers such as statice, helichrysum and acroclinium for drying for winter decoration. Achillea flower heads can also be dried for the same purpose. The flower stems should be tied into bunches and hung upside down in a cool, dry, airy place, away from direct sunshine which would make the flowers fade.

Dianthus cuttings which were taken last month (see p. 75) will have rooted by now, and can be planted out in their growing positions. They like a good-quality, well-drained soil of a non-acid nature and an open sunny position.

FRUIT

Young growths on Morello cherries trained on walls should be kept in place and any unnecessary growths pruned out. The Morello cherry carries its fruit on young wood made in the previous year, like the peach and the nectarine.

A good way of trapping woodlice, which can be troublesome on peach and nectarine trees, is to place hollow portions of broad bean stems among the branches along the wall. The insects will hide inside the stems during the day and each morning the traps should be inspected and the woodlice dislodged and destroyed.

Growths on wall-trained plums must be trained into position and either tied to the supporting wires or to nails in the wall. The leading growths on espalier-trained trees should also be tied into place where these are needed to extend the framework of the tree.

Good, strong-growing strawberry plants in pots can be selected for forcing under glass next spring. The best plants can be potted now into 6½- or 7-in. pots using the John Innes No. 3 Potting Compost, these afterwards being plunged in a cold frame as they should not be moved into the greenhouse until the middle of January (see p. 28).

Some of the early apples ripen quite suddenly and are apt to fall if they are not picked at just the right time. This is particularly true of the variety Beauty of Bath.

Look over the trees daily and test the ripeness of the fruits by lifting them carefully. A fruit which is ready to be picked will virtually come away in the hand as soon as light pressure is exerted in this way. When the fruits part readily from the branches, gather in the crop.

VEGETABLES

Marrows should be cut while they are young and tender and before the outer skin hardens and sets.

Seedlings of seakale beet and spinach beet raised from sowings made in July (see p. 77) should be thinned now to about 12 in. apart.

Gather French and runner beans regularly while they are young and before they become old and stringy. Not only will they be nicer to eat if picked at this stage, but the growing season will be extended into the autumn.

A sowing of lettuce can be made out of doors now for planting later in a garden frame. Good varieties for this sowing are Cheshunt Early Giant, All the Year Round and May Queen.

In the North the ground can be prepared for planting spring cabbages. Fork over the soil lightly to remove any plant remains and to level the ground, and apply a dressing of general organic-based fertiliser at the rate of 2 oz. per square yard. When the time for planting comes round in a month or so the ground should be nicely firmed – this can be ensured by treading.

As farmyard manure is scarce and expensive these days it is a good idea to sow a green manure crop now if there is any vacant ground in the vegetable garden or allotment. Rape or mustard are suitable plants and can be sown broadcast. All that is necessary is to fork over the soil, scatter the seed and rake it in. It is important to dig in the mustard or rape before the plants begin to flower (to prevent the formation of seed) and before they are cut back by frost.

GREENHOUSE

Double-flowered begonias should be watched carefully for signs of botrytis or the grey mould fungus which may appear on the stems and where dead flowers have been removed.

This disease is more common in cool, damp conditions and as well as dusting the infected parts with flowers of sulphur the atmosphere of the greenhouse must be kept drier, particularly at night, by careful ventilation.

Bulbs for Christmas flowering should be ordered without delay. Some of the easiest to have in flower early are the Roman hyacinths and Paper White and Grand Soleil d'Or narcissi. Specially treated, pre-cooled bulbs for forcing should also be obtained if flowers are needed for Christmas, and remember, it never pays to buy cheap bulbs.

If cyclamen seed was not sown in June (see p. 74), a sowing can be made now. Plants from this sowing will be in flower in 15 to 16 months' time.

Sow the seed very thinly in pans filled with seed compost and germinate in a temperature of 16°C. (60°F.). Watering must be done with great care as over-watering can easily cause the seeds to decay. Some seeds may take several weeks longer to germinate than others, so do not discard the pan of compost until the required number of seedlings has appeared. Move the resulting seedlings into boxes of John Innes No. 1 Potting Compost as soon as they can be handled safely, spacing them 2 to 3 in. apart each way, and keep them growing steadily in a temperature of 10 to 13°C. (50 to 55°F.).

This is the time to pot plants of *Primula obconica* and *P. sinensis* into their final 5-in. pots, using the John Innes No. 2 Potting Compost. Afterwards, return the plants to the cold frame in which they are spending the summer.

The fibrous-rooted, winter-flowering begonias can now be given their final move into 6- or 7-in. pots if really large plants are wanted. The John Innes No. 2 Potting Compost should be used for this move, and do not pot too firmly. Pick off any flowers which appear before the end of September or the beginning of October to build up the strength of the plants so that eventually a better display will be given. Winter-flowering begonias will need a minimum temperature of 16°C. (60°F.) if they are to flourish.

Prick out seedlings of Brompton stocks raised from a sowing made last month. Pot them into 3½-in. pots and use the John Innes No. 1 Potting Compost. Return the plants to the cold frame for a week or two. They can then be bedded out in the garden in their flowering positions except in very cold districts where it is safer to over-winter them in their pots in a cold frame, and plant them out in the garden in the spring.

When going on holiday, do your utmost to get somebody to look after your greenhouse plants. It is sad to see a whole year's work spoilt by a week or two of neglect.

August: fourth week

Plant border carnations. Prune rambler roses. Trim lavender bushes. Protect chrysanthemum blooms. Prepare compost heap. Remove strawberry runners. Sow winter lettuce. Prepare ground for winter cabbage. Start freesias and lachenalias. Disbud chrysanthemums.

FLOWERS

Border carnations and pinks (dianthus) layered during July should now be rooted and ready for planting in their flowering positions. Sever the young plants from their parents, and lift them with plenty of soil attached to the roots. Ordinary garden soil is quite suitable for planting, provided it is well drained, but it helps if a dressing of bonemeal is given, and moist peat worked into the soil is also beneficial.

In cold districts, however, it is best to pot the rooted layers and keep them in a cold frame for the winter, planting them out the following spring. In this case use 4-in. pots and the John Innes No. 1 Potting Compost.

As rambler roses finish flowering so they should be pruned. Disentangle the growths from the trellis work and cut out at ground level those growths which have carried flowers. This task is made much easier if you untie all the stems and spread them on the ground before you start pruning. Keep the new stems made this year and tie them neatly into place. These will bear flowers next year.

Cuttings of alpine plants put in earlier (see p. 72) and now rooted should either be planted out where they are to grow or be potted up and placed in a frame until the spring. If they are to be kept in pots in this way it is best to plunge the pots to their rims in sand, ashes or soil.

As soon as lavenders have finished flowering the bushes should be clipped back to prevent them becoming bare at the base. Bare branches of dead wood are usually caused by neglecting to clip back after flowering and then trying to cut back severely into old wood at a later date.

As soon as the petals on the flowers of outdoor chrysanthemums begin to show colour, protect them with paper bags or some kind of shelter – that is, if you want perfect blooms.

To be able to grow good plants the soil must contain liberal quantities of organic matter, and with farmyard manure so difficult to obtain nowadays it is most important that all waste green material from the garden should be saved for composting. From now on there should be quite a lot of garden waste and a compost heap can be built up in layers.

To ensure even decomposition of the heap, thoroughly soak each layer with water and sprinkle with a proprietary accelerator or with sulphate of ammonia. After a few weeks it will be necessary to turn the heap so that the unrotted material on the outside is thrown into the centre of the new heap. Keep the heap well watered.

FRUIT

It is wise to move back the foliage on cordon- and espalier-trained apples and pears so that the fruit is exposed to the sun to ripen.

Any side growths which appear on the

When border carnations layered last month are well rooted, they can be planted out in their flowering positions

young shoots of peaches and nectarines should be nipped out whenever they are seen.

As the melons being grown in frames begin to ripen, ventilate more freely. When the fruits begin to ripen a delicious scent is produced, and to assist ripening a warm, dry, atmosphere is needed. Damp, stuffy conditions may cause rotting.

Runners formed on ordinary strawberries should be removed as they are not needed. Any dead or diseased leaves should also be removed without delay. Strawberries are very prone to virus diseases, as I have already pointed out, and these are spread to a large extent by aphids. It is, therefore, wise to spray regularly to kill these insects and one of the best controls is malathion.

Water any newly planted strawberries to help them to become established in their new beds.

VEGETABLES

In the Midlands and South seed of winter lettuce may now be sown.

Outdoor tomatoes will need frequent feeding now, and watering if the weather is dry. To help the lower trusses of fruit to ripen some of the foliage may be removed, as I advised earlier, to expose the fruits to the sun.

Brussels sprouts and other winter greens will benefit from feeding with a sprinkling of a compound fertiliser around the plants. This will help to keep them growing steadily.

Protecting chrysanthemum blooms from sun and rain with the aid of paper bags and wire frames. This should be done as soon as the buds begin to show colour, if blooms of exhibition quality are required

Strawberry runners should be pinched out as they appear, unless they are required for propagation purposes

GREENHOUSE

Cinerarias in 3½-in. pots should now be ready for potting into their final 5- or 6-in. pots, using the John Innes No. 2 Potting Compost. The correct time is when the roots are beginning to fill the smaller pots. Good drainage is important for these plants at all stages of their development. With clay pots, this can be provided by crocks (pieces of broken flower pot) placed over the drainage hole, and if plastic pots are used, extra sand should be added to the compost. After potting, return the plants to the cold frame.

Leaf miner (which I referred to on p. 84 in connection with this plant) is the main foe to be guarded against at present. If left unchecked the maggots can soon ruin the appearance of the leaves. If this pest is seen, spray at once with malathion.

Use malathion, too, to control greenfly on calceolarias and other pot plants.

This is quite a good month in which to take cuttings of coleus, selaginella, pilea, tradescantia, zebrina, *Impatiens holstii* and its varieties. These need housing in a close propagating frame but not necessarily a heated one. However, if the weather is cold at night, a little warmth will encourage quicker rooting. All these plants can, in fact, be increased in this way between April and the end of this month.

Freesias and lachenalias are especial favourites with many gardeners, and they are indeed delightful plants. The corms and bulbs respectively should be potted within the next week or two.

To take the freesias first, place seven or eight corms in a 6-in. pot of John Innes No. 1 Potting Compost and cover with about 1 in. of the mixture. Then stand the plants in a cold frame under a thick layer of moist peat. Remove the peat after about six weeks – by which time the plants should have formed a good root system – and bring them into the greenhouse where they must be kept well ventilated. Such plants will flower in January.

With lachenalias, plant five to seven of the bulbs in a 5-in. pot of John Innes No. 1 Potting Compost and cover these also

Tradescantia cuttings will root very easily if inserted around the edge of a 3-in. pot of John Innes No. 1 Potting Compost

with about 1 in. of compost. Then move them to a shaded cold frame and water very carefully and sparingly until the leaves begin to develop. They must then be brought into a cool greenhouse with a temperature of 7 to 10°C. (45 to 50°F.). More water will be needed from this point onwards as the plants come into flower. The flowering period is from February until May, and with flowering completed the plants are dried off and the bulbs ripened in the sun.

The disbudding of chrysanthemums is a task requiring frequent attention. One flower bud per stem should be the rule except for those varieties grown as sprays.

Feeding outdoor tomatoes with a general fertiliser. Afterwards, it should be thoroughly watered in unless rain is expected

Adding waste plant material to the compost heap. Organic matter in the soil is essential if plants are to flourish, and well-rotted garden compost will provide an invaluable supply of this

September: first week

Take lavender and rose cuttings. Plant daffodils for cut flowers. Transplant violets. Prepare to store apples and pears. Gather French and runner beans and sweet corn. Remove early cyclamen flowers. Sow greenhouse annuals.

FLOWERS

The nights are getting longer and, one must assume, colder, so there will be a danger of fungi of one kind or another appearing on many of the bedding plants, particularly begonias. If dead flowers are left on the beds, these may act as centres of infection from which the fungi can affect stems and leaves and the later flowers.

This is the time to take lavender cuttings and those taken with a heel root most readily. They can either be rooted in a sunny, sheltered bed out of doors or in sandy soil in a cold frame. Outdoors, make a shallow trench for them and sprinkle this with plenty of sharp sand before inserting the cuttings and filling in. These cuttings can be planted out in the garden the following spring.

Cuttings of roses can also be inserted now. Rambler roses almost always grow well from cuttings and so do many of the old-fashioned roses and modern floribundas. One merit of roses on their own roots is that suckers become an advantage instead of being a nuisance.

Reduce the growth of herbaceous plants which have finished flowering but do not cut off too much foliage. Continue to tie and support other plants where this may seem necessary as a protection against the wind and rain we must expect at this time of year.

Cut flowers are being used more and more for indoor decoration and it is well worth while planting a few rows of daffodils in a spare part of the vegetable garden or allotment solely for the purpose of cutting.

Continue to take cuttings of bedding geraniums (pelargoniums) as described on p. 87. Cuttings of bedding fuchsias can also be taken and rooted in pots of compost in a garden frame, but there is some urgency about doing this job as the weather will soon be against quick rooting.

Violets which have been growing in a nursery bed since March will now be ready for transplanting into cold frames for winter flowering. Plant them so that the clumps are almost touching, and water them freely. Do not put the lights on the frames until there is a danger of frost occuring, and ventilate freely at all times.

FRUIT

Complete the planting of strawberries as soon as possible, otherwise the plants will not have time to establish themselves and build up strong crowns for fruiting next year. Strawberries can be planted in late summer, in early autumn or in March, but spring-planted ones should not be allowed to bear fruit during the first season.

If no proper fruit store is available – which is usually the case – other arrangements must be made, for the apples and pears are now starting to mature. Get hold of some strong boxes now, and make sure that they are clean. Tomato trays make ideal boxes for storing fruit in. It is also an advantage to wrap the long-keeping apples and pears individually, so buy some of the paper wrappers sold especially for this purpose.

You must pay some attention, too, as to how you store these boxes for they need to get plenty of air and they must be accessible so that the fruit can be inspected from time to time. Just one rotten apple can spread infection around in a very short time indeed.

Start to gather the early pears as they ripen.

VEGETABLES

Onions are late in ripening in some seasons, which is hardly surprising bearing in mind the unpredictable qualities of our climate. If the tops have not been turned over yet to expose the bulbs to all the sunshine available, do this now and lift the crop as soon as it seems reasonable.

Gather French and runner beans regularly and never leave any pods on the plants to become old and stringy unless

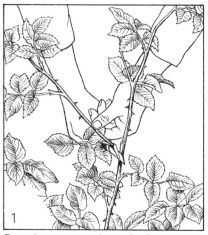

Preparing rose cuttings. **1.** Firm, young shoots will provide suitable material and should be removed with a heel of older wood. **2.** The heel of wood is trimmed neatly, and any soft wood at the tip of the shoot should be removed. The lower leaves are

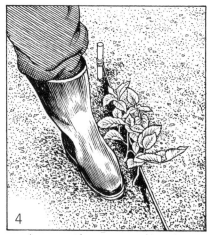

also removed and when completed the cuttings should be about 9 in. long. **3** and **4.** After dipping the ends in hormone rooting powder, the cuttings are placed in a shallow trench with sand in the bottom and then carefully firmed in position

Preparing cuttings of lavender from firm shoots of the current seasons growth, with a heel of older wood attached

Strawberry planting should be completed now if the plants are to build up strong crowns for fruiting next year. Space the plants 2 ft. apart in the rows with 2½ ft. between the rows

they are required for seed purposes, in which case they should be specially marked.

Continue to earth up celery, but remember that this should not all be done at once. It is far better to earth up the plants a little at a time.

Celery leaf spot can be a troublesome disease. It causes spotting on the foliage and this will shrivel and die in a bad attack. Spraying with a good proprietary copper fungicide will help to prevent the disease spreading.

Sweet corn should be gathered before the cobs begin to go too yellow. If the harvesting is left until later they may be rather mealy.

GREENHOUSE

The most forward cyclamen plants are now beginning to show some flowers, and these should be pulled off with a sharp tug. In this way, the flower stem should come away cleanly without leaving a piece at the base which could rot and cause trouble later on. At the same time remove any leaves which are showing signs of decay, again taking care not to leave any part of the stem attached to the crown of the plant. If this is not done disease may spread to the buds and younger leaves. Feed the plants regularly each fortnight with liquid fertiliser.

Keep young schizanthus plants as near to the glass as possible so that the seedlings grow sturdily and do not become drawn. They should be grown in cool conditions.

Insert cuttings of heliotrope and the verbenas Lawrence Johnston and Loveliness. These will root readily in a propagating frame with a minimum temperature of 15°C. (60°F.). A sandy compost should be used.

There are many annual flowers which make excellent pot plants for the cool greenhouse, flowering from April to July and sometimes into August. It cannot be said too often, though, that they do need cool conditions and a temperature of around 4°C. (40°F.), but not less, is just about the ideal. If they are given too much heat the plants will soon become weak and drawn and hardly worth the space they occupy.

Antirrhinums (which, although treated as annuals, are really biennials), Beauty of Nice and East Lothian stocks, clarkias, cornflowers, godetias, nemesias and salpiglossis are all excellent for this purpose. Seeds of these can be sown now in boxes filled with seed compost and germinated in a cold frame or on a shelf near the glass in a cool greenhouse. Ventilate the house carefully and do not allow the atmosphere to become cold and damp or damping off of the seedlings will be a strong likelihood.

As soon as the seedlings can be handled, prick them out into 3-in. pots of John Innes No. 1 Potting Compost and place them on a shelf near the glass to pass the winter. When they are ready for another move, repot them into pots of 5-in. size.

Some are better for stopping, the tips of the shoots being pinched out when they are about 4 to 5 in. high to encourage them to form a bushy habit.

If apples and pears are to be kept for several months in store, it is a good idea to wrap each fruit individually in the special paper wrappers that are sold for this purpose. These will stop the spread of infection, should it arise

93

September: second week

Plant bulbs for naturalising. Prune rampant climbers. Train climbing roses. Treat hydrangeas with colourant. Pick apples and pears. Grease band fruit trees. Ripen onions. Feed leeks. Pot cyclamen. Re-house arum lilies.

FLOWERS

If daffodils and narcissi are to be naturalised in grass, the sooner they are planted the better. There is an excellent tool available for this work which cuts out a neat core of soil to just the right depth for bulb planting. I find that it saves much time and labour.

Clear away all hardy annuals which have finished flowering. These old plants can be put on the compost heap and they will make useful garden compost.

Brompton stocks which have been raised in a cold frame can be bedded out now in all but very cold districts. In such places it is better to overwinter them in a cold frame.

Continue to protect the later chrysanthemum blooms outdoors. Although at this time of year the petals tend to be harder and, therefore, better able to stand up to bad weather than those of the very early chrysanthemums, they still, nevertheless, become marked by strong winds and heavy rain.

The growth of rampant climbers like some kinds of clematis, wisteria and ampelopsis can be cut back now if the plants are taking up too much room.

Tie in the long shoots which have been made during the past few weeks by climbing roses. They are the shoots which will flower most freely next year but they are rather brittle and easily broken by stormy weather.

Violas are best renewed frequently, either from seed or cuttings. Cuttings can be taken now and they should be prepared from young, non-flowering shoots. Insert them in sandy soil in a cold frame.

Outdoor hydrangeas should be treated now with one of the proprietary hydrangea colourants if blue flowers are required next year. Whatever preparation is chosen, it should be used as recommended by the manufacturer. The best blues come from those hydrangeas which, in alkaline soils, have pale pink flowers.

FRUIT

Continue to gather early apples and pears. Generally speaking, these early-maturing varieties are not long keeping so they should be placed where it is easy to get at them for they should be used as quickly as possible.

Melons in frames should now be approaching ripeness and must be cut as soon as they become fully ripe. They can be kept for a short time in a cool larder and once ripe will certainly do better there than if they are left in the frame.

Prepare the ground now for new plantings of raspberries and black currants. It is useless to retain diseased stocks of either of these fruits. Mosaic and reversion disease can soon ruin the cropping qualities of plants and if either trouble is apparent it is far better to clear out the whole bed and replant with healthy stock.

It is not wise to plant new stock on ground which has already been used for these fruits and a fresh site elsewhere in the garden should be chosen.

Now is the time to place grease bands around fruit trees. They are particularly serviceable on apples, but can also be used on pears, plums and other large fruit trees. They are especially effective as a control of the winter moth, the wingless females having to crawl up the trees in the autumn to lay their eggs on the branches. Broad bands of grease-proof paper are placed around the main trunk or each of the main branches and are coated with a sticky substance, and insects which crawl over these are trapped. Special bands and banding compounds are available at garden stores, and putting them on the trees is an easy operation.

Black currants in particular need a good, rich soil, and when digging over the ground generous dressings of farmyard manure, garden compost or peat should be worked in.

Unwanted laterals should be removed from peaches and nectarines for the last time this season.

VEGETABLES

Onions which have been harvested should be placed in the sun to be sure of thorough ripening, but put them somewhere where they will be sheltered from rain. If part of a frame is available this is ideal.

Prepare the ground for a planting of spring cabbages if this has not already been done last month, as suggested (see p. 89). Although this crop needs good soil it should not be too rich as this might encourage soft growth which could not withstand really hard winter weather.

Shallots need to be stored in a cool, dry place. Select good bulbs for planting next year and store these carefully, too.

Leeks can be fed with a general organic-based fertiliser at the rate of 2 oz. to the yard of row.

We have now reached what must be considered the latest date for gathering herbs for winter drying, so if this work has not already been completed it should be attended to immediately.

Marrows can be stored if there are too many for immediate use. A good way of keeping them is to hang them in nets in a place which is cool and frost proof.

When planting bulbs in grass for naturalising a bulb planter is a useful piece of equipment. This tool takes out a core of soil which can be replaced on top of the bulb after it has been positioned

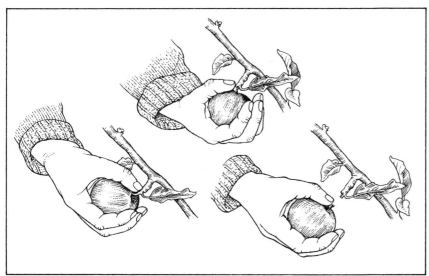

Fruit should not be picked until it parts easily from the tree. The correct method of picking apples is to hold the fruit from underneath, with the thumb on the stalk, and gently lever sideways, taking care not to bruise or damage the fruit

Tying a grease band firmly in position on an apple tree in order to control the wingless females of the winter moth

GREENHOUSE

As cinerarias, *Primula obconica*, and *P. sinensis* fill their 5-in. pots with roots they should be fed regularly with liquid or soluble fertiliser. Continue to feed them until the flower buds have formed.

Seedling cyclamen should be potted singly in small pots by now. If this has not been done do not delay any longer. Use the John Innes No. 2 Potting Compost with extra sand added to ensure good drainage.

If cyclamen plants are standing in a frame, leave the lights off at night so that the plants get the benefit of the heavy autumn dews.

Put in cuttings of the silver-leaved *Centaurea gymnocarpa*. The cuttings will root in a frame in sandy soil, and can be planted out next May or June. I find this plant most useful in bedding schemes.

Arum Lilies should be housed by now to avoid any possibility of frost damage. Water the plants sparingly until growth really gets under way. The temperature can be raised gradually to 13 to 16°C. (55 to 60°F.) as the plants develop if early flowers are desired. If you are prepared to wait longer for the blooms a temperature of 7 to 10°C. (45 to 50°F.) is all that is needed.

The Arum Lilies flower in spring and are much in demand at Easter time for floral decorations. Their botanical name is zantedeschia and the species most frequently grown is *Zantedeschia aethiopica*, which has white flowers. The pale yellow *Z. elliottiana* and the deep yellow *Z. pentlandii* are more tender than *Z. aethiopica* and need slightly higher temperatures.

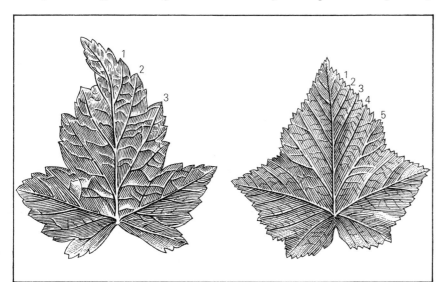

Blackcurrant leaves, showing the effect of reversion disease. On the left an infected leaf with only three veins to the lobe as opposed to a healthy leaf on the right with five veins

Before shallots are stored in a cool, dry place the bulbs should be carefully cleaned by rubbing away the loose outer skin

September: third week

Take cuttings of bedding calceolarias and penstemons. Protect alpines with panes of glass. Expose grapes to sun. Prune loganberries. Lift and store carrots and beetroot. Clear away greenhouse tomatoes. House cyclamen. Dry off begonias and gloxinias. Pot up bulbs.

FLOWERS

As the flower spikes of Red Hot Pokers (kniphofias) fade, cut them off for these soon begin to look unsightly.

This is about the time to take cuttings of both bedding calceolarias and penstemons. The cuttings should be prepared from non-flowering shoots and will root readily in sandy soil in a cold frame. They should be overwintered in the frame and planted out in April.

Winter-flowering pansies may already be producing some flowers but I prefer to pick off these early blooms and so help the plants to make stronger growth before the winter arrives.

Hardy primulas are all the better for being planted rather early in the autumn. *Primula japonica* and *P. pulverulenta* and their varieties look particularly attractive when planted near to water.

Choice alpines are best protected during the autumn and winter by a sheet of glass which will keep off excessive moisture. Dampness is the great enemy of these plants which are not averse to cold but cannot stand wetness at any price.

FRUIT

Different varieties of apples and pears reach maturity at different dates so it is important to watch each tree carefully, testing the fruits from time to time by lifting one here and there and noting whether it leaves the branch easily. If it does, this

Protecting alpines from winter rain and dampness with the aid of a pane of glass supported on wooden pegs

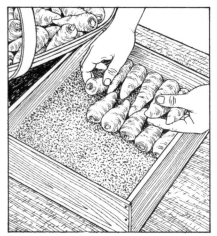

Storing carrots in boxes of dry sand or soil for use later on in winter when vegetables are scarce

is a sign that it is ready for harvesting. Do not gather the late-keeping apples like Sturmer Pippin, Ribston Pippin, Blenheim Orange and Bramley's Seedling too early or they will shrivel in store.

Young peach and nectarine trees sometimes become too vigorous and make a great deal of growth at the expense of fruit buds. This can be checked by lifting and replanting the trees now.

The ordering of fruit trees should not be left any later than this if they are required for planting in the autumn. However, if you intend to buy container-grown plants this is another matter.

Grapes on outdoor vines should be exposed to the sun by folding back the leaves or, in some cases, by actually removing a few of them.

Loganberries should be pruned by cutting out the canes which have just borne fruit and training in their place all the young canes which will fruit next year. The canes should be cut out at ground level so that no short stumps are left.

VEGETABLES

Carrots should be lifted and stored before the roots start to split, which they will do very quickly once the autumns rains begin.

For the same reason beetroot are better lifted and stored now – in boxes between layers of moderately dry sand or soil, the containers being housed in the garden shed or garage. The ideal size for a beetroot is about that of a cricket ball. Carrots can be stored in the same way as beetroot.

Lettuces sown last month (see p. 89) for frame cultivation should now be ready for planting, and more seed can be sown to provide a succession of plants throughout the winter months.

GREENHOUSE

Where possible, clear away the tomatoes now so that the house can be prepared for the autumn and winter flowers. Any unripened fruits can be put in boxes to ripen indoors.

Cyclamen which have been growing in a frame would be better in a greenhouse now as there will soon be a danger of frost at night. Keep the plants well ventilated and do not use any artificial heat yet.

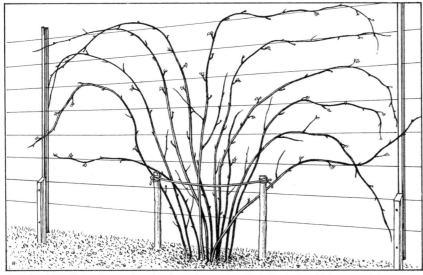

A well-trained loganberry, showing how the young canes should be tied in to the training wires in a fan shape. Canes which have already fruited should be cut right out at ground level

Tuberous-rooted begonias and gloxinias should be gradually dried off as they finish flowering. The pots can be placed on their sides under the staging to dry out. Do not dry the plants off too quickly though – wait until the leaves begin to turn yellow before starting this process.

All manner of spring-flowering bulbs, including daffodils, may now be potted or placed in bowls for late winter or spring flowering. You can have colour from Christmas until spring, for instance, in the cool greenhouse from daffodils (narcissi) and hyacinths.

For the earliest flowers of narcissi you need to grow varieties like Paper White or Grand Soleil d'Or, and remember that the attractive Roman hyacinths flower earlier than the large-flowered kinds. But pre-cooled bulbs of popular daffodil varieties will also be in flower by Christmas. Examples of treated bulbs include the lovely Tazetta variety Cragford, white, with a bright orange-red corona; and the Large-cupped variety Carlton, in two shades of yellow.

If these bulbs are grown in pots place them close together and use the John Innes No. 1 Potting Compost as a growing medium. With potting completed, the tips of the bulbs should be just above the surface of the compost.

If they are to be grown in bowls use bulb fibre, making sure that it is soaked well before use. Whichever method is used, do not pot too firmly or the roots may push the bulbs out of the compost.

For the next 8 to 10 weeks the pots or bowls should be stood in a cool, sheltered place out of doors – under a north-facing fence or wall is ideal. Give them a thorough watering before covering with a layer of sand, weathered ashes or peat. By the end of the period just suggested the bulbs should have made good root systems and be ready for moving, first to a cold frame and, subsequently, when the flower buds appear, into a greenhouse or warm room.

Young hydrangeas which are housed in cold frames should be covered with lights at night from now onwards. They must be returned to the greenhouse in October.

Prick out schizanthus seedlings singly into small pots filled with John Innes No. 1 Potting Compost. Place these plants on a shelf near the glass for they like all the light they can get.

Above: *Aster amellus*, an herbaceous perennial which is also used for bedding. It is closely related to the Michaelmas daisy

Below: Dwarf Rose, a late-flowering, reflexed decorative chrysanthemum, belonging to the medium-flowered section

September: fourth week

Propagate tender bedding plants. Lift gladioli. Sow sweet peas. Hoe strawberry beds. Earth up celery and leeks. Store onions. Lift maincrop potatoes. Pick outdoor tomatoes. House freesias, carnations and chrysanthemums. Prick out greenhouse annuals.

FLOWERS

The propagation of all the more tender bedding plants such as pelargoniums, fuchsias, iresines and so on must be completed before the first frosts arrive and the young growths are damaged. Cuttings can be prepared from any of the firm, non-flowering shoots and will root easily in a warm propagating frame.

Cuttings taken earlier will need potting now into 3½-in. pots of John Innes No. 1 Potting Compost. They should be brought into the greenhouse for overwintering.

It is not surprising that the large-flowered, tuberous-rooted begonias have become increasingly popular as bedding plants. These are, however, tender plants which even a slight frost will cut down, (though it will do no harm to the tubers tucked safely away beneath the soil) and it is time now to lift the plants and dry off the tubers so that they can be stored away for the winter. Dust the tubers with flowers of sulphur, store them in peat-filled boxes and keep them in a frost-proof place.

Seedlings of meconopsis raised from a sowing made in August should now be ready for pricking out into boxes. These should be overwintered in a cold frame and be planted out next April or May.

The earliest gladioli will die down soon and they should then be lifted carefully, ready for drying and storing. The drying off can be done in a frost-proof shed or greenhouse and the corms afterwards stored in a cool, airy place which is absolutely frost proof. When the foliage has died down it should be cut away and care should be taken to save the little cormlets or spawn which develop around the corm for growing on.

There are several ways of growing sweet peas and one is to treat them like autumn-sown hardy annuals, sowing the seed now out of doors where the plants are to bloom next year. A sheltered and well-drained border must be chosen, and the seed should be sown in a trench 2 to 3 in. deep so that they have adequate protection. Alternatively, sow 5 or 6 seeds in a 3-in. pot and germinate in a cold frame. The young plants will be potted in January.

FRUIT

Continue to pick apples and pears as the fruits become ready. This is when they

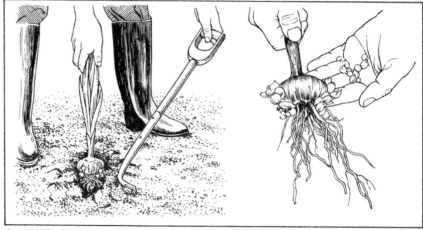

As gladiolus begin to die down, they should be carefully lifted and dried off before storing in a cool, frost-proof shed for the winter. The small cormlets which form around the corm can be saved and grown on next spring

part easily from the tree (see remarks on p. 89).

Storing pears can bring problems. I like to store mine where I can look over them at intervals of a few days, for pears have a habit of ripening and then going soft in two or three days. This is why there are so many complaints every year of pears being 'sleepy' before they are ripe. In fact, they were ripe first but this period of their development was missed.

When the soil is sufficiently dry, hoe between the strawberry plants in both the new and the established beds to encourage growth and help build up strong crowns.

The amount of pruning carried out on

Fruit trees should be picked over regularly so that no fruit is allowed to become over-ripe and spoil

damsons should be minimal, but when it is necessary this is a good time to do it, before the leaves fall.

VEGETABLES

Continue to earth up celery, a little at a time. If the earthing up is done too quickly it will tend to check growth unduly. Soil should also be pulled up along each side of the leek rows. Alternatively, if extra long, blanched stems are required, a couple of boards can be fixed on edge to each side of the row and the space in between filled with soil. Old potting compost is ideal for this purpose.

Onions can be stored in ropes or on

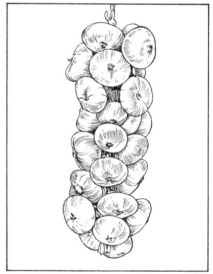

A good method of storing onions is to plait the withered leaves together with two or three strands of raffia to form a rope

Blanching endive by covering with a large flower pot. The leaves are likely to taste bitter unless this job is done thoroughly

An attractive way to grow crocuses is in a specially designed crocus bowl. As the bowl is filled with bulb fibre, one corm is placed over each hole and held in position by more fibre. Finally, three or four corms are planted at the top

slatted shelves in a dry, airy shed or room. Make sure that they are well cleaned (but not skinned) before storing.

Lift some plants of endive and place them in a frame, after which the hearts can be covered with upturned pots or saucers to blanch them.

When the skin of maincrop potatoes has set, that is when it cannot be easily rubbed off by pressure with the thumb, this is a sign that the tubers are mature and ready for lifting. It is always wise to make this test first.

Gather all outdoor tomatoes, even if they have not ripened yet. There is always a danger of frost from now onwards and the fruits would be ruined by even a degree or two, so it is far better to finish the ripening indoors. I find that a warm, dark place such as an airing cupboard, will quickly ripen green fruits.

GREENHOUSE

Seedling freesias, which up to now have been standing in a frame, will be better in a greenhouse. They should be given plenty of light and ventilation. The same thing applies to winter-flowering pelargoniums.

Perpetual-flowering carnations which have been in a frame or outside for the summer will also be better now in the greenhouse. They like plenty of light and air and a rather dry atmosphere, but not too much heat. If large flowers are required, the plants should be disbudded now, the side buds around the terminal bud being removed in each case.

As soon as the greenhouse has been properly cleared of tomatoes, the large exhibition chrysanthemums can be brought inside, and any other chrysanthemums as well which are showing really prominent flower buds. Before taking the plants into the greenhouse, though, remove all dead leaves and spray the plants with a combined fungicide and insecticide. When they are in their new quarters, allow them plenty of space and ventilate freely.

On cold, damp nights provide the greenhouse with a little artificial heat.

Pots of crocuses, chionodoxas, scillas and other early bulbs are always welcome in the spring. The corms or bulbs should be placed in pots or pans now and plunged out of doors under peat or sand until the plants have formed good root systems. Crocuses should not be forced before mid-January, when a temperature of 10°C. (50°F.) is sufficient.

Bring plants of *Azalea indica* back into the greenhouse as the nights become colder. They need cool greenhouse conditions with just enough heat to keep the air fairly dry, otherwise the blooms will be spoilt by dampness.

Bring cinerarias and plants of *Primula malacoides*, *P. obconica* and *P. sinensis* back into a cool greenhouse.

Annuals raised from a sowing made in the greenhouse at the beginning of the month will need pricking out into John Innes No. 1 Potting Compost. Keep the plants on a shelf near the light and provide them with cool conditions. If desired, they can be housed in a cold frame until the colder weather arrives.

Before pot-grown chrysanthemums are brought back into the greenhouse they must be thoroughly sprayed with a combined insecticide and fungicide. Decayed leaves should also be removed as these are likely to be a source of infection

A fine display of spray chrysanthemums and dahlias. Both these plants are ideal for use as cut flowers in the home, the chrysanthemums, in particular, lasting for a long time in water

October: first week

Rake lawns. Lift tender plants. Prune rambler roses. Thin raspberry canes. Take gooseberry cuttings. Plant lettuces in frames. Pick runner and French beans. Plant spring cabbages. House chrysanthemums and solanums. Pot pre-cooled bulbs for Christmas.

Above: The brilliant autumn colour of *Rhus typhina*, the Stag's Horn Sumach. This small tree is well suited to town gardens

Below: The delicate flowers of *Colchicum speciosum*, the Meadow Saffron, a plant which is ideal for naturalising in grass

FLOWERS

Damaging frosts may occur at any time now. Indeed, it is probable that even before October arrives frosts will have occurred in cold districts. Bearing this danger in mind, make the fullest possible use of all the flowers while they last.

Lawns will benefit from a good raking and aerating at this time of year, as well as a topdressing of equal parts of peat and loam brushed well into the surface.

If frost threatens, the more tender plants like pelargoniums (geraniums) and fuchsias must be brought inside. Some of the fibrous-rooted begonias (*Begonia semperflorens*) can also be lifted and put into pots, as they will go on flowering in the greenhouse or on a window-sill in the home throughout most of the winter. They will also provide stock for future use.

Rambler roses should be pruned and trained if this has not already been done. Cut out as much of the growth which has already flowered as possible, but remember that the application of this rule will vary from variety to variety as some ramblers, like Dorothy Perkins, Excelsa and American Pillar, make most of their new growth from the base whereas others, such as Emily Gray and Albéric Barbier, make very little basal growth. With the latter varieties, it is necessary to cut the old growth to a point just above that at which strong new growth starts, while in the case of varieties making strong basal growth the old stems can be cut out to ground level.

FRUIT

The gathering of apples and pears must continue as the various varieties become ready for picking. Sometimes it pays to pick over a tree several times at intervals of a few days as all the fruit may not mature together.

Handle all fruit with care and only store really sound fruits.

In a wet summer raspberries often throw up more basal growths than usual and it is wise to cut some of them away. Canes which will carry next year's crop must now be tied permanently in position.

Take gooseberry cuttings now from firm young growths produced this year. Make a clean cut above a bud at the top, and below a bud at the base, finishing up with a cutting of about 9 in. in length. All

Raking the lawn with a wire-toothed rake will remove dead grass and other debris, and also help to aerate the soil

the buds should then be removed, except the top three or four, to ensure that the bushes are grown on a short stem or 'leg'. After preparing the cuttings, insert them out of doors in trenches where the soil is light and well drained. It is also wise to place a layer of coarse sand on the bottom of the trench to encourage rooting.

VEGETABLES
Lettuce seedlings can be planted in the frame to give winter supplies. After planting put down a slug killer such as metal-

dehyde mixed with bran to make certain that slugs and snails do no damage to the young plants. The frames should be ventilated freely whenever the weather is mild.

Gather all sizeable, ripe marrows before there is any danger of frost and store them in a dry, frost-proof shed.

No matter what the season, the main-crop potatoes should be lifted and stored. It really pays to take advantage of every fine day and get this job done. As you pick up the tubers any that are noticed to be diseased should be kept away from those being stored.

Make the most of the last of the runner and French beans by picking all the size-able beans each day, particularly if frost threatens.

Late sowings of French beans made in June should be covered with cloches.

Take advantage of the dry weather which often occurs in early October to earth up celery for the last time. It is much easier to do this job when the soil is fairly dry rather than muddy and sticky.

Spring cabbages should be planted now. It is important to firm each one well in after planting. I like to draw out drills with a hoe and plant in these. Then a little later I draw the soil back into the drills, so pulling it around the stems of the cabbages.

GREENHOUSE
Continue to bring chrysanthemums into the greenhouse as the flower buds form. If

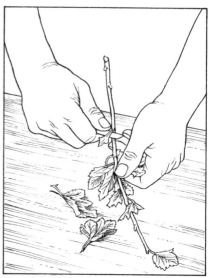

Preparing a gooseberry cutting. All the buds except the top three of four should be removed if the plant is to grow on a leg

frost threatens they should be brought inside at once whether the buds are showing or not.

The Winter Cherry, *Solanum capsicastrum*, is another tender pot plant which will need protection as soon as there is a danger of frost. In fact, it is wiser to bring the plants in a week or so too early than to risk having them damaged.

Ventilate the greenhouse freely to keep air on the move and prevent too damp an atmosphere occuring which might encourage disease.

From now onwards, cinerarias will need very careful watering. They must not be allowed to become dry, nor must they be kept constantly sodden.

Arum Lilies which are growing strongly will need adequate water supplies and should be fed generously. They respond to regular feeding once the pots are full of roots. To obtain really good flowers, feed with a liquid or soluble feed once every 7 to 10 days.

Make a regular practice of picking off dead or decaying leaves from pelargoniums (geraniums) for if this is neglected disease can spread to the stems themselves.

It is not normally possible to buy pre-cooled bulbs before this time, but as soon as they arrive, pot them up and stand them in a cool place, preferably under a north-facing wall, until the third or fourth week in November. Cover them over with peat or weathered ashes in the normal way.

A few weeks after planting, spring cabbages will benefit if the soil on either side of the row is drawn up slightly. This will help to protect them from the cold weather which is to come, and also prevent wind rocking which would loosen the roots

October: second week

Prepare ground for spring bedding. Pot up shrub cuttings. Complete picking of apples and pears and inspect those in store. Prepare ground for fruit trees. Prune blackberries. Dig in green manure. Store begonia and gloxinia tubers. House hydrangeas and freesias.

FLOWERS

This is the time to start planting out wallflowers, polyanthus, forget-me-nots, Sweet Williams, foxgloves and similar plants which are either biennial or are grown primarily for spring bedding displays. Do not retain summer bedding flowers so long that these plants which follow them have insufficient time to establish themselves before the winter sets in.

Before the spring- and early-summer-flowering plants are put in, the soil should be dug over to the depth of a spade or fork. A fertiliser can be used if the soil is not considered to be sufficiently rich, and it should be a slow-acting kind such as bonemeal and not one of the quick-acting spring or summer fertilisers. Use the bonemeal at the rate of about a handful per square yard. The soil must be made firm and should be raked level before planting. Firmness is really important as it helps the plants to establish themselves before the severe weather sets in.

Half-ripe shrub cuttings taken during July and August should now be rooted. I prefer to pot these at once into $3\frac{1}{2}$-in. pots and to keep them in a frame for the time being. When they are well established in the pots they can be plunged outside.

Lift plants of *Lobelia cardinalis* and *L. fulgens* now and box them up. Then place them in a cold frame for the winter as they are not completely hardy.

FRUIT

Apples and pears in store need careful watching as they may show signs of brown

Planting forget-me-nots for spring flowering. Such plants must have sufficient time to establish themselves before the winter

rot or other diseases, even if they appeared perfectly sound when gathered.

It should now be possible to complete the picking of all apples and pears. It is dangerous to leave them on the trees too long as violent storms could bring them down.

Do not delay in the preparation of sites for fruit trees which one intends to plant in November. The soil should be well dug and, if possible, enriched with some decayed manure as well as a good sprinkling of coarse bonemeal.

It would be wise to check up now on the newer varieties of all fruits, for you may well find some in which you are particularly interested. Trying these out is always interesting and often worth while.

This is the time to prune blackberries, the method adopted being exactly the same as that used for loganberries. All the old canes which have just borne a crop are cut right out and the young canes are trained in to take their place.

It is as well to remember that autumn gales are often severe and badly tied growths of blackberries and loganberries may often be broken with the inevitable loss of much fruit next year.

VEGETABLES

Keep a close watch on potatoes and onions in store and remove any which show the least sign of disease.

Choose any day when the soil is reasonably dry on top to hoe between spring cabbages and winter lettuces as this will help them a great deal.

The lifting and storing of late-sown carrots and beetroot should now be completed as there is no advantage to be gained by leaving them in the soil any longer. Both of these vegetables can be stored in a cool shed in boxes of sand or ashes.

This is a good time to dig in green manure crops like mustard. It is quite a good policy to sprinkle the crop with Nitro-chalk as it is turned in, as this helps it to decay quickly and improves the quality of the resultant manure.

In very exposed places it may be necessary to put stakes to the Brussels sprouts, especially after a wet summer and if the soil is light. Remove any yellowing leaves

As with carrots, beetroots are readily stored in boxes of dry sand in a frost-proof place. Beetroot tops are best removed by twisting them off rather than cutting, as this lessens the chance of bleeding

Begonia and gloxinia tubers should be dusted with flowers of sulphur before storing to protect them from fungus diseases

from the plants to prevent attack by fungus diseases.

GREENHOUSE

The latest flowering chrysanthemums should now be brought inside before they are damaged by frost. The same applies to fuchsias.

Make a regular practice of looking over cyclamen and removing any leaves which are showing signs of decay, otherwise diseases can spread easily to the young buds in the crowns. Continue to feed cyclamen plants with weak liquid manure at fortnightly intervals.

When the foliage of gloxinias and begonias has withered completely the tubers can be knocked out of their pots and the old compost shaken away. Then dust the tubers with flowers of sulphur before storing them in a dry, frost-proof place. This dusting will protect them from fungus diseases.

Calceolarias must not be allowed to become pot bound. Pot them on as soon as the small pots become comfortably filled with roots, and keep them as near to the glass as possible to prevent the growth from becoming drawn. The plants will be repotted into 5-in. pots at this stage, using the John Innes No. 1 Potting Compost.

Specimens of *Genista fragrans* will also need moving into 5-in. pots from the 3½-in. pots into which they were potted in August. The John Innes No. 2 Potting Compost should be used.

Hydrangeas in pots which have been housed in a cold frame during the summer should now be moved to the greenhouse. Well-grown plants can be potted on into 7-in. pots at this stage, again using the special compost referred to on p. 66.

Do not provide too much heat in the greenhouse at this time, but make a little warmth available when necessary to keep the air dry and on the move. This will prevent the atmosphere becoming damp and stagnant. Naturally, heat must be provided if tender plants are being grown.

Freesias raised from corms started into growth in August should now be moved from the cold frame into the cool greenhouse. They need support and twiggy sticks are ideal for this purpose, these being placed in among the growths so that they can grow up through them. These plants will come into flower in January.

Above: *Schizostylis coccinea*, the Kaffir Lily, flowers in the autumn and grows best when planted in a sheltered position

Below: *Rosa rugosa scabrosa*, one of many roses which have the added advantage of colourful hips in the autumn

October: third week

Plant spring bedding, aubrietas, alyssum and winter-flowering pansies. Take cuttings of shrubs and roses. Clean strawberry beds. Tie in raspberries. Prune and train morello cherries. Turn compost heaps. Lift seakale. Pot up lilies.

FLOWERS

When planting bedding material for spring, I want to emphasise how important it is to exercise great care and preserve as many roots as possible. This job is often done in far too much of a hurry, with the result that a lot of the roots are lost, and the plants suffer a severe setback.

Aubrietas and *Alyssum saxatile*, such excellent plants for rock gardens, dry walls and the tops of retaining walls, can now be planted safely. These plants will be transferred from the nursery bed in which they were pricked out in June (see p. 70). Winter-flowering pansies can be used for the same purpose and it is a pity that they are not better known for they are most attractive plants.

Dahlias can be left in the ground until their tops have become blackened by frost, but it is not essential to leave them that long. If the ground is wanted for other purposes there is no reason why they should not be lifted at once. The tops should be cut off 9 in. above the tubers, which must then be dried off thoroughly before they are stored.

Cuttings of a great many shrubs and roses may be taken now, and these can be rooted out of doors or in a frame. The cuttings may include those conifers like *Chamaecyparis lawsoniana* which are so useful for hedge making. It will be a full year before they are sufficiently well rooted to be lifted and planted out elsewhere, and the cutting bed should, therefore, be in a place where the cuttings can be left undisturbed throughout next spring and summer.

There are hardy heathers of varying kinds in flower throughout the year, and this is the best time to plant them. For winter flowering, *Erica darleyensis* can be relied upon to show its deep rosy-pink flowers from November onwards. Then, for winter colour also, there are all the varieties of *E. carnea*. These, like *E. darleyensis*, will grow in an alkaline soil provided plenty of peat is added. The varieties have a flowering period covering October to April. Plant them 1½ ft. apart and put plenty of the same variety together to get the best effect. Varieties I especially like include the pure white Springwood White and the bright pink Springwood Pink, both 6 to 9 in. tall; and the rich carmine Eileen Porter of similar height. This last

flowers the winter through, and the other two from January to April.

The many other heaths and heathers include *E. cinerea* and its varieties flowering from June to September; and the Cornish heath, *E. vagans*, and its varieties, flowering from August to October. Then there are the varieties of *Calluna vulgaris* for late summer and autumn (many with attractively coloured foliage), and the daboecias like *D. cantabrica atropurpurea* which flowers from early summer until early autumn.

All these need a lime-free soil.

FRUIT

Strawberry beds should now be cleaned up, all dead, diseased and damaged foliage being removed. Weeds should be eliminated at the same time, too. Then, if the soil is dry enough, hoe between the young plants. With strawberries, as with spring cabbages, it is an advantage to draw up a little soil along each side of the row. Alternatively, they may be topdressed with some well-rotted manure or garden compost.

Tie in raspberries but do not, as yet, cut back the tips, a job better left until mid-February. It is wise at the same time to make quite sure that the supports for the raspberry training wires are in good condition and not rotting at the base.

Prune and tie in Morello cherries. The object is to retain as many of the good young branches made in the past summer as possible and to reduce all older side growths which have already borne a crop.

When gathering the leaves of seakale beet it is best to take only a few from each plant, otherwise they will be weakened

Morello cherries, like peaches, bear best on year-old laterals.

Clean up the ground around fruit trees and bushes so that later on when the leaves have to be raked up this job is made easier.

VEGETABLES

I know just how difficult it is for most amateur gardeners to get supplies of animal manure these days, but I would stress again its value in the garden. As an alternative or supplement to manure, compost is excellent. Compost heaps made earlier in the autumn should now be turned, bringing the material on the outside into the centre and vice versa.

Lifting young wallflower plants prior to bedding them out for the spring display. Great care should be taken to ensure that a good ball of soil remains around the roots, otherwise the plants will have an unnecessary setback

Boxing up seakale crowns. By lifting and storing these crowns at this stage before the ground is frozen hard they will be readily accessible when they are required in December for forcing

When pulling the leaves of seakale beet take a few at a time from each plant. If the plants are stripped completely they will be weakened.

Seakale should be lifted and the strong crowns stored in sand. They will then keep in excellent condition until they are needed for forcing. The thick, fleshy roots (not the crowns) can be used for root cuttings. Cut them into pieces 6 to 8 in. long, making a flat cut at the top and a slanting cut at the bottom of each piece so that later on it will be possible to tell which end is which.

Then tie these in bundles and store them in moist soil or sand until March, when they should be planted (see p. 42).

(see p. 42)

GREENHOUSE

Dry off the last of the begonias and gloxinias growing in pots by turning the pots on their sides and giving the plants no more water. Achimenes in pots can also be dried off as these, too, must have a thorough rest during the winter before they are started again next year.

Gradually reduce the amount of water given to fuchsias, but do not allow these to become completely dry at any time. Rooted cuttings of fuchsias from which specimen plants and standards are to be formed should be potted on as necessary.

Another plant that may need potting up now is *Primula malacoides*, the dainty winter- and spring-flowering primula. They should be moved into $3\frac{1}{2}$-in. pots and the John Innes No. 1 Potting Compost should be used.

Pot up lilies such as *Lilium auratum* and *L. speciosum rubrum* required for the greenhouse. Both of the lilies mentioned are stem rooting and the bulbs, like others of their type, should be kept well down in the pots. These need not be filled completely yet as some topdressing will be desirable later. The pots should be put into a cold frame for the winter, and then returned to a cool greenhouse with a temperature not higher than 10°C. (50°F.) in March or April.

Now is a good time to propagate lilies from scales. Insert them upright in a seed box filled with a mixture of peat and sand, cover them to a depth of $\frac{1}{2}$ in. with a similar mixture, and move the boxes to a cold frame. By the following autumn bulblets will have formed at the base of the scales. These are removed and potted up or planted out in a nursery bed.

Generally speaking, the atmosphere in all greenhouses will have to be kept drier from now onwards.

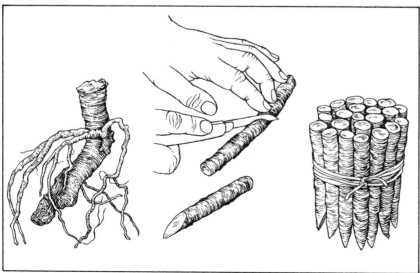

Preparing root cuttings of seakale, with a slanting cut at the bottom and a straight cut at the top to distinguish one end from the other. Afterwards, they are tied into bundles and stored in moist sand until required in the spring

A typical example of a stem-rooting lily. When grown in pots, space must be left for topdressing at a later stage

October: fourth week

Tidy the herbaceous border. Lift and store dahlia tubers. Complete bulb planting. Inspect fruit in store. Lift roots of parsley for winter use. Cut down asparagus. Pot roses for the greenhouse. Dry off cannas. Stop schizanthus.

FLOWERS

In many places autumn colour is now just about at its best, and this is a good season to bring out the garden notebook and jot down the names of shrubs which have especially attractive berries and autumn leaf colour. Some of these, perhaps, can be ordered for planting a little later on in one's own garden.

Now is the time to begin cleaning up the herbaceous border. I know that many gardeners argue that it is better to leave the dead tops on the plants for winter protection but I am not in favour of this. I think that it is much better to have all top growth trimmed back and the borders properly cleaned up before the winter. This makes for good health as well as tidiness, and the soil can be lightly forked over between the plants to destroy weeds and improve aeration. At the same time take up all the canes and sticks used for support and store them away in a dry place to prevent decay.

When frost has browned the tops of dahlias cut them down to within 9 in. of ground level. Tie a label to each stem so that the plants can be easily identified at planting time next year. Lift the tubers carefully and spread them out on the staging in a greenhouse or frost-proof shed for a time to dry before they are finally stored away for the winter. I find that it is best to keep dahlias stalk end downwards for a week or two to allow any surplus moisture to drain away from the stems.

Planting tulip bulbs between forget-me-nots for an attractive spring display. When planting bulbs they should rest firmly on the soil at the bottom of the hole and not have a pocket of air trapped beneath them

Most bulb planting should be completed as quickly as possible, although tulips can be left until November. Nevertheless, even with tulips, I think that better results are obtained from planting in October.

The best tulips for the average garden are the Early Single and Early Double varieties. The tulip species are also excellent, and these can be left in the ground from year to year. For example, *Tulipa kaufmanniana*, the Water-lily Tulip, has many fine March- to April-flowering hybrids. These have an excellent colour range, they are only 6 to 8 in. tall and are splendid flowers for the rock garden or the front of the border. Some of the best varieties are the creamy-white Johann Strauss, with a cream centre and red exterior to the petals; Scarlet Elegance; the red edged with yellow Glück; the carmine-red and golden-yellow César Franck; and The First, ivory-white with a yellow base and exterior markings of carmine edged white.

The April-flowering *T. greigii* hybrids (9 to 12 in. tall) are noted for their beautiful flower colours and handsome leaf markings; and there are the taller (1 to 1½ ft.) *T. fosteriana* varieties; the 6-in. tall *T. tarda*, yellowish-green and white; and the 9-in., scarlet-orange *T. praestans* Fusilier, among others.

After flowering, herbaceous plants should be cut down with secateurs and the soil between the plants lightly pricked over

When dahlias are cut back by frosts, the tubers should be lifted for storing. Before cutting away the tops, a label bearing the variety of the plant should be carefully attached low down on the stem

Removing yellowing leaves from Brussels sprouts. These must be cleared away to prevent possible attack by fungus diseases

FRUIT

Inspect all fruit in store and remove any which show signs of decay. By inspecting fruit regularly in this way it is possible to make use of much which would otherwise become rotten and would spread decay to healthy fruits.

It is a good plan to select some of the really sound, late-keeping apples such as Bramley's Seedling, Newton Wonder, Crawley Beauty and Laxton's Superb, wrap them separately and store them away for winter use.

Many small gardens have little room for top fruits, but there are few in which at least some soft fruits cannot be planted

with advantage. In a week or so it will be time to plant gooseberries, currants and the various cane fruits. Now is the time to get the ground ready for them by digging and manuring.

VEGETABLES

Lift a few roots of parsley carefully with plenty of soil attached and transfer them to a frame for winter use.

Cut all top growth from asparagus beds now as it turns yellow, and clear the beds of any weeds or other rubbish.

Brussels sprouts which show a tendency to be late and are not producing their buttons well can be encouraged by feeding now with a general fertiliser, and any leaves which have turned yellow should be removed. Winter cabbages, too, will benefit from a dressing of general fertiliser.

The top growth of Jerusalem artichokes can now be cut down to ground level. Celeriac, by contrast, should be lifted and stored in damp sand in a shed or other sheltered place for winter use.

Round-seeded peas can be sown under cloches in flat-bottomed drills 8 in. wide and 2 in. deep. Sow the seeds 2 to 3 in. apart in three rows.

GREENHOUSE

At this time of year one appreciates more than ever having shelves in the greenhouse quite near to the glass. Such a shelf is the ideal place in the autumn for young schizanthus plants, calceolarias and various annuals being grown for spring flowering. I would like to emphasise the importance

Potting up a rose for greenhouse flowering. As the compost is added, it should be firmed with the aid of a wooden rammer

of this for it is vital that growth should be strengthened and hardened now if the plants are to be extra good when in bloom.

Roses can be lifted and potted for flowering in the greenhouse during the spring. Any roses already in pots should be pruned back fairly hard and some of the old soil removed with a pointed stick from the top of the pot and replaced with fresh, rather rich compost.

Cannas, those brightly coloured plants which can be grown in pots in the greenhouse or as bedding plants in the garden during the summer, should now be gradually dried off. Very shortly they will need no more water until they are restarted into growth in the late spring. With green or bronze foliage and flowers in orange, red, pink and yellow which are borne throughout the summer these are plants well worth growing.

Cinerarias need all the air possible at this time of year, and as long as they are not frozen they are far better when kept cool, so give them as much ventilation as you can. The tops of some of the plants can be pinched out, if desired, to delay flowering and so give a longer overall period of display.

Pinch out the tips of the tallest schizanthus seedlings to encourage the formation of bushy plants.

Pot plants must be fed less and less frequently now, with the exception of cyclamen and primulas.

During the winter months it is sometimes difficult to give young plants enough light. A shelf above the staging in the greenhouse will bring plants closer to the glass and help to overcome this problem

November: first week

Tidy up the garden. Lay turf. Plant lilies. Protect tender shrubs. Clean and grease lawn mowers. Prune red and white currants. Ridge heavy soils. Lift Jerusalem artichokes, parsnips and horseradish. Pot up lilies-of-the-valley.

FLOWERS

Before the weather becomes too bad to do any serious gardening, it is a good idea to get as much tidying up done as possible. I consider this very important because to look at an untidy garden for the whole of the winter is an annoyance and probably a worry.

This is the ideal time to lay turf. It must be said, however, that making a lawn from turf is much more expensive than making a lawn from seed, and good turf is difficult to get hold of. This last point is important for one wants a turf containing fine grasses and one which is reasonably free of weeds. Of the two factors, the fine grasses should be the main consideration as weeds can be eliminated later by using a selective weedkiller.

Lily bulbs are now being offered for sale and can be planted when conditions are suitable. The only lily which needs planting at a different time is *Lilium candidum*, which should be planted in August (see p. 83).

Lilium regale, the Regal Lily, is a species I am particularly fond of, and others include *L. auratum*, the Golden-rayed Lily of Japan, *L. tigrinum* and *L. tigrinum splendens*. I also like the many splendid hybrid lilies now available, the majority of them coming from the United States of America. These last include the Mid-Century Hybrids, $2\frac{1}{2}$ to 4 ft. tall; the Golden Clarion Strain, $3\frac{1}{2}$ to 4 ft. tall; and the Bellingham Hybrids, which are 7 ft. or more tall, with Turk's-cap flowers.

Lilies like to be planted in a well-worked soil with good drainage. They also need a cool root run, so the lower parts of the stems should be shaded from strong sunshine. Such cover can be provided by interplanting with herbaceous plants or low-growing shrubs, with which lilies associate admirably. The bulbs must not come in contact with manure and if the soil needs feeding in this way it is essential to put the manure down in the second spit out of harm's way. Heavy soil can be lightened by digging in peat, leafmould or coarse sand.

Stem-rooting lilies (those which form roots on the lower part of their stems as well as on the bulbs) must be planted rather deeper than non-stem-rooting kinds – at a depth of 8 to 9 in. as opposed to 5 to 6 in. And to avoid trouble with bulb rotting, it is always a good idea to put a little sand in the bottom of the planting hole on which the bulb can rest. I also like to plant the bulbs in groups of three or four of the same kind as the flowers look more impressive in this way. Set the bulbs a few inches apart within each group.

Shrubs which are a little tender, like crinodendrons, the evergreen ceanothus and the hebes should be protected now. Bracken is ideal for this purpose as it is light and does not retain rain water like straw. If bracken or straw is unobtainable, though, sacking may be tied to stakes around the shrubs.

Hydrangeas of the Hortensia type (varieties of *H. macrophylla*) grow best along the west coast of Britain – in the west of Scotland, in Cornwall, Devon and Wales. In less favoured places it is often a good idea to plant them in the shelter of a wall, but $1\frac{1}{2}$ to 2 ft. away from it. *Hydrangea petiolaris* is a vigorous and very tall self-clinging climber which bears prominent, flat corymbs of white flowers in early summer. There are also those other splendid hydrangeas to consider, *H. paniculata grandiflora*, with its large panicles of creamy-white flowers in late summer, which will grow some 8 ft. tall and 6 ft. through; and *H. villosa* which is an extremely decorative shrub with its greyish-green, long leaves and pale blue, lacecap flowers which are borne in late summer.

The blue-flowered agapanthus likes a well-drained position which is also open and sunny. It is another of those plants which needs winter protection. I grow it

Planting lily bulbs on a bed of sand. For the most effective display they should be planted in groups of three or four

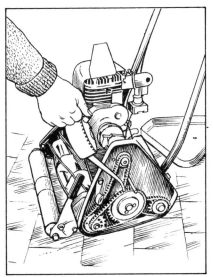
Before putting lawn mowers away at the end of the grass-cutting season, they should be thoroughly cleaned and oiled

out of doors at Shrewsbury, but before really severe weather arrives I always put bracken, straw or peat around and over the crowns.

Now that the mowing season has finished the lawn mower, of whatever type, should be cleaned, greased all over and put away in a dry place. If it appears to need an overhaul or if the blades need sharpening, now is the time to get this done.

FRUIT

Ground should now be prepared for the planting of all kinds of fruit trees, bushes and fruiting canes. Dig the soil over as deeply as possible and work in some manure. This is particularly important in the case of black currants.

Fruit trees trained to walls, fences and so on should be pruned now. After pruning see that all branches and shoots are securely tied.

Inspect the posts carrying wires for raspberries, blackberries and other fruit to make sure that they are still sound. Where posts have decayed at ground level they can be made good by driving into the soil a length of angle iron and bolting this to the base of the post just above ground level.

When contemplating the purchase of new fruit trees do not forget that a quince tree may be a useful addition to the garden, not only for the value of the fruits for jellies and flavouring but also for the attractive foliage effect of the tree. Some of the crab apples have the same good points, and are very colourful in the flowering season.

Now is the time to prune red and white currants. Cut back the leading shoots to leave about 6 in. of the new season's wood, and cut back the sideshoots to leave one bud. This treatment helps to build up the spur system which is desired, for these fruits produce their berries on the spurs of mature branches.

Cuttings of red, white and black currants can be taken now. These hard-wood cuttings, made from the current season's wood, should be about 10 in. long and be planted in a trench of sufficient depth to cover all but the top three or four buds when the trench is filled in. Often, the lower buds of red and white currants are removed so that the plants will grow on a leg, but this is not done with black currants. Space the cuttings 9 in. apart and firm the soil well around them.

VEGETABLES

It will be possible to work heavy clay soils more easily next spring if they can be ridged now or turned over and left as rough as possible so that a large surface of soil is exposed to the weather. Basic slag is one of the cheapest fertilisers to use on this kind of soil and as it is slow acting it can be put on now at the rate of 4 oz. to the square yard.

Keep an eye on lettuces under cloches and in frames, and do not let quick-growing weeds like chickweed smother them. Lettuces need plenty of air circu-

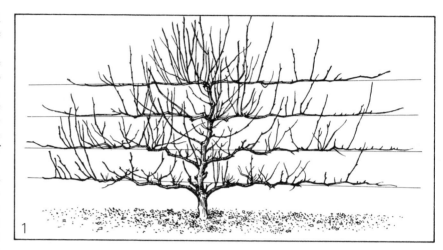

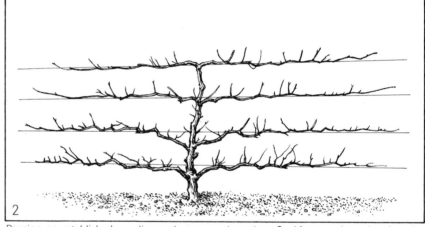

Pruning an established espalier apple tree. Careful pruning is important with all trained fruits if they are to maintain their correct shape and produce a good crop. **1.** Before pruning, there are many overgrown laterals which should be reduced in size or cut out altogether. **2.** After pruning, showing the laterals cut back to two buds to encourage the formation of fruiting spurs. All branches should then be tied in securely to the training wires to prevent damage by wind or rain

lating around them to keep them healthy.

Lift and store Jerusalem artichokes in the same way as potatoes so that they are accessible if the ground freezes and makes digging difficult.

Lift a few roots of parsnips and horse-radish and store these in damp peat or sand in a shed for use later on if the ground should become frozen so hard that it is impossible to continue to dig.

If it is too wet to work outside, this is a good time to give all the cloches a thorough wash and clean. This job is too often neglected. Light transmission is a vital factor in plant growth.

GREENHOUSE

Crowns of lily-of-the-valley can be bought now and potted or boxed in John Innes No. 1 Potting Compost to flower early in the spring in a cool greenhouse. Just cover the crowns with soil.

Cyclamen and winter-flowering primulas are already coming into flower and will benefit from feeding once a fortnight with weak liquid manure. Never feed them when the soil is dry. Remember, first water and then feed.

Be careful with all watering under glass at this time of year. Keep most plants a little on the dry side. The whole success of greenhouse gardening in winter depends on avoiding over-wetness and the careful balance of heating and ventilation.

Pot schizanthus as soon as they have filled their pots with roots. Then place them near the glass to prevent them becoming drawn.

Potting up lily-of-the-valley crowns for spring flowering. When potting is complete the crowns should be covered with compost

November: second week

Lift and protect outdoor chrysanthemums. Plant lily-of-the-valley crowns. Protect kniphofias. Plant hedges. Prune apples and pears. Plant fruit trees. Lift and store scorzonera and salsify. Sow broad beans and hardy peas. Cut down chrysanthemums.

FLOWERS

The roots of outdoor chrysanthemums should be carefully labelled and then lifted and brought into the greenhouse or frame for the winter. I put mine in boxes, cover the roots with a little soil or peat and then place them in a frame until the new year, after which they can go into the greenhouse to provide cuttings for propagation purposes. I do exactly the same with the Korean chrysanthemums, even though these are reputed to be hardier and can be left in the ground.

If no greenhouse or frame is available, the chrysanthemums may be kept quite safely if the boxes are placed under the shelter of a wall and covered over with a little straw, bracken or even sacking during periods of severe weather.

Lily-of-the-valley crowns can now be planted out of doors. They do well in a partially shaded position such as under a north-facing wall or even beneath the shade of trees. Plant the crowns singly, 9 in. apart with the points just below the surface. They need good, fairly light soil, and heavy soil can be made suitable for them by digging in a generous dressing of leafmould, garden compost or peat. They should not be disturbed after this until the bed becomes overcrowded.

Cut the dead flower spikes from Red Hot Pokers (kniphofias), then draw up the foliage over the centre of each plant and tie it together. The foliage will then look rather like a tent and will help to keep moisture away from the crowns and so prevent losses due to rotting off during the winter. In very exposed gardens it is a good idea also to put straw or bracken over the crowns as an added protection.

This is a good time to plant hedges. Quickthorn makes a good boundary hedge, but the hedging plant *par excellence* is *Cupressocyparis leylandii*, a cross between *Cupressus macrocarpa* and *Chamaecyparis nootkatensis*. This conifer grows extremely quickly, has the most handsome deep green foliage and will make a splendid formal hedge measuring anything from 8 to 25 ft. in height in a relatively few years.

Other attractive conifers for hedging purposes are the Lawson's Cypress (*Chamaecyparis lawsoniana*) and certain of its varieties like Green Hedger; and the Western Arbor-vitae, *Thuja plicata*. I do not like privet because it robs the soil of nourishment and needs clipping at least three or four times during the growing season.

For hedges inside the garden, the rose species have a high claim for consideration. *Rosa rugosa* will make a really big hedge and provide a display of flowers for many weeks in summer. Also very vigorous and good as a hedging plant is the hybrid tea rose Peace, with pale to deep yellow flowers, marked with cerise-pink on the edges of the petals.

For smaller hedges there are numerous

Tying the foliage of Red Hot Pokers together to protect the crowns from excessive moisture during the winter

floribundas which are excellent, as well as some shrub roses. Floribundas include the very popular, soft pink Queen Elizabeth with flowers almost like a hybrid tea; the splendid white Iceberg; the rich yellow, very vigorous Chinatown; and Shepherd's Delight, flame, orange and yellow. Decorative shrub roses for this purpose include the creamy-salmon hybrid musk Penelope; and the modern shrub roses Elmshorn, carmine; Will Scarlet, brilliant scarlet; Nymphenburg, pale salmon-pink with yellow at the base of the petals; and Wil-

Planting a conifer hedge. **1.** Before planting the ground must be thoroughly dug and well manured. A hole is then dug out for each plant, spacing them about 2 ft. apart. **2.** The plants are placed in position with the roots well spaced out in the planting hole. **3.** After filling in the hole with soil, the plant is carefully firmed in position

helm, crimson. An old garden rose to consider is the rose-pink Frau Dagmar Hastrup. The freely produced flowers are followed by large crimson hips.

For seaside hedges there is no better shrub than *Euonymus japonicus*, a tough evergreen with deep green, glossy leaves which can withstand a salt-laden atmosphere. This will make a formal hedge 10 to 12 ft. high.

A splendid formal hedge for general purposes is the Common Beech, *Fagus sylvatica*. The leaves persist on the branches throughout the winter and their rich brown colouring is extremely attractive. Again, for general purposes, the Common Box makes what I consider to be the best formal evergreen hedge of up to 15 ft. And for a very dense hedge some feet taller than this there are the hollies – varieties of *Ilex aquifolium* – like the yellow-marked Golden King and the silver-variegated *argenteomarginata*.

FRUIT

This is the time to start pruning apples and pears. Cordon-trained trees will need a good deal more pruning than bush trees. In many cases bush trees are badly overpruned with the result that they make too much new leafy growth the following year and do not fruit well. It is far better to thin out the branches than to cut back every shoot.

The sooner the planting of fruit trees

Boxing up stools of outdoor chrysanthemums. After covering the roots with compost, they can be put in a cold frame

and bushes can be done the better. This will allow them to become established before the severe weather sets in. But planting can continue until March, if necessary – during suitable weather of course.

If your garden is small, be sure to obtain apples and pears on dwarfing or semi-dwarfing rootstocks. Single-stemmed cordons or small bush trees are much more suitable than large bushes or standards, and usually produce high-quality fruit.

Where there are fruit trees which for one

reason or another do not pay for the space they occupy, I think that it is wise to replace them. I know that this is not an easy point to decide, but it is as well to consider it.

VEGETABLES

Two rather uncommon root vegetables, scorzonera and salsify, should be lifted now and stored in sand or peat for winter use.

Get as much of the winter digging done as possible before the soil becomes too wet and sticky. Do not overlook the advice already given to leave the ground as rough as possible, especially if the soil is heavy. The greater the surface area exposed to frost, wind and rain the better. Never under any circumstances, though, try to work the soil when it is in an unsuitable condition for this can do much damage to its structure.

In many parts of the country where the winters are not too severe, broad beans can now be sown out of doors. Choose one of the varieties which are specially suitable for autumn sowing, such as Aquadulce. This crop needs a rich, well-manured soil and the drills should be made 3 in. deep and 2 ft. apart, the seeds being set 4 to 6 in. apart in the drills.

This is also a suitable time to sow a hardy, round-seeded pea such as Meteor, or Feltham First, but again a sheltered position and a well-drained soil are essential for success.

GREENHOUSE

The October-flowering chrysanthemums have now finished their display and the growths should be cut down to within 9 in. of the pots. These stools will later provide young shoots from which cuttings can be made (see p. 25).

Remember that calceolarias should be quite dry before they are watered again. Indeed, this remark applies to all pot plants at this time of the year except those which are in full and rapid growth in heated greenhouses.

Two plants which must not be allowed to dry out for they are easily spoilt are Christmas-flowering azaleas and solanums (Winter Cherries). And if peaty composts are used for potting, these must be watched carefully, for once they have dried out they are very difficult to moisten again.

Digging over empty ground in the vegetable garden. The soil should be left in large lumps to expose it to the beneficial action of frost and rain during the winter. This job must not be attempted if the soil is very sticky or frozen hard

November: third week

Plant ornamental trees and waterside plants. Prune neglected fruit trees. Rake up fallen leaves. Plant red and white currants. Hoe between lettuce and onions. Cut savoy cabbages. Bring pots of bulbs out of plunge beds.

FLOWERS

All this month while the weather remains open and the soil is in good condition the planting of trees and shrubs may continue. It is important to stake all standard trees firmly and I like to drive a stake into the planting hole before the tree is put in position. This not only results in firm staking but it also ensures that the stake will not be driven through the roots, damaging them in the process. While it is advisable to have manure or compost in the soil this should not come in contact with the roots. Put it down below them so that the new roots can go in search of it.

Good flowering trees for gardens include most of the ornamental crabs such as the purple *Malus lemoinei*; the rosy-crimson *M. eleyi* with purplish-green leaves; and *M. floribunda* with crimson buds and pink flowers. These flower in April and May. Attractive dark-coloured fruits are carried later in the season by *M. lemoinei* and *M. eleyi*. The Japanese cherries are among the best of all flowering trees for the garden for to their display of flowers in spring must be added their delightful leaf tints in

autumn. Young trees will need staking at first. Three popular varieties are the rose-pink Hisakura; the erect-growing Amanogawa; and the double-flowered Shirofugen, pink when in bud and white later. Then there is the attractive Autumn-flowering Cherry, *Prunus subhirtella autumnalis*, which will bear its delicate little semi-double, white flowers on and off (depending on the weather) from this month until March; the pink-flowered *P. cerasifera atropurpurea* (better known as *P. c. pissardii*), with pink flowers in spring and reddish-purple foliage; and the double, rosy-pink-flowered, gooseberry-leafed *P.c. blireiana*. These are just a handful of the huge number of varieties to choose from.

Waterside plants such as astilbe and trollius can be planted now, but this is not a good time to move the true aquatics. A host of good astilbes is available nowadays from varieties such as *A. chinensis pumila* and *A. simplicifolia* between 6 and 12 in. high, to the much taller varieties like the clear pink Betsy Cuperus, the dark red Fanal, Red Sentinel and White Gloria in the 2- to 3-ft. range. Other good waterside

Below left: The golden-yellow, translucent berries of *Viburnum opulus xanthocarpum* appear in the autumn and persist

well into the New Year. **Above:** Another shrub which bears its berries over a long period is *Pyracantha coccinea lalandii*, one

of the Firethorns. **Below right:** *Hebe* Autumn Glory, a slightly tender, evergreen shrub for late summer and autumn flowering

When planting trees, whether fruit or ornamental, it is important that they should be securely staked. If the stake is driven into the planting hole before the tree is placed in position, this will ensure that the roots are not damaged

plants are the giant ragwort, *Ligularia clivorum* (*Senecio clivorum*) and the pink and white forms of *Anemone hupehensis* (*A. japonica*) which are particularly welcome in late summer. *L. clivorum* is a plant some 4 ft. tall which needs plenty of room. Its bold heads of orange-yellow flowers are very decorative and are carried above large, heart-shaped leaves in late summer.

The compost heap will need turning regularly to mix the material thoroughly.

FRUIT

This is a suitable time to deal with old and neglected fruit trees. With these, there should be no snipping of innumerable small shoots, but rather the complete removal of a branch here and there to open up the centre of the tree and let in light and air. All large wounds made in this way should be trimmed carefully with a sharp knife and then painted to prevent disease from getting into the tree. Look carefully for canker wounds on these old trees and cut out the affected parts. Then paint the wounds over with a bituminous paint.

Fork very lightly around fruit trees and bushes to get rid of weeds, but do not dig deeply as this would destroy many of the feeding roots near the surface.

By now most of the leaves should have fallen from fruit trees and these can be raked up and placed on the compost heap. This will be another stage in the pre-winter clearance I have already mentioned.

This is a good time to plant red and white currant bushes in ground prepared during October (see p. 108).

Continue the winter pruning of apples and pears.

VEGETABLES

In frosty weather it is a good plan to wheel all manure or compost onto the ground now, in preparation for digging in later on. Do not spread it out but leave it in large heaps until the digging is carried out.

Hoe between winter lettuces whenever soil conditions permit, and also between rows of autumn-sown onions. Even in winter, weeds can grow surprisingly quickly if there are a few mild days.

Remove any yellowing leaves from Brussels sprouts and leaves which have fallen to the ground. When picking sprouts, gather only a few at a time from each plant. Start from the bottom and work upwards.

Early savoy cabbages are now coming into season and my advice would be to use these first and leave the sprouts as long as possible.

GREENHOUSE

By now the weather will, no doubt, be wet, cold, and, in many places, foggy as well. This is often very trying for plants under glass and I want to emphasise the importance of avoiding an excess of atmospheric humidity. Stop damping the floors of the greenhouse, do not overwater the plants and do all you can to keep the air dry.

The earliest varieties of evergreen azaleas – not to be confused with *Azalea indica*, the Florists' Azalea – which may be expected to bloom by Christmas or soon after, should now be brought inside.

Strawberries in pots at present plunged out of doors should have their yellowing and dying leaves removed as well as any late runners which have formed. The plants do not need a great deal of water now, but they should not become really dry.

Bulbs in pots which have been plunged or grown in cool conditions for 8 to 10 weeks may now be brought out into the light. They should not be given too much warmth straight away, and a cold frame would be an ideal position. Give them a further week or so to become accustomed to the change and then take them into the increased warmth of the greenhouse to bring them into flower. I like to see the flower buds above the bulb before I begin to force them in the greenhouse.

When the shoots of pot-grown bulbs are showing above the rim of the pot, they may be moved from the plunge bed and brought into the light. They should not be forced too quickly, though, and a cold frame is the best place for the next week or so

114

November: fourth week

Repair and re-lay garden paths. Plant rhododendrons and azaleas. Protect Christmas roses. Plant raspberries, blackberries and loganberries. Protect trees from mice. Inspect fruit and potatoes in store. Force rhubarb and chicory. Reduce water given to cacti.

FLOWERS

This is a good time to inspect the garden paths and repair or re-lay any which are in need of such attention. Old gravel paths will be greatly improved by the addition of a little fresh gravel. If you are planning new paths it is wise to remove the soil to a depth of several inches along the length of the path, using it to build up beds, borders and so on, and to replace this with stones, broken bricks or other hard rubble which will make a good solid foundation for the path.

Fork lightly between shrubs to get rid of weeds, aerate the soil and work in any leaves which may be lying on the surface. There is no need to remove annual weeds in a mistaken enthusiasm for cleanliness, as forked in they will rot and make excellent humus. But do not fork more than 2 in. deep.

Rhododendrons and azaleas may be planted now, but do not plant these shrubs where there is any free lime in the soil. If you are in doubt on this point, have a sample of soil tested or test it yourself by putting a handful of soil in a jam jar and pouring a little dilute hydrochloric acid over it. If the fluid effervesces there is lime in the soil, but if there is no reaction there is no free lime present. There are also excellent, inexpensive soil-testing kits on sale which will give you more precise indications of the soil's acidity or alkalinity.

Put frame lights or cloches over some of

Winter is the best time of year to do constructional work in the garden. Here, a concrete path is being levelled with the aid of a flat piece of wood. Note the hardcore used as a foundation for the path

the Christmas roses (*Helleborus niger*) to bring the flowers on for Christmas and keep them free of mud splashes.

FRUIT

This is a good time to plant raspberries, blackberries and loganberries. For those who object to thorns, there are thornless varieties of both these fruits. Malling Promise, Malling Jewel and Malling Enterprise are all good varieties of raspberry. Merton Thornless is a very good blackberry. It is not too vigorous and the fruit is

of excellent quality. Another good one is Himalaya Giant. Blackberries are very useful for continuing the soft fruit crop through into the autumn. LY59 is the strain of loganberry usually grown.

Now, or at any time between this month and March is a suitable time to propagate all three of these fruits, the raspberries by division of mature plants and the blackberries and loganberries by layering.

Watch young fruit trees, particularly those planted in grass, for any signs of barking by voles, field mice, or in country districts, rabbits. If such damage is allowed to take place it can easily prove fatal to the trees. Sacking dipped in animal oil and lightly placed on the ground around the trees, but not actually touching them, should keep these pests away.

Make an inspection of fruit in store, particularly late pears, and remove any which show signs of even the slightest damage. Pears which are beginning to mellow should be taken indoors for use.

Get on with the winter pruning of fruit trees and bushes as weather permits. Many fruit growers prefer not to prune plums, damsons and cherries in winter as there is then a greater danger of infection by silver leaf disease.

VEGETABLES

It may appear that I repeat myself rather about looking over stored potatoes, but it

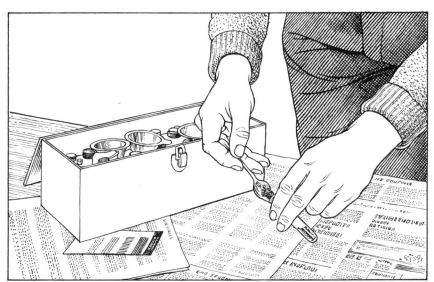

Soil testing kits of varying complexity are available from gardening centres. These are extremely useful for the gardener who would like to know the exact acidity or alkalinity of his soil, and will save a lot of guesswork when applying fertilisers

Above: Two Dogwoods with attractive bark for winter months are the red *Cornus stolonifera* and the yellow *C. s. flaviramea*

Below: For winter colour variegated-leaved shrubs such as *Elaeagnus pungens aureo-variegata* should not be forgotten

is so important to do this that it bears repetition. Look them over now and remove any diseased specimens, remembering that in a week's time – if this job is left – there may be twice as many spoilt.

Take every favourable opportunity to get on with winter digging, particularly on heavier soils. If you are bothered by couch grass, remove the roots while digging.

Lift a few crowns of rhubarb for forcing and leave them on top of the ground for a week or so before taking them inside and putting them under the greenhouse staging. The crowns can be packed close to one another and a little moist soil should be worked in among the roots. Forcing is more successful if light is excluded and to do this sacking can be hung from the top of the staging to the floor below.

Chicory can also be forced now. Strong roots are lifted and packed, 2 to 3 in. apart, in deep boxes or large flower pots with some light soil. Old potting compost is very suitable for this purpose. They are then brought into the greenhouse or even into a shed or cellar in which they can be kept dark and fairly warm. The blanched shoots are cut off at ground level.

GREENHOUSE

Rooted pelargonium (geranium) cuttings may be potted immediately or, if preferred, left in their pots until February.

With the exception of the Christmas- and Easter-flowering Cacti all cacti should be kept almost dry now. They need little or no water until the end of February.

The Christmas Cactus, *Schlumbergera buckleyi*, (also known as *Zygocactus truncatus*) and the Easter Cactus, *Rhipsalidopsis gaertneri*, must be kept slightly moist during the winter months. They flower from November to January and from February to April respectively.

Young plants and cuttings should be kept on a shelf as near to the glass as possible. On my shelves at this time of year are schizanthus, antirrhinums, various annuals, seedling cyclamen, *Primula malacoides*, and rooted cuttings of heliotrope. None of these need much artificial heat, but they should be protected from frost. Schizanthus will need staking now.

This is the time to move specially prepared bulbs from the plunge bed into a cold frame. They should stay there for one or two weeks.

December: first week

Half prune roses. Ventilate plants in frames. Protect delphiniums from slugs. Repair fences. Control big bud on black currants. Prune outdoor vines. Lift celery. Earth up spring cabbages. Box up chrysanthemum stools. Bring pots of bulbs into greenhouse.

FLOWERS

Frosts in November usually finish off the last of the rose blooms, and to avoid them looking untidy during the winter I always cut the flowering growths on mine halfway back. This does not mean that the roses have already been fully pruned but that the soft top growth with a few buds and frosted flowers have been removed. The rose beds look all the better for this tidying-up treatment and there is also the added benefit that the bushes are less likely to be rocked by winter winds and have their roots loosened.

It is really very unwise to attempt to plant trees and shrubs when the soil is wet and sticky. As I said a few weeks ago in connection with the vegetable garden (see p. 112), it is best to keep off the soil altogether at such times, at least on medium to heavy soils. If the soil is light and quick-draining there is not the same problem and one can work these even though it is impossible to cultivate the heavier, clay types.

If there is plenty of. humus-forming material in the soil this will help to rectify deficiencies of soil texture – and this applies whether the soil is too heavy or too light. In the first case it keeps the soil more open and improves drainage and in the second it acts as a sponge-like medium to retain more moisture. Farmyard manure, peat, leafmould, spent hops and garden compost will all have this beneficial effect and may be worked in at any time during the winter.

This is a difficult time of year for plants in frames as these structures will probably have to be covered at night to keep out the frost, and on frosty days it is not wise to uncover them at all. They should, therefore, be ventilated whenever possible.

Herbaceous plants sometimes suffer badly during the winter from slug damage, and delphiniums are particularly likely to be victims. A good preventive is to scrape some of the soil away from around the crowns of the plants and replace this with sharp cinder ashes.

This is a good time to repair rustic fences, arches and similar structures, if such attentions are necessary. You will be far too busy to attend to these matters in the spring.

At this time of year, too, I always think that it is a good idea to look at the garden with a cool eye and make up your mind if there is anything you want to change – or some new feature which you wish to introduce. Everybody these days is looking for ways in which to reduce maintenance work and any fundamental replanning on these lines could well be done at this stage.

Shrubs of any kind are labour saving in so much that they need a minimum of attention, and if the ground-covering kinds are grown as well then even more can be achieved in this direction. Heaths (ericas and daboecias) and heathers (callunas); *Cotoneaster adpressus praecox* and *C. horizontalis*; varieties of *Potentilla fruticosa*; the prostrate *Euonymus fortunei*; *Ruscus aculeatus* (Butcher's Broom); the late-winter-flowering *Sarcococca humilis*; and *Vinca major* and *V. minor* (the Peri-

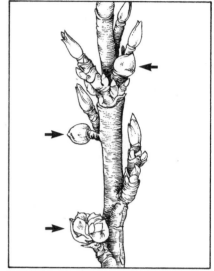

A black currant shoot showing swollen buds affected by the big bud mite. These should be removed and burnt

winkles) are just a few of those useful for this purpose.

Then, of course, there are herbaceous plants like the hostas, so showy with their bold, often variegated foliage; the bergenias, again with bold foliage and handsome flowers; *Stachys macrantha superba*, with dark green, wrinkled leaves and rosy-purple flowers in June; tiarellas, tellimas, pulmonarias, herbaceous geraniums, astilbes and a host of others.

If new plant features incorporating this kind of plant are to be created, then the planting should all be completed between now and next spring.

FRUIT

There is not much work to do in the fruit garden at this time of year, but if pruning has not been completed press on with this as quickly as possible. I, personally, like to see this job completed before Christmas.

It is now very easy to distinguish the buds on black currants which are affected by the big bud mite, for these buds will be large and globular in contrast to the smaller and more pointed healthy buds. All affected buds should be picked off and burnt. It is important to do this job very thoroughly.

Outdoor vines can be pruned now and it should not be thought that this will in any way harm them. I know that some people fear that they may kill their plants but so long as it is not actually freezing all should

Covering frames with hessian as a protection against frost. These covers can usually be taken off during the day, unless the frost persists. Whenever the weather is at all favourable, plants in frames will benefit from careful ventilation

be well. Cut back all last year's branches to two eyes and remove all thin and useless wood, and the results should be good. There are many outdoor vines which would be better dealt with in this way – in other words, their owners should be really severe with the annual pruning to keep the plants under control.

VEGETABLES

Celery should be lifted as it is required for use. Remove the paper 'collars' which were placed around the plants and cut off all the fibrous roots before taking them into the house. This saves a lot of work in the kitchen.

Take the opportunity, when the ground is dry, to pull a little soil around the stems of spring cabbages. This is really a mild form of earthing up. I find that it helps to bring the plants through the winter more safely and gives them a better anchorage as well.

In gardens of any size – say those over a quarter of an acre – rotary cultivators can make work much easier and help to keep the garden in a better state of cultivation. Some machines are fairly inexpensive and are capable of cultivating to a depth of 7 to 9 in. Most can be fitted with attachments to cut grass, trim hedges and do other useful jobs like spraying. These machines can be hired rather than bought if they are only wanted for occasional use.

GREENHOUSE

The average amateur gardener has little room to spare and so, as more and more

If large areas have to be cultivated each year in the vegetable garden, or if starting a new garden from scratch, a rotary cultivator will make the task much easier. There are many models to choose from, and they may be hired as well as bought

chrysanthemums finish flowering, these should be cut back and the stools put as near to the glass as possible. Alternatively, they can be put into a frame until they are needed.

I make it a practice to take all the stools out of their pots, shake the soil away from them and then pack those which I wish to keep as a source of material for cuttings close together in boxes, covering the roots with fresh potting compost. I am always very careful about labelling the stools as I cut them down for boxing up, to prevent any confusion over varieties when it comes to taking cuttings.

Cyclamen should now be almost at their best, and they must be watered with care. The best time to water them is during the early part of the day so that surplus water can dry off before evening – and they should only be watered when the soil has become dry. Keep the spout of the watering-can well down in the pot and water the soil, not the leaves. Watch for signs of botrytis in the crowns or centres of the plants. Pull out any leaves showing signs of decay and dust the crowns with flowers of sulphur to prevent the spread of the fungus.

Examine all bulbs plunged in ashes or in dark places because, by now, some of them may be an inch or so high and they will be ready for moving into a cold frame before going on, when ready, to the greenhouse for forcing.

Bulbs which have been out of the plunge bed for some time can be brought into a warm house or heated frame, but it pays to be patient even if it means waiting another week or two before this is done. It is best to bring them in in stages, a few at a time, so that a succession is maintained as far into the spring as possible. I like to see the flower buds showing well above the bulbs before I even start to force them, otherwise the flowers may not develop properly.

Specially prepared, pre-cooled bulbs should be moved into the warm greenhouse to bring the flowers on for Christmas display.

Lifting celery. Note the paper collar which was tied around the plant before earthing up to keep soil away from the heart

Dusting a cyclamen with flowers of sulphur to control an attack by botrytis. Any affected leaves or buds should be removed

December: second week

Treat wooden fences with preservative. Cut winter-flowering shrubs for the house. Continue to plant trees and shrubs. Screen newly planted evergreens. Order winter washes. Inspect grease bands. Force seakale. Protect broccoli. Sow onions. Sponge foliage plants.

FLOWERS

Many winter-flowering shrubs start to bloom early in certain years and in my part of Shropshire both *Viburnum fragrans* and *V. tinus*, the familiar Laurustinus, often make a lovely picture at this time. Although many flowers may be damaged by November frosts other buds soon open and the bushes are once more a mass of bloom. *Erica carnea*, the winter-flowering heather, and some of its varieties like the rosy-pink King George, are usually in flower, and trees of *Prunus subhirtella autumnalis* – which I consider the best of all winter-flowering trees – can always be expected to bloom just now.

Wooden trellis work and fences should be examined and, if necessary, treated with a good wood preservative. Do not under any circumstances use creosote as this is liable to damage plants growing nearby.

Twigs of numerous trees and shrubs, including those of the yellow-flowered *Jasminum nudiflorum*, will be in flower by Christmas if cut and put in water and brought into a warm room now. When cutting trees and shrubs in this way, take care not to disfigure them but cut small pieces here and there where they will not be missed. The yellow jasmine, incidentally, is an ideal plant for training on a wall or fence and it will thrive in shade as well as in sunny places.

As long as the weather remains open and the soil conditions are good the planting of trees and shrubs can continue. Make sure that all trees are properly staked and that climbing plants are tied securely to their supports.

Especial care should be taken when staking trees for if the trunk is allowed to move in the wind and rub against the stake then the whole exercise is wasted. The proprietary plastic tree ties one can buy nowadays are, I think, especially good, for they hold the trees securely, well away from the stake, they are easy to put on and they are not expensive.

Establishing evergreen trees and shrubs is always a little tricky for they have no proper resting period and are in a particularly vulnerable position until their roots are active again. It helps tremendously if a screen of some kind is erected on the wind-sheltered gardens. **Above:** The attractive flowers of *Iris unguicularis* appear between November and March. **Below right:** *Ilex*

aquifolium Golden King, a female variety of holly, bearing a plentiful crop of berries

Below left: The most spectacular of the mahonias is *M. lomariifolia*, but it is slightly tender and can therefore only be grown in

ward side after planting and left in position for at least the first winter. This could be made out of wattle hurdles or hessian, and the idea is to break up the force of the wind, which is one of the most damaging causes of moisture loss through the leaves. Also, of course, a strong wind always tends to rock plants – even if they are well staked – and a tree or shrub struggling to re-establish itself will not like this at all.

The other important thing to check frequently, therefore, is the firmness at the roots, and I like to look round new plantings after every period of rough weather and firm the soil where necessary.

FRUIT

Tar oil or DNOC winter wash should be ordered now because winter spraying is a job which must be started soon. It can only be done efficiently in fairly still, dry weather, and often there are not many suitable days during late December and January.

Prepare ground for the late planting of fruit trees, bushes and so on. The ground should be deeply dug and some manure worked in, and a dressing of basic slag or bonemeal could also be given with advantage at this time.

Burn all tree prunings as some may be infected with disease or be carrying the eggs of aphids or other pests.

Inspect all grease bands on fruit trees to make sure that they are still doing their job efficiently. Remove any leaves found sticking to the grease bands and renew the grease if necessary.

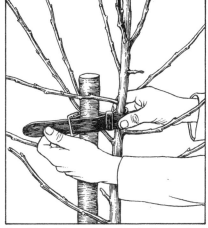

An efficient type of tree tie. As the trunk of the tree expands, the buckle on the tie can be loosened

VEGETABLES

Seakale crowns can be forced and blanched in the same way as chicory which I described on p. 116, and blanched endive may be lifted and brought inside to give variety to the winter salad bowl.

See that frame lights are properly tied down or firmly fixed in some other way for at this time of year they can easily be blown off and broken by strong winds. Cloches are usually able to take care of themselves, but some of the lighter types may require something to hold them down such as a length of wire securely fastened to stakes. It may be necessary to protect frames and cloches with sacking or straw at night if the weather is frosty.

The gathering of Brussels sprouts should be in full swing now. Do not remove the tops of the plants until the sprouts have all been gathered and only pick a few of the best.

Some of the winter broccoli are beginning to form their curds now. Turn in the leaves to protect the curds from frost and cut regularly, as once they have reached their full size they soon begin to spoil.

If seakale beet plants are covered with cloches they will provide leaves for winter use.

GREENHOUSE

If you want really large exhibition onions next year now is the time to sow a variety like Selected Ailsa Craig, Flagon or Premier. Sow the seed very thinly in a seed box filled with seed compost and germinate in a greenhouse with a temperature of 13°C. (55°F.).

Sponge the foliage of large-leaved evergreen plants such as dracaenas, codiaeums, ficuses and palms. If half a teaspoonful of milk is stirred into a cup of water it will put a nice gloss on the leaves. Alternatively, use a proprietary leaf-shining preparation.

Do not start to take chrysanthemum cuttings too early. There is sometimes a temptation to do this when good-looking shoots begin to appear on the stools in December. I prefer to leave all chrysanthemum propagation until early January and I am certain that the plants are the better for it.

Light is especially important in the greenhouse at this time of year, and the glass should be washed – particularly on the outside – to remove any grime.

Evergreen trees and shrubs are often difficult to establish and are particularly vulnerable to strong winds which tend to dry the leaves up and rock the plants. A wind-break of hessian supported by stakes would help to overcome this problem

Sponging the leaves of a ficus. It is surprising how much the appearance of such plants will be improved by this treatment

December: third week

Shake snow off shrubs and trees. Paint garden frames. Firm cuttings.
Apply winter wash to fruit trees, and feed. Lift leeks and heel in.
Force rhubarb. Prepare ground for runner beans. Prune vines and
peaches under glass. Take carnation cuttings.

This week embraces Christmas and I hope
that all readers will have a happy time.

While comfortably seated beside the
fireside there is an opportunity to consider
what the garden has been able to contribute
towards the Christmas festivities. Are
there a few chrysanthemum blooms, one or
two pot plants or even some flowering
shrub material which can be used? What
vegetables has the garden provided for the
Christmas table? Are there Brussels
sprouts, cabbages, beetroot, onions and
parsnips? Are there a few late dessert
apples, or some culinary apples for cooking purposes? If not, now is the time to
think ahead and make preparations so that
you will have your own flowers, fruits and
vegetables for Christmas next year.

FLOWERS
If snow comes early to give a white Christmas, do remember the damage that this
can do to trees and shrubs on occasions.
After a heavy fall get out into the garden
and dislodge any large accumulations,
especially on conifers which can be permanently disfigured if too weighed down.

If some of the more difficult alpines in
the rock garden have been covered with
panes of glass, examine these occasionally
and make sure that dead leaves have not
collected under the glass to the detriment
of these small and easily smothered plants.
Clear away any such leaves or rubbish and
make certain the glass is secure.

Garden frames should be painted regularly
to preserve the wood. Those made from
cedar should be oiled rather than painted

Feeding a wall-trained fruit tree with a
dressing of sulphate of potash applied at
the rate of 4 oz. per tree

When cutting evergreens for Christmas
decoration use a sharp pair of secateurs
and cut in such a way as not to disfigure the
tree or shrub. Either cut so that the shape
of the specimen will be made more pleasant
or cut pieces from here and there so that it
will not be noticed anyway.

Garden frames should be painted regularly to keep them in good condition.

If frost has loosened the soil around
cuttings these should be firmed in.

FRUIT
As soon as Christmas is over make preparations for winter spraying. Tar oil washes
are particularly valuable for clearing the

trees of lichen and moss. DNOC winter
wash is even more effective than tar oil
against some of the overwintering pests,
but it does not clean the bark of the trees to
the same extent. For these reasons it is
quite a good policy to alternate the use of
these winter sprays, using tar oil one year
and DNOC the next.

Apply sulphate of potash to fruit trees
at the rate of 4 oz. per tree. This is a fertiliser which all fruit trees appreciate as it
encourages fruitfulness and good ripening.

I have no doubt that readers have much
to do at the moment in connection with
Christmas, but it is worth making a special
effort to get everything tidied up and the
pruning finished. It is particularly important to clear up all tree prunings within as
short a time as possible in the interests of
garden hygiene.

VEGETABLES
It is a good plan to lift a few leeks and heel
these in somewhere handy so that they can
be reached easily if the weather turns really
severe. Treated in this way they will keep
in good condition for many weeks. It
might be wise to lift some celery, too, and
put it in a frost-proof place just in case
severe weather sets in.

More roots of rhubarb can be brought
into the greenhouse for forcing. The best
place for them, as I have already said, is
under the staging where light can be
excluded with sacking, polythene, boards
or other suitable material.

Many gardeners use the same part of the
garden each year for growing runner beans

Heavy snow falls can do much damage in
the garden, particularly to conifers, where a
broken branch can permanently spoil the
shape of a tree. After such a fall, it is a good
idea to shake branches carefully to dislodge
the snow

and there is no harm in this provided the soil is well prepared. Make the trenches 2 to 3 ft. wide and 1½ to 2 ft. deep, and ridge the soil up on each side of the trench now. This will leave it open to the beneficial effects of the winter weather.

GREENHOUSE

Vines under glass should now be pruned. All side growths or laterals are cut back to two buds. The spurs carrying these shortened growths should be well spaced – at least 15 to 18 in. apart – on the main rod so that there is no overcrowding in the summer. After pruning, lower the rods to encourage even growth later on.

At this time, also, rub off the loose bark on vines as this forms an ideal hiding place for overwintering eggs of aphids and red spider mites. Scrape this loose bark carefully with a knife or twist it off with the hands. Care must be taken not to expose the green rind underneath.

Peach trees under glass must also be pruned now, the method used being to cut out some of the older branches and train in younger wood in its place. Any diseased branches should also be cut out.

Fuchsias are now dormant and they should be inspected periodically. Do not allow them to become too dry – just keep the soil slightly moist. Those plants being trained as standard specimens should be tied to canes already placed in position so that the leading shoot grows straight up.

Lifting leeks in preparation for severe weather. **1.** The plants are lifted from their growing position before the ground becomes too hard to dig. **2.** Heeling the plants in closely together in the shelter of a wall until they are required for use

In heated greenhouses – even those heated by hot water pipes and more so in those with electrical heating – I find it advisable to sprinkle water under the staging occasionally to prevent the atmosphere becoming too dry.

Start to take cuttings of perpetual-flowering carnations and continue to take these in batches until March. What is wanted is firm growths taken from non-flowering sideshoots, and those from midway up the flowering stems are best. These cuttings will root best of all in pure sand in a propagating frame provided with a temperature of 16°C. (60°F.). If sand is used as a rooting medium, the cuttings must be potted as soon as they have rooted into a growing mixture like the John Innes No. 1 Potting Compost, for sand on its own contains no nutrients.

The seed lists start to come through the letter box round about now, and some time should be spent looking through them over the holiday period. With seed orders in particular, it is always best to get off to an early start.

Forcing rhubarb under the greenhouse staging. Sacking or black polythene is hung from the staging to exclude light

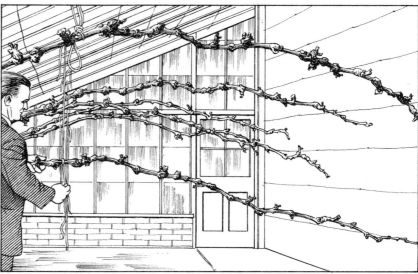

After pruning greenhouse vines, the rods should then be lowered and supported by strings from the roof of the house. This will encourage even development of shoots along the whole length of the rods, and not just at the tips

December: fourth week

Order flower seeds. Dig over annual borders. Check protective material used on tender plants. Protect fruit against bird damage. Manure wall-trained fruit trees. Force mint. Prepare onion bed. Cut back pelargoniums. Clean greenhouse thoroughly.

FLOWERS

So we reach the last week in the year when we must begin all over again and plan and work for the year ahead. My advice to everybody is to try and arrange things so that work is reduced to a minimum, without loss of efficiency. Then the garden becomes a quiet retreat from the bustle of life.

If the roots of hardy primulas have been exposed by heavy rain or lifted by frost, topdress the plants with a compost consisting of loam, peat and sand.

The flower seed order will probably contain half-hardy and hardy annuals as well as, possibly, some perennials, many of which come readily from seed sown outdoors in May or early June.

Half-hardy annuals I would not be without include zinnias, stocks, asters, French and African Marigolds, ageratum and petunias. The hardy annual order can scarcely omit sweet peas, calendulas, candytuft, godetias, clarkias, the annual chrysanthemum and coreopsis, nasturtiums, scarlet flax and sweet alyssum.

Perennials which can be very successfully grown from seed are Oriental Poppies, geums, gaillardias, *Campanula persicifolia*, lupins, delphiniums, anthemis, *Lychnis chalcedonica*, pyrethrum and aquilegias. Nor must we forget, of course, hollyhocks and Sweet Williams, which many gardeners prefer to treat as biennials, and foxgloves and Canterbury Bells which are genuine biennials.

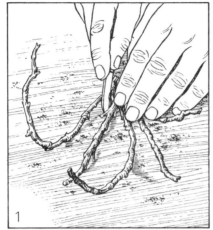

Preparing mint for early picking. **1.** Mint roots are lifted from the garden and cut up into pieces 3 to 4 in. long. **2.** The pieces are

I find that people with gardens of all sizes are using plants in all these categories more adventurously nowadays than they used to. Perhaps it has all followed on from the popularity of the mixed border. It is certainly nice to come across a display of good plants like those I have mentioned in positions which show off their attractive features to perfection – say an angle by a bend in a path or in a bed at the end of a short vista.

But to return to more practical matters, now is the time to dig over borders and beds in which hardy annuals are to be sown in the spring. I do not recommend the use of any manure on such sites as long

then laid flat on the surface of a box filled with potting compost. (Old compost may be used.) **3.** After covering the cuttings with

more compost, the boxes should be put in the greenhouse or in a frame to encourage the early production of shoots

as the soil is reasonably good. Annuals flower best in a soil which is not too rich. Over-fed, they produce mostly foliage.

Inspect all the sacking, bracken, straw and other material being used to protect tender plants and make sure that these protective materials are still in position and capable of doing their job.

FRUIT

Discontinue planting fruit trees and bushes if the weather becomes too severe.

Watch carefully for bird damage on fruit trees. Gooseberries and plums are particularly liable to suffer in this way, and sometimes birds will pick out all the buds. With small fruits a fruit cage is really the ideal answer, but sometimes it is possible to make the buds distasteful to birds by

Some plants are not sufficiently hardy to survive the winter except with the aid of a protective covering. Bracken is an ideal material for this purpose, and may be held in place over the plant with the help of split bamboo canes

Pruning and repotting a pelargonium. **1.** The tall stems should be cut back to a bud or joint 6 to 9 in. above the rim of the pot.

2. After knocking the plant out of its pot, some of the old soil is teased away, taking care not to damage the roots. **3.** The plant

is then placed in the smallest sized pot that will accommodate the roots, and topped up with fresh compost

spraying them with a bird repellent, applied as directed by the manufacturer.

Wall-trained fruit trees are always liable to suffer from lack of moisture during the summer months and it is a good idea to fork manure, compost or peat in around the trees now to make the soil more moisture retentive. This is one of those jobs which must be done carefully, though, for it is all too easy to damage the roots, so fork the material in only lightly.

If the weather is favourable – which means in this case not frosty or windy – complete winter spraying with tar oil wash.

VEGETABLES

Lift a few roots of mint, place them in a fairly deep seed box, cover them with potting compost (old potting compost will do) and then put them in a frame or greenhouse to provide shoots for early picking.

If the onion bed has not already been dug and manured, no time should be lost in completing this task. It will then be broken up by the hard frosts which are still to come. Dig in manure deeply if this is available, otherwise use any humus-forming material like compost or peat in its place. Spread bonfire ash liberally over the top if this is available, as well as bone-meal and hoof and horn, each of which should be applied at the rate of 4 oz. to the square yard. The fertilisers will be worked in later when the seed bed is prepared.

GREENHOUSE

Cut back old pelargonium plants, shortening the growths to a joint or bud 6 to 9 in.

above the pot. Then repot the plants, shaking all the old soil from the roots and replacing them into the smallest pots which the roots can comfortably be fitted into. Use the John Innes No. 1 Potting Compost.

I begin preparations for seed sowing in the greenhouse now by thoroughly cleaning all the pots, boxes and crocks and making certain that suitable supplies of seed sowing composts are available. It is at this time of year that the value of a seed raiser or warm propagating frame for raising seedlings is most appreciated. What is needed is something in which a temperature of 16 to 18°C. (60 to 65°F.) can be maintained.

Now that the chrysanthemums have finished flowering there is more room to move around and the greenhouse can be thoroughly washed down, section by section, with a solution of disinfectant. Make sure that you get the scrubbing brush well into all the cracks and crevices and thoroughly clean the glass, both inside and out.

Continue to pick the dead leaves off plants in frames and in the greenhouse as these can encourage fungi and cause the plants to rot.

I hope that you have enjoyed a profitable year's gardening and that you have found these notes useful.

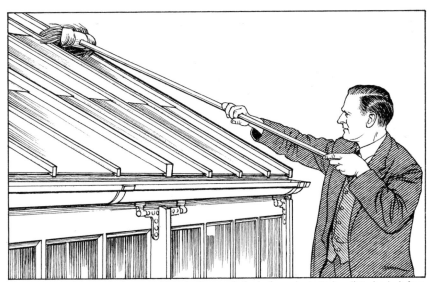

Both the inside and the outside of the greenhouse should be thoroughly washed down at this time of year when there are relatively few plants to be disturbed. A few drops of detergent added to the water will help to remove grime

Plants
for
Every
Month

Name	Type and Size	General Remarks

JANUARY

Name	Type and Size	General Remarks
Azaleas (Indian)	Cool greenhouse shrub. Up to 5 ft. tall	The Indian azaleas (forced specimens of *Rhododendron simsii*) are first-rate plants for January to April display. The annual repotting after flowering should be done with a mixture of 2 parts moist peat and 1 part coarse sand, and as this contains little food, regular feeding is essential.
Begonias (Lorraine type)	Warm greenhouse, fibrous-rooted perennials. 1 ft. tall	The fibrous-rooted Lorraine begonias which flower in winter are graceful plants. They need a minimum temperature of 16°C. (60°F.).
Eranthis tubergenii (Winter Aconite)	Tuberous-rooted perennial. 3 to 5 in. tall	The bright, golden-yellow flowers appear in January to March. *E. tubergenii* is a hybrid between *E. cilicica* and *E. hyemalis* and is especially handsome. (See illustration p. 27.) Likes shade and grows well in grass and under trees. Plant in September or October 2 in. deep and 2 in. apart. No special soil requirements.
Erica carnea (Heath)	Evergreen flowering shrub. 9 to 12 in. tall	This species and its many varieties are a delight in the winter garden from mid-December to April. Include colours from carmine and pink to white. *E. carnea* and its varieties, unlike most heaths and heathers, will tolerate limy soils. Need well-drained conditions, preferably with plenty of peat or leafmould.
Freesias	Cool greenhouse, bulbous plants. 12 to 18 in. tall	These beautiful flowers are a delight from January until spring. Their scented flowers in colours like orange, crimson, yellow, white and lavender are borne on wiry stems. See weekly notes for cultivation.
Galanthus nivalis (Common Snowdrop)	Bulbous plant. 6 in. tall	Few flowers are more eagerly awaited than the common snowdrop, *Galanthus nivalis* which makes its appearance in January and February. S. Arnott and *atkinsii* are fine varieties. All have white flowers with green markings.
Garrya elliptica	Evergreen shrub. 8 to 12 ft. tall	Impressive silvery-green catkins in January and February, 9 in. or more long on male plants, shorter on female specimens. (See illustration p. 31.) Needs sunny position sheltered from cold winds. Best trained against sunny wall. Ordinary soil.
Hamamelis mollis	Deciduous shrub or small tree. Up to 20 ft. tall	Scented, yellow flowers with strap-like petals in January and February. The variety *H. m. pallida* is especially attractive with large, sulphur-yellow flowers. Plant in good loamy soil in sunny, sheltered position.
Iris histrioides major	Cormous plant. 3 to 4 in. tall	This splendid little iris bears rich blue flowers with white and gold markings on its petals in late January and early February. Grow in a gritty mixture.
Lonicera fragrantissima	Partially evergreen shrub. Up to 8 ft. tall	Produces creamy white flowers in winter. A hybrid between this species and *L. standishii*, named *L. purpusii*, is also a good winter shrub with flowers of similar colour. Any ordinary soil will suffice.
Mahonias	Evergreen shrubs. 2 to 8 ft. tall	The mahonias are extremely useful shrubs and include the very easily grown *Mahonia aquifolium*, a splendid ground-cover plant with yellow flowers in spring; and the choice *M. japonica* with long racemes of fragrant lemon-yellow flowers in February and March. For gardens in warmer parts of the country there is also *M. lomariifolia* which flowers from December to March. (See illustration p. 120.)
Viburnum tinus (Laurustinus)	Evergreen shrub. 7 to 10 ft. tall and through	This is one of the best-known winter-flowering shrubs with its white flowers–pink in the bud–studding the bush from January to April. It likes a good, loamy soil and an open, sunny position.

FEBRUARY

Name	Type and Size	General Remarks
Camellia japonica and varieties	Cool greenhouse, or garden evergreen shrubs. Generally 6 to 8 ft. tall but up to 20 ft.	*Camellia japonica* and its varieties are excellent flowering shrubs for the greenhouse from which frost is excluded. They can also be grown out of doors in sheltered positions, and are very suitable for a north wall. (See illustration p. 31.) They need a lime-free soil.

Name	Type and Size	General Remarks
Crocus tomasinianus	Cormous plant. 9 to 10 in. tall	Mauvish-blue flowers in February and March. Delightful varieties include Whitwell Purple, mauvish-purple, and Taplow Purple, reddish-purple. (See illustration p. 31.) Plant corms in September or October 3 in. deep and 3 in. apart in well-drained soil. Splendid for borders, the rock garden or for naturalising in grass.
Daphne mezereum (The Mezereon)	Deciduous shrub. 4 ft. tall	Perhaps my favourite early-flowering shrub. Its sweetly scented, purple flowers are a delight in February and March. It needs a moist but free-draining soil.
Hellebores	Herbaceous perennials. 1 to 1½ ft. tall	*Helleborus niger* has large, white, saucer-shaped flowers from December to February. They are easily weather damaged and best covered with cloches. *Helleborus corsicus* has clusters of attractive, greenish-yellow flowers in February and March and handsome foliage. (See illustration p. 31.) Both need rich, loamy soil and a cool, shady position.
Lachenalias (Cape Cowslips)	Cool greenhouse, bulbous plants. Up to 1 ft. tall	The many species and varieties have a good range of colours and flower from February to May. Two popular kinds are *Lachenalia aloides nelsonii*, golden-yellow; and *L. bulbifera* with red, yellow, purple and green shades in its flowers.
Matthiolas (Stocks)	Cool greenhouse annuals, or summer bedding plants. 18 in. tall	In addition to being fine half-hardy annuals for the border, these colourful stocks are excellent for flowering in pots in late winter and early spring in the cool greenhouse.
Primula kewensis	Cool greenhouse perennial, but treated as an annual. 1 ft. tall	This yellow-flowered hybrid blooms in spring. Seed is sown in February or March and germinated in a temperature of 16°C. (60°F.). Once established it needs lower temperatures than other greenhouse primulas – just enough heat to keep the frost out. (See illustration p. 30.)
Sarcococca humilis	Evergreen shrub. 2 ft. tall .	Excellent winter-flowering shrub for shade which provides good ground cover. It has shiny, dark green leaves, willow-like in appearance, and small white flowers.
Scilla sibirica (Siberian Squill)	Bulbous plant. 4 to 6 in. tall	The bright blue flowers of the Siberian Squill are particularly welcome in February, normally such an unpleasant month for weather. Plant in ordinary soil between August and November, 2 to 4 in. deep and 4 in. apart. (See illustration p. 46.)

MARCH

Name	Type and Size	General Remarks
Abutilon **Fireball**	Cool greenhouse, evergreen shrub. 4 to 6 ft. tall	This excellent shrub (see illustration page 43) will flower throughout most of the year given a winter temperature of 7 to 10°C. (45 to 50°F.) and a temperature of 16 to 18°C. (60 to 65°F.) from March to September.
Anemone blanda	Rhizomatous plant. Up to 6 in. tall	Deep blue to mauve, pink and white flowers in March and April. (See illustration p. 42.) Prefers sunny position and sheltered site. Soil should be well drained.
Bergenia cordifolia	Herbaceous perennial. 1 ft. tall	The large-leaved bergenias are particularly useful plants for growing beside a pool or path. The flowers of *B. cordifolia* are rose-magenta.
Brunfelsia calycina	Cool greenhouse, evergreen shrub. 2 ft. tall	This flowering shrub is an excellent plant for the cool greenhouse, sun lounge or conservatory. The lavender-purple flowers are borne intermittently throughout the year but the main flowering period is late winter and spring.
Chaenomeles speciosa	Deciduous shrub. 6 ft. tall	The many varieties of *Chaenomeles speciosa* in shades of red, pink and white are especially good as wall shrubs for March to April flowering. (See illustration p. 42.) Grows well in almost any soil in sunny or partially shaded position.
Chionodoxa luciliae (Glory of the Snow)	Bulbous plant. 6 in. tall	This pretty plant has blue, white-centred, star-shaped flowers. It is best in a sunny position and needs a well-drained soil.
Clivia miniata (Kaffir Lily)	Warm greenhouse, fleshy-rooted, evergreen plant. 1 to 2 ft. tall	The forms of *Clivia miniata* bear lily-like flowers of orange, red or yellow between March and June – the higher the temperature the earlier the flowering. Pot in February and place in a sunny position providing a temperature of 13°C. (55°F.). Minimum winter temperature 7°C. (45°F.).
Forsythias	Deciduous shrubs. 10 to 12 ft. tall	These are, without doubt, the best-known shrubs of spring, and they are very easily pleased, growing well in most soils and in sun or partial shade. The most widely grown varieties are *Forsythia intermedia spectabilis*, with golden-yellow flowers; *F. i.* Lynwood, with numerous bright yellow flowers; and the semi-pendulous *F. suspensa* which is a splendid plant for a north-facing wall.

Name	Type and Size	General Remarks
Magnolia stellata (The Star Magnolia)	Deciduous shrub. 8 to 12 ft. tall and through	A fine shrub for the small garden; it bears star-shaped, white flowers in March and April on the bare branches. An excellent lawn specimen for lime-free soil.
Pilea cadierei	Warm greenhouse perennial. 6 to 12 in. tall	*Pilea cadierei*, which has green leaves boldly marked with silver, is a decorative plant much used in the home these days. It needs a temperature of 13 to 16°C. (55 to 60°F.) and liberal amounts of water the year round.
Polyanthus	Hardy perennial. 9 to 12 in. tall	The polyanthus (varieties and forms of *Primula polyantha*) are superb bedding plants for spring display and can be left undisturbed for as long as they continue to grow well. They prefer a shady position and need a soil which does not dry out.
Ribes sanguineum (Flowering Currant)	Deciduous shrub. 8 to 10 ft. tall and through	Easily pleased, the flowering currants will succeed in any ordinary soil in sun or in partial shade and their flowers are a welcome sight in March and April. Two of the best are the crimson King Edward VII and Pulborough Scarlet.
Zantedeschia aethiopica (Arum Lily, Calla Lily)	Cool greenhouse perennial. 2 to 2½ ft. tall	This plant, with its pure white spathes and prominent yellow spadices provides a splendid display from March to early summer. See weekly notes for cultivation.

APRIL

Name	Type and Size	General Remarks
Alyssum saxatile	Rock garden perennial. Up to 12 in. tall	Attractive, yellow flowers borne in abundance from April to June on walls or in rock gardens. The double-flowered, golden-yellow *A. s. flore pleno* is popular.
Aubrietas	Rock garden, evergreen perennials. 2 to 3 in. tall	You see these plants everywhere—like the alyssum—but how cheerful they are in early spring. For growing in the rock garden and on walls they are ideal trailing plants. Attractive varieties include the pale rose-pink Maurice Prichard; the deep red Barker's Double; and the lavender Studland.
Calceolarias	Cool greenhouse biennials. 10 to 15 in. tall	The colourful, pouched flowers of these plants make them attractive greenhouse subjects. If seed is sown in May the resultant plants will flower the following April. A minimum winter temperature of 7°C. (45°F.) is all that is needed.
Cheiranthuses (Wallflowers)	Perennials, but treated as biennials. 1 to 1½ ft. tall	Delightfully cheery colours characterize the wallflower (*Cheiranthus cheiri*) with their flowers of orange, red and various shades of yellow. Dwarf varieties, such as Tom Thumb Mixed, are only 9 in. tall and useful for edging.
Doronicum plantagineum	Herbaceous perennial. 2 to 3 ft. tall	Cheerful, yellow flowers (see illustration p. 51) in April and May. Two excellent varieties are the golden-yellow Harpur Crewe, 2½ ft.; and the bright yellow Miss Mason, 2 ft. Plant in any ordinary soil in sun or shade.
Fritillaria imperialis (Crown Imperial)	Bulbous plant. 3 to 4 ft. tall	This decorative plant is suitable for a partly shaded border. The nodding, bell-shaped flowers are borne in April in a circle at the top of the stem and may be yellow, red or orange. Plant the bulbs in September, 4 in. deep and 18 in. apart.
Fritillaria meleagris (Snake's-head Fritillary)	Bulbous plant. 1 ft. tall	Beautifully marked flowers in April (see illustration p. 51) in various shades of purple. Plant bulbs in September, 4 in. deep and 6 in. apart.
Gardenia jasminoides	Warm greenhouse, evergreen shrub. 1 to 6 ft. tall	This strong-scented, lime-hating shrub bears its white flowers in spring, summer and autumn. The best blooms are borne on one- or two-year-old plants but older specimens flower freely. It needs a winter temperature of 13 to 18°C. (55 to 65°F.).
Grevillea robusta (Silk Oak or Silk Bark Oak)	Cool greenhouse evergreen tree, or summer bedding plant. Generally 2 to 4 ft. tall	This handsome foliage plant with finely cut, fern-like leaves is decorative the year round and is extremely useful as a foil for flowering plants. It is also used for summer bedding. It likes cool, airy conditions under glass.
Maluses (Ornamental Crabs)	Deciduous trees. 15 to 30 ft. tall	Like the flowering cherries, the ornamental crabs are enjoyed for their floral beauty in spring. The lovely Japanese Crab, *Malus floribunda*, for instance, bears a profusion of pink flowers in late April and May. Other crabs are grown mainly for their handsome fruits—Golden Hornet, with bright yellow fruits; and John Downie, with spectacular orange and red fruits are two notable examples.
Myosotis (Forget-me-not)	Perennial, but treated as a biennial. 6 to 12 in. tall	This popular old flower is lovely to see in the garden in April and May. Forms of *Myosotis alpestris* in various shades of blue are freely available and there is an attractive carmine-rose variety named Carmine King.

Name	Type and Size	General Remarks
Narcissi (for naturalising)	Bulbous plants. 6 to 12 in. tall	The narcissi or daffodils are superb plants for naturalising in grass, around shrubs or in rose beds to provide a colourful display in early spring. The best sites are those which are sunny and open but they will also grow in semi-shade.
Primulas	Herbaceous perennials. 3 in. to 3 ft. tall	Of the many fine primulas, none is more garden-worthy than the lovely rich red *Primula pulverulenta*, 2 to 3 ft. tall, and its pink-flowered Bartley Strain. The Candelabra primulas, 1 to 3 ft. tall, bear flowers in whorls all round the stem. Then there is the round-headed *P. denticulata*, 1 ft. tall, with pale purple, lavender or white flowers in early spring. A dainty primula is the rose-coloured *P. rosea*, 6 in. tall and *P.* Wanda, 3 in. tall, has reddish-purple flowers.
Prunus persica	Deciduous tree. Up to 15 ft. tall	This small tree is particularly lovely in its form Aurora, which bears rosettes of rose-pink flowers throughout April. Other good varieties include the semi-double, bright pink Helen Borchers and the semi-double, pink Windle Weeping.
Pulmonaria saccharata	Herbaceous perennial. 1 ft. tall	A valuable plant for light shade with pink flowers–turning blue with age–in April and May, and attractive, fresh green foliage marked with white. The rose-coloured Mrs Moon is a good variety. Needs a fairly moist soil.
Pulsatilla vulgaris (Pasque Flower)	Herbaceous perennial. 1 ft. tall	Beautiful flowers (see illustration p. 43) of various colours from purple and red to mauve and white during April. Needs well-drained soil and a sunny position.
Schizanthus (Poor Man's Orchid)	Cool greenhouse, half-hardy annual. 1 to 4 ft. tall	Several strains provide beautiful flowers in colours from purple to red and pink. Particularly suitable for a small greenhouse is the Dwarf Bouquet strain.
Sweet Violets	Herbaceous perennials. 4 to 6 in. tall	The Sweet Violet, *Viola odorata*, needs a rich, well-worked soil and partial shade. The fragrant flowers, borne in April and May, are violet, pink or white.
Tulipa tarda	Bulbous plant. 6 in. tall	*Tulipa tarda* produces its yellow flowers with yellowish-green markings in late April and early May. The bulbs are not lifted each year at the end of the season like those of the bedding tulips but are allowed to stay where they are. Plant 3 in. deep in well-drained, moderately rich soil in October or November.

MAY

Name	Type and Size	General Remarks
Anthuriums	Warm greenhouse, evergreen perennials. 1 to 3 ft. tall	These plants with spathes of white, pink, red or orange are decorative in all seasons but most of all from May to September. Two popular kinds are *Anthurium andreanum* with heart-shaped leaves and *A. scherzerianum* with long, narrow leaves.
Campanula medium (Canterbury Bell)	Biennial. 2½ ft. tall	This popular plant flowers in May and June in a variety of colours from violet-blue to lavender, rose and white. (See illustration p. 68.) They like a rich soil.
Ceanothus thyrsiflorus	Half-hardy evergreen shrub. Up to 25 ft. tall and wide	Pale blue flowers in May and June, and one of the most hardy of the evergreen ceanothus–but it still needs the protection of a wall in all but the most favoured parts of the country. (See illustration p. 65.) Well-drained soil and a sunny, sheltered position against south- or west-facing wall or fence.
Cheiranthus allionii (Siberian Wallflower)	Herbaceous perennial, but treated as a biennial or an annual. 1 ft. tall	Seed sown out of doors at the end of May will provide plants for flowering in a year's time. An early spring sowing will give flowers in the same year.
Clematis Lasurstern	Deciduous climbing shrub. Up to 10 ft. tall	A handsome clematis (see illustration p. 55) which flowers on the young wood in May and June and again later in the summer. Grow in full sun with roots in cool, moist soil shaded by other plants or a piece of flat stone.
Clematis montana	Deciduous climbing shrub. Up to 20 ft. tall	One of the loveliest of all climbers with its mass of flowers in May. The most popular variety is *rubens* with rose-pink flowers, but the white *grandiflora* is also excellent. Elizabeth, delicate pink in colour, has fragrant flowers.
Erythronium revolutum (Trout Lily)	Bulbous plant. 8 to 12 in. tall	A beautiful flower which appears in April and May. The rosy-pink blooms of the species have a delightful foil in the mottled foliage and there is also a white variety, White Beauty. (See illustration p. 54.) Plant the bulbs in August or September, 2 to 3 in. deep and apart in a soil rich in humus and in semi-shade.
Helianthemums (Sun Roses)	Evergreen shrubs. 6 to 18 in. tall and up to twice as much through	These pretty little shrubs, mostly varieties of *Helianthemum nummularium*, have orange, red, pink, yellow or white flowers in May and June. They grow best in light, sandy soil. Fine named varieties are the golden-yellow Ben Fhada; the crimson, double-flowered Cerise Queen; and the lemon-yellow Wisley Primrose.

Name	Type and Size	General Remarks
Heucherellas	Herbaceous perennials. 1 to 2 ft. tall	Two of these lovely plants are quite widely grown – *H. tiarelloides* with panicles of rose-pink flowers on 1-ft. stems and the rather taller *H.* Bridget Bloom which bears pale pink flowers in May and June and again in August and September.
Hoyas	Warm greenhouse, evergreen shrubs. 1½ to 8 ft. tall	Two hoyas are commonly grown – the climbing *H. carnosa* with waxy, pink and white flowers and glossy green leaves, and the much smaller, pendulous *H. bella* with white, crimson- or violet-centred flowers. This last is grown in hanging baskets or as a pot plant and it needs a rather higher temperature than *H. carnosa*. For preference, *H. carnosa* should be grown in the greenhouse border and it needs a winter temperature of 7 to 13°C. (45 to 55°F.).
Irises (Tall Bearded type)	Evergreen, rhizomatous perennials. 2½ to 4 ft. tall	The tall bearded irises bring distinction to the May-June border but they need positioning with care if their rather prominent foliage is not to be an embarrassment for the rest of the year. They must be planted so that the sun can fully ripen the rhizomes and well-drained soil is essential.
Laburnum vossii	Deciduous tree. Up to 30 ft. tall	This variety is notable for its especially long racemes of yellow flowers in late May and June. Like all laburnums it grows well in any soil.
Lupins	Herbaceous perennials. 3 to 4 ft. tall	Named Russell varieties of lupins are available in such colours as golden-yellow, lemon-yellow, cerise, rosy-lilac and red and there are many others with mixed colouring. They like a well-drained soil but make sure it is not too rich or they are liable to form fleshy roots which are easily damaged by frost and damp.
Pieris formosa forrestii	Evergreen shrub. 8 ft. tall and up to 12 ft. through	This splendid shrub with its bright red young growths and panicles of white, lily-of-the-valley like flowers is a delight in April and the earliest part of May. (See illustration p. 54.) It must have a lime-free soil, preferably containing liberal amounts of peat or leafmould. Suitable for growing in sheltered shrubbery or thin woodland.
Pyrethrums (Coloured Marguerites)	Herbaceous perennials. 2 to 2½ ft. tall	These attractive members of the chrysanthemum tribe are excellent both for garden display and cutting. They need a well-drained soil and sunshine to do well.
Rhododendrons (Hardy Hybrid type)	Evergreen shrubs. 6 to 8 ft. tall	This large genus is of special interest to gardeners with lime-free soil and a few hardy hybrids of merit are Britannia, crimson-scarlet; Pink Pearl, rose-pink; and Purple Splendour, deep purple with black markings. In addition to being lime-free the soil should, for preference, be moist, peaty and fairly light.
Weigela **Abel Carrière**	Deciduous shrub. 5 to 6 ft. tall and through	This excellent variety (see illustration p. 55) bears its rose-carmine flowers during May and June. All weigelas need a good soil and a sunny, open position.
Wisterias	Deciduous climbing shrubs. Up to 100 ft. tall	The wisterias need sunshine and a fairly rich soil. The most popular species is *Wisteria sinensis* with mauve flowers, and *W. floribunda macrobotrys* has very large racemes, 2 to 3 ft. long, of lilac flowers.

JUNE

Name	Type and Size	General Remarks
Acanthus mollis (Bear's Breeches)	Herbaceous perennial. 4 to 5 ft. tall	This is what is called an 'architectural' plant with large, thistle-like leaves and spikes of white and purple flowers from June to September. It likes good soil, and a sunny or semi-shaded position.
Allamanda cathartica	Warm greenhouse, evergreen climber. 5 to 10 ft. tall	This plant bears golden-yellow, trumpet-like flowers from June onwards. It needs a winter temperature of at least 13°C. (55°F.). Attractive varieties are *hendersonii* with orange-yellow flowers and *grandiflora* with pale yellow flowers.
Antirrhinums (Snapdragons)	Herbaceous perennials, but treated as half-hardy annuals. 4 in. to 3 ft. tall	These useful garden plants flower from June until autumn. They come in shades of red, pink, orange and yellow and also white. See weekly notes for cultivation.
Browallias	Cool greenhouse annuals and perennials. 1 to 2 ft. tall	The half-hardy annual *Browallia demissa* with blue or white flowers from June to October and the perennial *B. speciosa major* with blue or violet flowers, from June to September are good greenhouse plants. Sow seeds in March, or if winter-flowering plants are required, in July.
Cannas (Indian Shot)	Warm greenhouse, rhizomatous perennials, or summer bedding plants. 3 to 4 ft. tall	These bold-leaved plants with their orange, red or yellow flowers and bronze or green foliage are a cheery sight from June to September.

Name	Type and Size	General Remarks
Delphiniums	Herbaceous perennials. 3 to 7 ft. tall	The Elatum delphiniums are striking border plants. There are many varieties, all of which flower in June and July. (See illustration p. 72.) More dainty are the freely branching Belladonna varieties. The flowers, in delightful soft colours, are borne in loose sprays in June and July. All need a rich, well-drained soil.
Deutzias	Deciduous shrubs. Up to 10 ft. tall and 6 to 7 ft. through	These easily grown shrubs are useful for early summer colour. Good varieties are the rose-pink *Deutzia rosea carminea*; Mount Rose of similar colouring; and Avalanche with white flowers. Plant in ordinary soil in a sunny position.
Dianthus allwoodii varieties	Herbaceous perennial. 6 to 9 in. tall	*Dianthus allwoodii* resulted from a cross between the typical garden pink and a perpetual-flowering carnation. It makes an excellent border plant, and needs a good-quality, well-drained soil of a non-acid nature.
Dianthus barbatus (Sweet William)	Herbaceous perennial, but treated as a biennial. 1 to 1½ ft.	Sweet Williams grow well in any rather good soil in a sunny position. The dwarf forms, only 6 to 9 in. tall, are especially attractive.
***Digitalis* Excelsior Hybrids** (Foxglove)	Biennials. 4 to 5 ft. tall	These hybrids have flowers all round the stem (usually they are on one side only) which are carried almost at right angles and so show off their lovely markings. (See illustration p. 68.) Grow in shade. They do well in dry conditions.
Escallonias	Evergreen shrubs. 6 to 12 ft. tall	These are especially useful shrubs for seaside gardens. Some, however, are not hardy in colder, inland parts of the country. Good varieties include C. F. Ball, with rose-crimson flowers and growing to a height of about 10 ft.; Donard Seedling, pale pink in the bud and then white, up to 12 ft.; and *E. langleyensis*, with rose-crimson flowers on arching branches, 8 ft.
Gloriosa rothschildiana	Warm greenhouse, bulbous climber. 6 ft. tall	This tender climber has distinctive crimson flowers with spotted, wavy and recurved petals from June to August. It needs a winter temperature of 13°C. (55°F.).
Heleniums (Sneezeworts)	Herbaceous perennials. 2 to 5 ft. tall	These attractive plants need a sunny position and will then do well in any ordinary garden soil. The varieties of *Helenium autumnale* include the rich red Moerheim Beauty, 3 ft. tall and flowering from July to September; and the rich yellow Butterpat, also 3 ft. and flowering from August until autumn.
Lilies (modern hybrids and forms)	Bulbous plants 2½ to 7 ft. tall	There are many superb hybrids and forms available, like the June-flowering Mid-Century Hybrids in pale yellow, red or orange; and the splendid Golden Clarion Strain which produces its yellow or orange trumpet flowers in July and August.
Meconopsis betonicifolia (The Blue Poppy)	Herbaceous perennial. 3 ft. tall	This short-lived perennial is a most beautiful plant with sky-blue flowers in June and July. It takes from 12 to 18 months to come into flower and is best grown in partial shade in moist, well-drained soil.
Mimosa pudica (Sensitive Plant)	Cool greenhouse perennial, but treated as an annual. 1 to 1½ ft.	This is a 'fun' plant in the sense that the leaves droop when touched, hence the common name. The round heads of purplish flowers are of secondary importance.
Nerium oleander (Oleander)	Cool greenhouse, evergreen shrub. 10 ft. tall	This shrub, with its willow-like leaves bears clusters of white or pink single or double flowers from June to October.
Nymphaeas (Water Lilies)	Aquatic, tuberous-rooted perennials	There are many varieties of nymphaeas available for planting in water varying in depth from less than a foot to 2½ to 3 ft. James Brydon, with red flowers, suitable for depths of 1½ to 2 ft. is one of the most popular. Another is the red Escarboucle, also for medium water depths. Mrs Richmond has large, rose-pink flowers, flushed white, with prominent golden-yellow stamens. (See illustration p. 76.) It needs a planting depth of 2 ft.
Peonies	Herbaceous perennials. 1 to 3 ft. tall	Peonies need a deeply dug, rich soil which has been well manured before planting. Quite apart from the superb single and double flowers in June and July, there is another interest in the attractive colour the leaves turn in autumn.
Philadelphuses (Mock Oranges)	Deciduous shrubs. 6 to 8 ft. tall	The handsome, white-flowered, fragrant philadelphuses, are among the best of the summer-flowering shrubs of medium height. The double-flowered variety Virginal and the lovely Beauclerk are especially fine. The compact *Philadelphus microphyllus*, only 3 ft. tall, is excellent for small gardens.
Plumbago capensis	Cool greenhouse, evergreen shrub. 10 to 15 ft. tall	Although not a climber, this plant is excellent for growing on walls if trained on trellis work. It can also be trained on canes or a wire 'umbrella'. The pale blue flowers, so freely borne, are a delight from June until the end of August.
Streptocarpus (Cape Primrose)	Warm greenhouse, herbaceous perennial. 1 to 1½ ft. tall	Many fine hybrids are available, in colours from purple and blue to red, pink and white. One of the best is the mauvish-blue Constant Nymph.

Name	Type and Size	General Remarks
Streptosolen jamesonii	Cool greenhouse, evergreen, climbing shrub. 4 to 6 ft. tall	This tender shrub bears orange flowers from June to September and needs a minimum winter temperature of 7°C. (45°F.).

JULY

Name	Type and Size	General Remarks
Achimenes (Hot Water Plant)	Cool greenhouse, tuberous-rooted perennial. 9 to 12 in. tall	Decorative plants for pot cultivation and for hanging baskets, with flowers in shades of purple, blue, red, pink and white. See weekly notes for cultivation.
Agapanthus (African Lily)	Herbaceous perennial. 2 to 4 ft. tall	The handsome agapanthus, which make excellent plants for growing in containers as well as in borders, vary in hardiness. *Agapanthus orientalis* with its blue flower heads in July can be damaged in severe weather if not well protected, whereas the Headbourne Hybrids with flowers in various shades of blue are much hardier.
Ageratums	Half-hardy annuals. 4 to 9 in. tall	These are valuable bedding plants, varieties like Blue Blazer and Blue Mink being especially desirable. Traditionally, these plants are blue, but there are now also white, pink and purple varieties.
Aphelandra squarrosa louisae	Warm greenhouse, evergreen shrub. 1 to 2 ft. tall	Popular as a house plant, this aphelandra is better in the greenhouse for it dislikes dry atmospheric conditions and fluctuations in temperature. It is a very handsome plant with its white-veined, dark green leaves and bright yellow bracts. A minimum winter temperature of 13°C. (55°F.) is needed.
Astilbes	Herbaceous perennials. Generally 2 to 3½ ft. tall but also dwarf forms	It would be difficult to omit the gaily plumed astilbes from any border well supplied with soil moisture. I am particularly fond of the *arendsii* hybrids, in a wide range of pinks and reds, and white.
Buddleia davidii **varieties**	Deciduous shrub. 12 ft. tall	Valuable shrubs for late-summer flowering, putting up a show from July to October. The reddish-purple Royal Red and Dubonnet, deep purple, are two good varieties.
Calendulas (Pot Marigolds)	Hardy annual. 1 to 2 ft. tall	The calendulas are among the most popular of all annual flowers and the double-flowered Geisha Girl, illustrated on p. 72, is one of the best.
Campanula pyramidalis (Chimney Bell Flower)	Cool greenhouse perennial, but treated as a biennial. 4 ft. tall	This delightful campanula with blue or white bell-like flowers may be grown in the greenhouse in 6- to 10-in. pots. Seed is sown in a cool greenhouse or cold frame in March or April. The resulting plants are hardened off and spend the summer out of doors and are then overwintered in a cold frame. They come into flower in July and continue to bloom for many weeks.
Celosias (Cockscomb, Prince of Wales' Feathers)	Cool greenhouse annuals, or summer bedding plants. 9 to 18 in. tall	There are two celosias which are excellent for greenhouse decoration in summer: *C. cristata*, the Cockscomb, with crested red flowers; and *C. plumosa*, with plumes of red or yellow flowers.
Clarkias	Hardy annuals. 2 ft. tall	These are useful plants both for border display and cutting with a multitude of small, double flowers in such colours as purple, scarlet, pink and white. They continue to flower until autumn, and are suitable for semi-shade or full sun.
Crocosmia crocosmiiflora (Montbretia)	Cormous plant. 2 to 3 ft. tall	The modern, large-flowered hybrids in colourful orange, crimson and bright yellow are splendid garden plants. Compared with the old cottage-garden montbretias, though, they can be a little tender and may need protecting with bracken or straw in the autumn or lifting and overwintering in a frame. They need a sunny position and well-drained soil.
Echinops **Taplow Blue** (Globe Thistle)	Herbaceous perennial. 6 to 7 ft. tall	The handsome Globe Thistle is seen at its best in the variety Taplow Blue which has thistle-like flower heads of a striking deep blue colour in July and August. Excellent for cutting. Plant in ordinary soil in full sun.
Eschscholzias	Hardy annuals. 1 ft. tall	If you do not mind them seeding themselves freely – always a possibility – these are splendid flowers for late summer colour. Flowers like small poppies in colours from orange and red to rose, yellow and white are borne against a background of grey foliage. These are sun lovers.
Gladioli	Half-hardy cormous plants. 1 to 4 ft. tall	The Large-flowered varieties and the Primulinus and Butterfly varieties are splendid for colour from late July until the end of August or September. They demand good drainage and an open, sunny position. The Large-flowered type have spikes of large flowers set close together; the Primulinus type have hooded flowers set quite widely apart, and the Butterflies are the equal of the Large-flowered kind in height (2 to 4 ft.) but have smaller flowers, usually in contrasting colours.

Name	Type and Size	General Remarks
Hebe Midsummer Beauty	Evergreen shrub. 3 to 4 ft. tall and 6 ft. through	The hebes were formerly included in the genus *Veronica* and they are unfortunately rather tender. One of the most attractive, and hardier than many, is Midsummer Beauty, which bears lavender-purple flowers from July to September. (See illustration p. 76.) Likes ordinary, well-drained soil and a sheltered position.
Heliotropiums (Heliotropes)	Cool greenhouse shrubs, or summer bedding plants. 1 to 1½ ft. tall	This is an extremely useful pot plant for the greenhouse and a popular bedding plant. Named varieties in shades of blue and purple are available. They need a winter temperature of 10 to 13°C. (50 to 55°F.).
Impatiens (Busy Lizzie)	Cool greenhouse perennial, but treated as a half-hardy annual. 6 in. to 3 ft. tall	The gay impatiens flower throughout summer and autumn and into winter and bring colour to the greenhouse with their orange, red, pink and white flowers. The two kinds most often grown are *Impatiens holstii* and *I. sultanii* and their varieties.
Ipomoea tricolor (Morning Glory)	Cool greenhouse, half-hardy annual climber. 8 to 10 ft. tall	A first class plant with blue, white or dark red trumpet-shaped flowers. Correctly called *Pharbitis tricolor*, but still listed by most nurserymen as ipomoea.
Lapageria rosea	Cool greenhouse, evergreen climber. 15 to 20 ft. tall	A delightful plant with pink, bell-shaped flowers from July to October. It is best of all grown in a greenhouse border and trained up trellis work but it can be grown in a large pot or tub and trained around canes. A minimum winter temperature of 7 to 10°C. (45 to 50°F.) is needed.
Larkspurs (Annual Delphiniums)	Hardy annuals. 1 to 3 ft. tall	These plants will grow in any fairly good soil. Seed should be sown where the plants are to flower, in August or early September or in March or April. Colours include blue, crimson, lavender and white, and the flowers are splendid for cutting.
Lilium regale (Regal Lily)	Bulbous plant. 3 to 6 ft. tall	This is one of the easiest and, I think, one of the best of all lilies with its handsome trumpet flowers in July. Marked with pinkish and maroon shades on the outside, the flowers are white on the inside with yellow markings on the throat. It likes sun, except at the roots, and is not averse to lime.
Lobelia cardinalis	Half-hardy, herbaceous perennial. 2 to 3 ft. tall	This showy perennial, with its scarlet flowers and fresh green leaves, is a splendid plant for a moist position in sunshine or semi-shade. Excellent, too, is the variety Queen Victoria with crimson foliage and scarlet flowers. Plants are best lifted in October, boxed or potted and stored in a cold frame until May when they can be planted in the border again.
Mesembryanthemum criniflorum (The Livingstone Daisy)	Half-hardy annual. 3 to 4 in. tall	This showy plant, with its daisy-like flowers in such colours as purple, mauve, red, yellow and white, needs a sunny position and well-drained soil. It is a splendid plant for providing colour from July until the autumn.
Nemesias	Half-hardy annuals. 6 to 12 in. tall	The compact strains of *Nemesia strumosa*, only 6 to 9 in. tall, include named varieties in red, blue, orange and yellow as well as mixed hybrids. They make excellent bedding plants.
Nicotianas (Tobacco Plants)	Half-hardy perennials, but treated as half-hardy annuals. 1½ to 3 ft. tall	These have an extremely pleasing fragrance to accompany the decorative crimson, pink and white flowers. Not so long ago it was only possible to obtain kinds which opened their flowers in the evening, but now one can get strains such as Sensation Mixed and Dwarf White Bedder with flowers which are open in the daytime.
Penstemons	Half-hardy, herbaceous perennials. 1 to 3 ft. tall	In most gardens these showy plants are best raised annually from cuttings. They can, however, thrive out of doors for many years in mild districts.
Petunias	Half-hardy, herbaceous perennials, but treated as half-hardy annuals. 6 to 15 in. tall	These are the bedding plants *par excellence* with a wonderful exuberance and colours from purple and blue to red, pink and white. The F_1 hybrids with their size of flower and freedom of flowering are particularly desirable.
Phlox drummondii and varieties	Half-hardy annuals. 6 to 12 in. tall	The annual phlox, with their flowers in colours from purple and violet to red, yellow and white, are wonderful bedding plants for the period July to September.
Phlox paniculata varieties	Herbaceous perennials. 2 to 4 ft. tall	Given a rich soil and shade from the strongest sunshine, the herbaceous phlox are among the best of border plants for July to September flowering. Colours include purple, red, carmine, pink and white.
Poppies (Annual)	Hardy annuals. 2 to 3 ft. tall	These plants are derived from *Papaver rhoeas* and *P. somniferum* and have an excellent colour range and an attractive rather delicate habit. The Peony-flowered strain have immense double flowers resembling herbaceous peonies.
Salpiglossis sinuata	Cool greenhouse annual, or summer bedding plant. 1½ to 3 ft. tall	This pretty plant, with its large flowers reminiscent of alstroemerias, is fine for summer bedding or for growing as a pot plant.

Name	Type and Size	General Remarks
Salvia splendens and varieties	Herbaceous perennials, but treated as half-hardy annuals. 9 to 12 in. tall	The brilliantly coloured Scarlet Sage, as *Salvia splendens* is called, is a popular plant for creating an eye-catching display from July until autumn. Of its varieties, one of special worth is Blaze of Fire.
Salvia superba	Herbaceous perennial. 3 ft. tall	This is a valuable border plant with spikes of bluish-purple flowers. A sunny position and ordinary garden soil are all that are needed.
Smithianthas	Warm greenhouse, tuberous-rooted perennials. 1½ ft. tall	Extremely attractive plants with large, heart-shaped, velvety leaves, and spikes of tubular flowers in shades of orange, red, yellow and apricot from July to December. The tubers should be started into growth in March.
Tagetes (French and African Marigolds)	Half-hardy annuals. 6 in. to 3 ft. tall	Probably the most popular bedding plants of all, with cheerful flowers in yellow, orange or maroon from June until autumn. A great favourite is the dwarf single French variety, Naughty Marietta, with golden-yellow flowers blotched with maroon.
Tibouchina semidecandra	Warm greenhouse, evergreen shrub. Up to 10 ft. tall	An extremely handsome plant which bears rich purple flowers with a velvet-like texture from July to October. The growths can be trained to wires or canes, but I prefer to restrict its size to form a bush by cutting back after flowering.
Tropaeolums (Nasturtiums)	Hardy annuals. 6 to 15 in. tall	Especially easy plants to please and, given sunny conditions, no other plant produces such a display of brilliant colour in poor, dry soil. One of the best dwarf double varieties is Jewel Mixed with gay flowers carried well above the foliage.
Ursinias	Half-hardy annuals. 9 to 15 in. tall	The orange, daisy flowers with contrasting centres make ursinias extremely attractive annuals. They like a warm, sunny position and also make fine pot plants.
Veronica incana	Herbaceous perennial. 1½ ft. tall	This is an easy plant for a sunny position, flowering in July and August. The dark blue flowers are set off by the grey foliage.
Violas (Pansies)	Herbaceous perennials, but treated as biennials. 6 to 9 in. tall	These plants need no introduction. Some of the most attractive are the Clear Crystals mixture, which have self-coloured flowers in yellow, purple, scarlet, blue and violet. Then there are the winter-flowering pansies like the pale blue Celestial Queen and the yellow Helios which can be raised from a sowing made in June.
Zinnias	Half-hardy annuals. 6 in. to 3 ft. tall	There is a wide range of zinnias to choose from, these including the Dahlia-flowered and Chrysanthemum-flowered types, and the Gaillardia-flowered and Pumila kinds. There are also dwarf varieties, such as Thumbelina. All need sun.

AUGUST

Name	Type and Size	General Remarks
Anemone hupehensis (Japanese Anemone)	Herbaceous perennial. 2½ ft. tall	The Japanese Anemones are particularly welcome bearing, as they do, their graceful pink, red and white flowers from August to October. What is more, they grow well in partial shade which so many other plants find disagreeable.
Caryopteris clandonensis	Deciduous shrub. 2 ft. tall	The small, verbena-like flowers are extremely pretty when seen in conjunction with the greyish foliage. Its flowering period is August and September. Likes sun. Heavenly Blue, with bright blue flowers, is usually grown.
Coleus blumei	Warm greenhouse perennial, but suitable for sun lounge in summer. 1 to 2 ft. tall	Coleus can now be raised from seed (previously the fine leaf colouring could only be obtained by raising them from cuttings) sown in February. The plants need plenty of light to develop good colouring.
Dimorphothecas	Hardy annuals. 6 to 12 in. tall	Daisy-like flowers in shades of orange, apricot, buff, salmon and yellow. (See illustration p. 81.) Seed should be sown in March or April in any ordinary, well-drained soil and a sunny position.
Hibiscus syriacus (Tree Hollyhock)	Deciduous shrub. Up to 10 ft. tall	The varieties of *Hibiscus syriacus* are useful for providing colour in August and September. They include the attractive Woodbridge, rose-pink with maroon centre; and Blue Bird, violet-blue with a darker eye. A rich, light, loamy soil suits them best and they need a sunny, sheltered position.
Hydrangeas	Deciduous shrubs. 2½ to 10 ft. tall	The two hydrangeas shown in the illustration on p. 80 are fine representatives of an interesting genus–a Hortensia variety of *H. macrophylla* and the large panicled *H. paniculata grandiflora*. The first is excellent for the border or for growing in containers, the second is an outstanding specimen shrub, flowering from late July until the end of August. Hortensia hydrangeas can be grown in sun or partial shade, but *H. paniculata grandiflora* prefers sun. Both like a rich soil.

Name	Type and Size	General Remarks
Hypericum elatum Elstead	Deciduous shrub. Up to 6 ft. tall	There are numerous excellent hypericums but one of particular interest is *H. e.* Elstead which flowers in late summer and bears clusters of brilliant salmon-red fruits in September together with the flowers. Grows in any well-drained soil.
Kniphofias (Red Hot Pokers)	Herbaceous perennials. 3 to 5 ft. tall	The kniphofias, so useful for late summer and early autumn colour, need a deep, fairly rich soil and a sunny sheltered position to be really successful. *Kniphofia uvaria* is commonly grown (see illustration p. 84) and splendid varieties include the yellow and scarlet Royal Standard; the White Maid of Orleans; and the early-flowering Bee's Sunset, orange-red, which comes into flower in June.
Leycesteria formosa	Deciduous shrub. Up to 8 ft. tall	The unusual blooms of this shrub consist of small white flowers surrounded by reddish-green bracts. (See illustration p. 81.) They are succeeded by dark purple berries in the autumn. Grows in any ordinary garden soil, in sun or shade.
Lilium auratum (The Golden-rayed Lily of Japan)	Bulbous plant. Up to 8 ft. tall	A species of great distinction with huge fragrant white flowers, lined with gold and spotted with crimson in August and September. (See illustration p. 85.)
Nerines	Cool greenhouse, bulbous plants. 1 to 1½ ft. tall	These lovely plants bear clusters of flowers–up to a dozen in a cluster–from August to November. They flower best when pot bound.
Pernettya mucronata	Evergreen shrub. 3 to 5 ft. tall	This decorative shrub needs a moist, lime-free soil. The showy berries in pink, purple, red and lavender shades appear in late summer and last well into winter. There are also small, white, bell-like flowers in spring.
Rudbeckias (Coneflowers)	Herbaceous perennials. Generally 2 to 3 ft. tall	The herbaceous rudbeckias are invaluable plants for late-summer and early-autumn colour. Some especially good ones are *Rudbeckia fulgida* Goldsturm with large deep yellow flowers with black centres; the lemon-yellow Goldquelle; and Herbstonne, golden-yellow, which is 6 ft. tall and splendid for the back of a border.
Sedum spectabile	Herbaceous perennial. 1 to 1½ ft. tall	A familiar sight in August and September are the flat, pink flower heads of *Sedum spectabile*. The variety Brilliant has attractive rose-pink blooms. All need a deep, rich, loamy soil and a sunny position.
Solidago (Golden Rod)	Herbaceous perennial. 6 in. to 5 ft. tall	These are especially useful border plants for they are easy to grow and do well in sun or shade. One of my favourites is the golden-yellow Goldenmosa, 2½ ft. tall with mimosa-like flowers. Another excellent small variety is 2-ft. Lemore, with pale yellow flowers. These will make a show throughout August and September. Even smaller is Crown of Rays, bright yellow and only 1 ft. tall. At the other end of the scale is the 5-ft. Ballardii, with golden-yellow flowers.
Vallota speciosa (Scarborough Lily)	Cool greenhouse, evergreen, bulbous plant. 2 to 3 ft. tall	The showy, scarlet trumpet flowers and the large strap-shaped leaves make an excellent contribution to the cool greenhouse during August and September.

SEPTEMBER

Name	Type and Size	General Remarks
Ampelopsis brevipedunculata	Deciduous climbing shrub. Up to 20 ft. tall	Vigorous climber bearing bluish grapes in autumn if exposed to reasonable amounts of sunshine. The leaves are hop-like. Suitable for ordinary garden soil.
Aster amellus	Herbaceous perennial. 2 to 2½ ft. tall	This purple-flowered species is the parent of several lovely varieties like the violet-blue King George, the pink Brilliant and Mauve Queen. They are excellent bedding plants which flower from August until October. (See illustration p. 97.)
Asters (Michaelmas Daisies)	Herbaceous perennials. 9 in. to 4 ft. tall	The *novae-angliae* and *novi-belgii* Michaelmas daisies, 2½ to 4 ft. tall, are superb garden plants but perhaps the best of all for small, modern gardens are the dwarf varieties, which range from 9 to 18 in. in height. Varieties like the pink Countess of Dudley, the white Snow Sprite and the violet-purple Jenny are especially pleasing when in flower. Grow in any good garden soil in an open position.
Colchicums (Autumn Crocus or Meadow Saffrons)	Cormous plants. 4 to 12 in. tall	The colchicums are good plants for growing in sun or semi-shade, preferably in light, well-drained soil. The flowers, which appear before the leaves, are purple, rose or white in colour. *Colchicum autumnale* is 4 to 6 in. tall and *C. speciosum* (see illustration p. 101) is 9 to 12 in. in height.
Kniphofia galpinii	Herbaceous perennial. 1½ to 2 ft. tall	Much more dainty than the typical border kniphofias (Red Hot Pokers), *Kniphofia galpinii* has grass-like foliage and bears delightful orange flower spikes in September and October. It needs a sunny, sheltered position and good drainage, and is an excellent plant for the rock garden or the front of the border.

Name	Type and Size	General Remarks
Nerine bowdenii (Guernsey Lily)	Bulbous plant. 1½ ft. tall	A handsome plant to grow at the foot of a warm, south-facing wall is *Nerine bowdenii* which bears heads of pink flowers in September and October. It is not a plant, however, for colder gardens and this is the only species of nerine which can be considered hardy enough for garden cultivation.
Physalis franchettii (Chinese Lantern or Cape Gooseberry)	Herbaceous perennial. 1½ ft. tall	The orange-red fruits of *Physalis franchettii*, which ripen in September, are much in demand for drying for winter decoration. Their common name, Chinese Lantern, is very descriptive. They like rich soil in a sunny, well-drained border.
Physostegia virginiana (The Obedient Plant)	Herbaceous perennial. 4 ft. tall	The variety Vivid is an admirable plant for the front of the border, for it bears its rose-coloured, tubular flowers on 1½-ft. stems at a time when this is especially appreciated – from September into the autumn.
Scabiosa caucasica	Herbaceous perennial. 2 ft. tall	The varieties of *Scabiosa caucasica* are excellent plants for late summer colour in the border and for cutting for the house. By far the most widely grown is the variety Clive Greaves, which bears mauve flowers from July to October. (See illustration p. 84.) These plants need an open, sunny position and a well-drained soil, preferably containing lime.

OCTOBER

Name	Type and Size	General Remarks
Arbutus unedo (Strawberry Tree)	Evergreen tree. Generally 15 to 20 ft. tall but up to 40 ft.	This is one of my favourite trees. The panicles of white flowers and the red, strawberry-like fruits are borne together in October and November. The leaves, too, are handsome – glossy and dark green. Although ericaceous, it does well on limy soil. It must be given a sheltered position.
Aucuba japonica variegata (Spotted Laurel)	Evergreen shrub. Up to 10 ft. tall, and as much through	This is a valuable plant for a sunless position, growing well in any soil. Aucubas come in male and female forms, and the females will give a fine crop of red berries in the winter if there is a male plant nearby for pollination.
Hebe Autumn Glory	Evergreen shrub. Up to 3 ft. tall	An excellent but rather tender shrub for providing colour in late summer and autumn. The flower spikes are violet-blue in colour and the leaves bluey-grey. Plant in full sun in well-drained soil. (See illustration p. 113.)
Pyracantha coccinea lalandii	Evergreen shrub. 10 to 12 ft. tall	Fine shrubs for a north wall. Particularly valued for their autumn and winter berries. This variety has small white flowers in May and June and orange-scarlet berries from August until January or February. Grow in ordinary, loamy soil. (See illustration p. 113.)
Rhus typhina The Stag's Horn Sumach	Deciduous shrub or small tree. 12 to 15 ft. tall	Splendid foliage plant with large pinnate leaves, 2 to 3 ft. long, which turn orange-red in autumn. (See illustration p. 101.) This shrub grows well in towns and does not need any special soil.
Schizostylis coccinea (Kaffir Lily)	Rhizomatous perennial. 1½ ft. tall	This handsome plant bears red flowers in autumn. The pink variety Mrs Hegarty flowers in September and October, and Viscountess Byng, also pink, in November. Grow in loamy soil and protect in hard weather. (See illustration p. 104.)
Viburnum opulus xanthocarpum (The Guelder Rose)	Deciduous shrub. 10 to 12 ft. tall	This variety has white flowers in June and July but its glory is its golden-yellow berries which are borne for an extensive period in autumn. Plant in a good, loamy soil in full sun. (See illustration p. 113.)

NOVEMBER

Name	Type and Size	General Remarks
Asparagus (Ornamental types)	Cool greenhouse perennials. Generally 1 to 3 ft. tall	Of especial value for decoration throughout the year, particularly in winter, are the feathery-foliaged *A. plumosus*, *A. asparagoides* with long, green shoots – both are suitable for growing in pots or in the greenhouse border – and *A. sprengeri* which is excellent for growing in hanging baskets. It has needle-like, drooping foliage. All need a minimum winter temperature of 10°C. (50°F.).
Codiaeum variegatum **varieties** (Crotons)	Warm greenhouse, evergreen shrub. 3 to 10 ft. tall	These are splendid plants for year-round interest in the greenhouse with their ornamental, variegated foliage. They need a minimum winter temperature of 13°C. (55°F.) and plenty of light to bring out the colour in the leaves.
Euphorbia pulcherrima (Poinsettia)	Warm greenhouse shrub. 1 to 6 ft. tall	This is the plant whose brightly coloured bracts are so appreciated at Christmas time. Although specially treated plants are now available for display all the year round, I still think it is best as a plant for November to February display.

Name	Type and Size	General Remarks
Iris unguicularis (*I. stylosa*)	Rhizomatous perennial. 1 ft. tall	Beautiful deep lilac flowers, with yellow keel and white suffused lilac throat from November to March. (See illustration p. 120.) Plant in a sunny, sheltered position, preferably below a south wall. The soil should not be too rich.
Jasminum nudiflorum (Winter Jasmine)	Deciduous shrub. 10 to 12 ft. tall	A superb wall shrub with bright yellow flowers borne on leafless stems from November to February. It will grow in almost any soil which is well drained, and is suitable for a north-facing wall.
Jasminum polyanthum	Cool greenhouse, evergreen, climbing shrub. Up to 10 ft. tall	Popular climber bearing clusters of white, fragrant flowers from late November to March. Place pot-grown specimens outside for the summer to ripen the wood.
Prunus subhirtella autumnalis	Deciduous tree. Up to 25 ft. tall	The winter-flowering cherry is a delightful small tree which bears its semi-double, white flowers intermittently from November to February. It likes reasonably good soil and an open position.
Tradescantias (Wandering Sailor, Wandering Jew)	Cool greenhouse perennials. 6 to 12 in. tall	The attraction of these plants is their variegated foliage and their graceful trailing habit. A good variety is Quick Silver, which is less likely to become straggly than others. *Tradescantia zebrina quadricolor* (correctly called *Zebrina pendula quadricolor* now) has leaves marked with cream, green, grey and red.
Viburnum fragrans	Deciduous shrub. Up to 9 to 10 ft. tall and 7 to 8 ft. through	An excellent winter-flowered shrub with fragrant, pink-tinged, white blooms. Puts up a good display from early November till March and will provide sprays for cutting and bringing indoors. Grow in loamy soil in an open, sunny position.

DECEMBER

Name	Type and Size	General Remarks
Chimonanthus praecox (Winter Sweet)	Deciduous shrub. 8 to 10 ft. tall	Pale yellow and purple, sweetly scented flowers from mid-winter until March, sometimes from November. Likes well-drained soil, against a sheltered wall.
Cinerarias	Cool greenhouse perennials, but treated as annuals. 9 in. to 2½ ft. tall	Excellent plants for a greenhouse with a minimum winter temperature of 7°C. (45°F.). For the smallest greenhouses the best choice are the Multiflora Nana strains, but with more room the Grandiflora hybrids and the Stellata type are better.
Cornus alba (Dogwood)	Deciduous shrub. 9 to 10 ft. tall and as much through	The coloured bark of *Cornus alba* and its varieties make them valuable shrubs for the winter garden. The species itself has red bark, and that of its variety *sibirica*, known as the Westonbirt Dogwood, bright crimson. *C. stolonifera* is a vigorous, suckering species with dark red shoots (see illustration p. 116), and its variety *flaviramea* with yellow stems is known as the Yellow-barked Dogwood.
Dracaenas	Warm greenhouse, evergreen perennials. 1 to 6 ft. tall	These decorative foliage plants need a minimum winter temperature of 13°C. (55°F.). Particularly attractive are the trailing *D. godseffiana*, which has dark green leaves marked with cream spots, and *D. sanderiana* with sword-like leaves of green, margined with silver.
Elaeagnus pungens aureo-variegata	Evergreen shrub. 12 to 15 ft. tall and as much through	This variety, with its bright green and creamy-yellow variegated leaves, is a splendid shrub for winter colour in the garden. (See illustration p. 116.) Grow in well-drained soil in sun or semi-shade.
Hyacinths	Cool greenhouse, bulbous plants. 9 to 12 in. tall	These popular spring flowers are excellent for forcing in time for Christmas. The Roman hyacinths, with spikes of fragrant white and pink flowers, are also suitable for an early show.
Ilex aquifolium (English Holly)	Evergreen tree. Generally 10 to 15 ft. tall, but up to 70 ft.	The common English Holly has many varieties, some of great decorative value, like the silver-variegated *I. a. argenteo-marginata pendula*, a weeping variety which carries a good crop of berries; and *I. a.* Golden King, also free-berrying, and with gold-margined leaves (see illustration p. 120). Hollies are not fussy about soil and will grow in sun or shade.
Primulas	Cool greenhouse perennials, but treated as annuals. 6 to 18 in. tall	The three primulas most often grown under glass are *Primula obconica*, whose main display season is winter and early spring; *P. malacoides*, with whorls of flowers in shades of red, pink, and lilac; and *P. sinensis* with many colours and flower forms. These, too, are winter flowering. See weekly notes for cultivation.
Solanum capsicastrum	Cool greenhouse shrub. 9 to 15 in. tall	Popular plant with red berries from October to February and especially welcome at Christmas. It is easy to grow, given a minimum temperature of 7°C. (45°F.).

Index